Reading Development
in a Second Language:
Theoretical, Empirical,
and Classroom Perspectives

Second Language Learning

A Monograph Series Dedicated to Studies in Acquisition and Principled Language Instruction

Robert Di Pietro, Series Editor

The Catalan Immersion Program: A European Point of View, by Josep Maria Artigal

A Developmental Psycholinguistic Approach to Second Language Teaching, by Traute Taeschner

Reading Development in a Second Language: Theoretical, Empirical, and Classroom Perspectives, by Elizabeth B. Bernhardt

in preparation
The Metaphorical Principle in Second Language Learning, by Marcel Danesi

Reading Development in a Second Language: Theoretical, Empirical, and Classroom Perspectives

Elizabeth B. Bernhardt

Associate Professor
Foreign and Second Language Education
The Ohio State University

ABLEX PUBLISHING CORPORATION
NORWOOD, NEW JERSEY

Second Printing 1993

Printed in the United States of America

Library of Congress Cataloging-in-Publication Data

Bernhardt, Elizabeth Buchter.
    Reading and development in a second language: theoretical,
empirical, and classroom perspectives / submitted by Elizabeth B.
Bernhardt.
      p. cm.—(Second language learning)
    Includes bibliographical references and index.
    ISBN 0-89391-675-7 (cloth); 0-89391-734-6 (ppk)
    1. Language and languages—Study and teaching. 2. Reading.
I. Title. II. Series.
P53.75.B47   1991
418'.007—dc20
                                    91-264
                                    CIP

Ablex Publishing Corporation
355 Chestnut Street
Norwood, New Jersey 07648

To the memory of my mother,
Elizabeth Brady Buchter

Table of Contents

Series Editor's Introduction

Second Language Learning is intended for the publication of research into second language acquisition and instruction. This series is distinguished from others that address similar topics by two major features. First of all, the volumes in the series are focused in their orientation. They may be authored by one or more persons but in all cases, their findings come from theoretically coherent and unified research projects. Secondly, they are motivated by the drive to uncover principles of acquisition and/or instruction rather than by a wish to fulfill some immediate classroom need.

Elizabeth Bernhardt's *Reading Development in a Second Language* clearly demonstrates the two features critical to this series. While the topic under discussion is reading in a second language, the results reported are cast so that they are interpretable within the general framework of reading research. Bernhardt's intention is not to provide a "methods-based approach," but rather a view of the second language reading process that is based on principles arising from a synthesis of empirical data. By the sixth chapter, Bernhardt is able to set forth a number of well-grounded principles to guide the second language instructor in the teaching of reading.

The reader will find much substance in this volume. It contains one of the most extensive surveys of published studies on second language reading to be found anywhere in print. This survey is organized in a way to facilitate understanding of the theoretical orientation of each study and the results obtained by it. The style is clear and unencumbered by pedantry. The book is so constructed as to allow the reader to experience a mounting excitement as Bernhardt builds towards her final statements about the nature of reading in a second language. We are pleased to welcome *Reading Development in a Second Language* to the *Second Language Learning* series.

Robert J. Di Pietro
Series Editor

Preface

Reading Development in a Second Language attempts to provide a thorough account of what is known about the acquisition of reading abilities in a second language. Its aim is to foster more principled research and instruction in second language literacy. In order to reach the aim, discussion is set forth from a variety of perspectives: first, through examinations of theoretical models of the reading process and their application to a second language context; second, through a synthesis of the empirical database from 1973 to the present; third, by means of descriptions of reader-based interactions with second language texts; and finally, through concepts of curriculum, instruction, and assessment.

The book is an outgrowth of a research program begun in 1983. That research program, heavily influenced by a psychological approach to the study of reading advocated by the Center for the Study of Human Learning at the University of Minnesota, had its inception in an instructional design study—one that compared the impact on comprehension of oral and silent reading modes. Since that initial study, the research program has grown. It now includes analyses of microlevel cognitive behaviors manifested during reading measured through eye movement; applications of immediate recall both to test and to teach second language text comprehension; experiments with a variety of assessment mechanisms and scoring devices to measure comprehension; examinations of teacher and student behaviors in classroom settings that seem to either facilitate or impede text understanding; and considerations of the efficacy of contemporary reading curricula within a variety of learning needs and contexts.

Reading Development in a Second Language has two readerships in mind. The first readership consists of those interested in the phenomenon of second language acquisition; for that group the book hopes to provide new perspectives and alternative ways of thinking about how second language learners learn to understand and how they understand what they learn. The second readership consists of those interested in reading phenomena, including issues such as word recognition, orthographic switch, syntactic processing, semantic encoding, and cross-cultural conflict; for that group the book intends to provide insights into readers who embody extreme sociocultural and cognitive differences when compared with native readers. The book argues that an analysis of second language readers documents the reading process as language-*dependent* rather than as *universal*.

The book is not intended for those who seek a list of classroom activities designed to facilitate "reading skills." Indeed, where applicable, the book attempts to discuss the classroom implications and classroom applications of particular theories and/or research findings. The author does not subscribe to a "methods-based" approach, but rather to a principled one that clearly reflects what is known about second language reading and that is sensible, reasonable, and workable within *individual* classroom environments.

Reading Development in a Second Language is a personal statement based on the author's own theory and research as well as that of others. It provides the author's view on merging what is known about reading in a second language into a coherent and useful perspective both for research and instruction. The view in the book was generated by examinations of *adult* second language readers who were for the most part already mother-tongue literate. This influence implies, therefore, that discussions of child learners who are not literate in either first or second languages are not extensive.

The book is divided into eight chapters. Chapter One is entitled "The Nature of Second Language Reading." This chapter offers a broad sketch of variables that must be considered in any discussion of second language reading. These variables include reader factors such as *Who are second language readers?* or *Are they different from readers who speak a nonstandard dialect?* The variables also include differences in theoretical perspectives in both instruction and research. A discussion of the nature of second language reading within this domain involves explications of cognitive and social models of the reading process. It also explores their applications within second language settings as well as the development of second language specific models. This initial chapter is heavily influenced by the thoughts of the late H. H. Stern who adamantly maintained that principled language teaching and research can only stem from "a good theoretical understanding" (Stern, 1983, p. 1).

Chapter Two is entitled "The Data Base in Second Language Reading." This chapter is the result of a multiyear study that examined the entire database in second language reading. The first part of the chapter examines theoretical frameworks in which second language research has been conducted and indicates a heavy reliance upon the so-called psycholinguistic model and considerably less awareness of other research models. The data outlined in Chapter Two also indicate a relatively disproportionate number of clinical versus research-based articles.

Each research study conducted since 1973 is outlined for the convenience of the reader, providing variables, subject group descriptions, as well as results of each study: The bulk of the chapter is organized around the topics of *word recognition*; *background knowledge*; *text-structure analyses*; *oral-aural factors*; *syntactic factors*; *cross-lingual processing strategies*; *metacognitive strategies*; *assessment*; and *instruction in second language reading*.

The final portion of this chapter highlights the difficulties in synthesizing these studies. It argues that the difficulties lie in the wide array of subject groups studied, the experimental tasks involved, as well as in theoretical and methodological inconsistencies.

The theory presented in Chapter One and the research base presented in Chapter Two set the stage for the remaining portions of the book. The next two chapters examine, in depth, individual variables in the second language comprehension process.

Chapter Three is entitled "Text-Driven Operations in Second Language Reading." This chapter explores variables in text comprehension such as word recognition, vocabulary density, syntax, phonology, and text structure and the ways in which second language readers either control and/or cope with these variables. The chapter discusses these factors in light of previously unpublished findings on the behaviors of second language readers. The discussion of word recognition, for example, explores, among other things, the impact of orthographic switch for significant numbers of learners: *How do native readers of a character system cognitively adapt their processing strategies when reading in an alphabetic system; how do readers of different alphabetic systems learn to cope?* The discussion of phonological factors questions the extent to which second language readers need an *accurate* phonological base for processing the second language and how readers of character systems can acquire a phonological base. The discussion of syntax cites eye movement research conducted on readers of German, French, Chinese, Japanese, and English. It outlines and illustrates crosslingually the manner in which many second language readers at different developmental levels learn to cope with the reading of a second language. The principal objective of this chapter is to examine text-based factors from a variety of perspectives, to suggest a number of synthesizing generalizations about second language reading, as well as to cite directions for further investigations.

Chapter Four is entitled "Knowledge-Driven Operations in Second Language Reading." Chapter Four discusses readers and the series of features that define them such as their knowledge of the world, their cultural knowledge, their shared versus idiosyncratic knowledge, their feelings and opinions. These extratext-based features all have an impact on the eventual comprehension products of second language readers. As noted in Chapter Two the bulk of second language reading research has focused on these features, especially cultural background knowledge.

Chapter Five, "A Synthesis of Perspectives," attempts to unify the discussions in the previous chapters. In so doing, it illustrates the second language reading process as integrative in nature, not componential. It argues that only through a well-understood holistic view can truly principled second language reading instruction develop. Chapter Five forms the bridge to Chapters Six and Seven which focus on classroom applications and implications. Chapter Six is entitled "Classroom Factors in Second Language Reading Comprehension: How is Comprehension Taught and Learned?" and Chapter Seven is called "Assessing Second Language Reading Comprehension."

Chapter Six overviews traditional second language reading curricula including concepts of controlled vs. authentic texts, readability, and expository vs. literary prose. It also examines the reading component in teacher education, by examining the suggestions made by frequently-used "methods" textbooks such as Chastain (1988), *Developing Second-Language Skills*; Allen and Valette (1979), *Classroom Techniques*; and Omaggio (1986), *Teaching Language in Context: Proficiency-Oriented Language Instruction*. In addition, this chapter examines a number of real classroom interactions meant to shed light on how teachers and students cope with the "reading lesson." In essence this chapter probes the question of whether the use of authentic texts in a foreign language classroom is not just another instance of procedural display or "pretense" on the parts of both teacher and students.

Chapter Seven provides, first, an outline of how comprehension is traditionally assessed in second languages: namely, using cloze, direct "content" questions, and multiple choice. The chapter then provides an alternative view on the assessment of comprehension using immediate recall. It outlines data whereby students were assessed on the same passage using a variety of assessment methods and discusses the relative utility and efficiency of each methodology. Finally, the chapter outlines a variety of assessment technologies for scoring based on propositional analysis schemes. Chapter Seven is based principally on a research projected funded by the Mellon Foundation and administered through the National Foreign Language Center in late 1988.

Chapter Eight concludes *Reading Development in a Second Language* and is entitled "Recommendations for Theory, Research, Curriculum, and Instruction." This chapter attempts to bring the multidimensional, highly interdependent process of reading comprehension back into focus *as such*—not compartmentalized as chapters in a book seem to make it. The reader should leave the book fully informed about the current state of information concerning the second language reading process, and appreciative of its complexity as a process. This appreciation should lead the reader toward a more principled approach to research and instruction in second language reading.

Support for the writing of this book has come from a variety of sources. Initial research was conducted in the Institute of Child Development at the University of Minnesota and funded by grants awarded to Professor Albert Yonas. Since that time grants from the Ohio State University, the Spencer Foundation, the Mellon Foundation, and the United States Department of Education programs in International Research and Studies, and the Office of Postsecondary Education have supported the research that is highlighted and explicated in this book.

Support for the writing of a book is not only financial. It comes in many ways: from students who actually seem interested in eventually reading the book especially Craig Deville, Sherry Taylor, Barbara Schmidt-Rinehart, Leslie Schrier, Pete Brooks, Diane Tedick, and Mike Everson; to family members who ask when they will be able to "show the next-door neighbor;" to secretaries who really wonder whether "all these bibliographic entries are all that necessary"; to former professors who call to say hello. Many people are in these groups and have the author's appreciation. Special thanks, however, go to Mary Armentrout, who typed the manuscript, and to Victoria Berkemeyer who read, reread, and rere-read it, and did much of the analysis in Chapter Five. They shared certain special frustrations with the author.

And a very special thanks goes to Michael L. Kamil, who somehow managed to critique this manuscript as a reading researcher and as my husband all at the same time.

I. B. Singer, Nobel laureate, has said on a number of occasions that individuals met early in an experience tend to take on important roles in later life. I hold first-hand evidence for Singer's belief. In September, 1984, I met H. H. Stern and Robert Di Pietro on the same day in the same place. In the years that followed these two men provided the most significant mentoring roles in my career. Although David Stern died in 1987, much gratitude is expressed posthumously; and to Bob Di Pietro, general editor for the series, a warm thanks not only for the opportunity to write this book, but for his encouragement and interest.

1

The Nature of Second Language Reading

INTRODUCTION

Interest in second language acquisition particularly as it relates to literacy skills in second language has burgeoned in the past decade. Several reasons appear to account for this growth. First, there are obvious *social-political* interests raised by the tremendous influx of nonnative readers, speakers, and writers of majority languages into developed countries throughout the world. Rarely does a primary or secondary school *not* contain at least several children who do not speak the majority language natively. These learners require content instruction in the majority language, and are, therefore, dependent on reading and writing skills in a language other than their own for success in school. In addition, a large portion of nonnative learners in classrooms throughout the world are adults who either need employment for survival and, therefore, must attain functional literacy skills *or* are graduate students seeking advanced degrees at universities who must attain very sophisticated literacy skills. The education of these adults has serious social and economic implications: On the one hand, there are concerns over potential additional strains on already strained economies; on the other, there are the acknowledged advantages of large international student populations that may pay higher tuition rates at universities or that are needed to provide cheap instruction or laboratory assistance in university courses.

A second reason for the general interest in literacy skills in second language is *pedagogical*. The ability to *read* is acknowledged to be the most stable and durable of the second language modalities (Rivers, 1981). In other words, learners may lose their productive skills yet still be able to comprehend texts with some degree of proficiency. In addition, written texts are highly accessible and cheap sources of second language materials. Even with advanced telephone and video materials, written language in hard copy provides the most feasible and cheapest source of contact with a second language. In a sense, then, reading is the most cost-effective of the second language skills that are taught throughout the world.

A third reason for this interest is *cognitive* in nature. The learning of two encoding systems is inherently interesting. Intriguing questions involve whether there are two separate, yet parallel cognitive processes at work or whether there are generic language and, more specifically, generic discourse processing strategies that accommodate both first *and* second languages. These questions in isolation—that is, apart from political or pedagogical considerations—are interesting to the educational research community in general. In other words, analyses of second language literacy acquisition may lend insight into the Universals Hypothesis (Goodman, 1968).

Despite these interest areas, second language research on reading, writing, speaking, or listening is frequently dismissed as being marginal and derivative from first language. Researchers ask questions such as: *Isn't reading in a second language merely a slower, bastardized version of doing the same task in the native language? Isn't writing in a second language the process of putting down words written in different ways in a different order from the mother tongue?* and *Aren't listening and speaking in a second language slower, mispronounced versions of the parallel tasks in a first language?*

Such comparisons imply that the task of a nonnative or novice is to become a native or expert. What the comparisons do not imply is that a nonnative may well become an expert without becoming a "native." Such comparisons also imply a simple solution: that second language tasks must be, in essence, mapping tasks—that is, replacing one mode of behavior with another. This book holds as its thesis that second language *anything* and, in this case, *second language reading* in particular, is a phenomenon unto itself—not just a less accurate version of something else. The intention of this chapter is to begin examining the phenomenon of second language reading by outlining the array of complexifying variables that constitute it. Only through the development of an understanding of these variables can second language reading research and instruction be truly principled. A first step in this development is, borrowing an expression from Stern (1983), to "clear the ground" with some definitions.

WHAT IS A SECOND LANGUAGE AND WHO ARE ITS READERS?

Second language refers to "the chronology of language learning; a second language being any language acquired after the native" (Stern, 1983, p. 12). This definition implies a firmly developed and entrenched native language. In addition, the term *second language* refers to "a non-native language learned and used *within* one country" (Stern, 1983, p. 16). Generally, second language refers to a language that is not spoken in the home, and yet, may be the language of wider communication.

While these are fairly common definitions, two additional fundamental distinctions must be drawn. First, the *differential* nature of second languages must be considered, whereby there is little if any commonality with the language of wider communication. In other words, the second language may contain a linguistic base that is syntactically, phonetically, semantically, and rhetorically distinct from the language of wider communication. Nonexamples of second language would be Black English or Appalachian English that are indeed heavily based on English, the language of wider communication. Examples of second languages within an English-speaking context would be Hmong, German, or Spanish. Secondly, the *accessibility* of the language of wider communication distinguishes second languages. While indeed there are children in schools who do not speak a middle-class *school* language, and are, therefore, at a disadvantage in school, this book concerns those learners who do not have access to *any* form of school language. In other words, learners who do not speak "school language" are still able to access comprehensible language via television or radio; second language speakers who have no form of the language of wider communication at all are barred from *any* access.

The notion of subculture vs. second culture warrants discussion, too. A subculture, by definition, is a recognized *part* of a culture. In fact, the majority culture or "culture" would not be the *same* "culture" if it did not contain the subculture. Examples of subcultures in North American society are Afro-American culture or Irish American culture—cultures that share many of the *same* values as well as basically common linguistic systems. A second culture—that may or may not share a common language such as British or American culture or Swiss or Austrian culture—contains a unique set of cultural assumptions and behavioral norms. While a second culture may share a value system that overlaps to an extent with another culture, it does not share exactly the same sociopolitical history. It can be defined most of the time as a national entity in and of itself such as German culture or Norwegian culture or Indonesian culture.

A follow-up question to these definitions is: *Who fits these definitions?* The answer to this question is complex and multifaceted. A terse, simplistic answer is anybody who has a dominant language and who engages with texts in a secondary language. This answer, however, does not provide significant insights into variables that need to be considered when coming to an understanding of second language reading since second language groups are so diverse. Figure 1.1 outlines some salient features.

A first group of second language readers consists of school children. This group may be subdivided into two, consisting of minority and majority children. As a result of political upheavals throughout the world, it is a rare primary or secondary school that does not contain at least several children from the former group. These are children who do not speak the majority language of the classroom natively. These second language speakers require content instruction in the majority language, and are, therefore, dependent on reading and writing skills in a language other than their own for ultimate educational attainment. The

Figure 1.1.   Groups of second language readers.

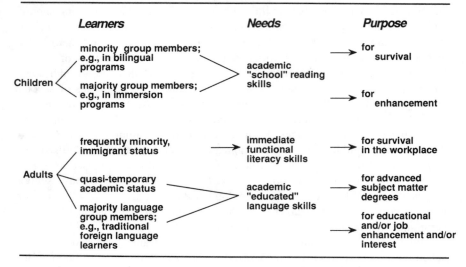

latter group consists of majority language-speaking children. These children are found in immersion programs placed therein to enhance their education. It is important to note that the education of this latter group is enhanced, not determined, by success in the second language. The same cannot be said about the former group. A unifying characteristic of both groups is that their members are still undergoing the process of language development in their own language.

A second group of second language readers consists of adults who need literacy skills in a language other than their dominant one. These adults constitute a multifaceted group. First of all, many of them, depending again on the political circumstances that bring them to a second language environment, need employment for survival and, therefore, must attain immediate functional literacy skills. An additional group of adult readers of second languages, however, is comprised of highly educated learners who seek advanced degrees at foreign universities. These readers require extremely sophisticated literacy skills—more sophisticated than those achieved by the majority of native speakers of a language.

A final group of adults attaining literacy skills in a second language is constituted by students who received their educations in their mother tongues, but who also receive second language instruction. The impetus behind such instruction is that it is either a required portion of a humanities-based curriculum, a personal interest, or needed for acquiring additional job enhancing skills. These learners are generally characterized as "traditional foreign language learners." A unifying characteristic of these learners is their fully-developed and entrenched native language competence as well as a wealth of life experience.

The three groups of adults and the two groups of children who could be termed "second language readers" are very different, one from another. Indeed, these differences make a synthesis statement on the "nature of second language reading" extremely difficult since that *nature,* as illustrated in Figure 1.1, is context-dependent. Yet recognizing the differences between and among these groups lends an initial step toward developing nongeneric, more principled language instruction. Admittedly, the descriptions offered here are still far too generic. Chapter Four, which addresses social and affective variables, will provide a fuller discussion of the nature of second language *readers.*

WHAT IS READING?

Webster's Seventh New Collegiate Dictionary (1971) offers seven principal definitions of the verb *to read.* These definitions range from *"to receive or take in the sense of (as letters or symbols) by scanning;"* to *"to understand the meaning of (written or printed matter);"* to *"to attribute a meaning or interpretation to (something read)."* Key terms in these definitions are "to take in," "to understand," and "to attribute an interpretation." Indeed, these phrases succinctly capture the essence of the act of reading: taking written information in and understanding it. Yet this simple definition is anything but straightforward. Just like definitions of any complex process, one has to stop and reread it, and say: "Now, what does it *really* mean? What does "take in" mean in the real world? What does "to understand" really imply?"

In a sense, if the question *What is reading?* could be answered in the pages of this book, most educational researchers could retire or select alternative careers. Thousands of academicians have been concerned with the process of reading for thousands of years. This concern has yielded many insights and much data, but no clearly stated, empirically supported, and theoretically unassailable definition.

Insights and data generated about reading generally fall under one of two rubrics: cognitive or social, implying in essence, that reading is a meaning-extracting or a meaning-constructing process. Clearly, these perspectives imply a dichotomous view. For the purpose of its initial introduction in this chapter, that dichotomous view will be maintained. The task in the initial stages of this chapter is merely to probe what these concepts imply about the nature of reading. As the book progresses, it will become clear that supporting or maintaining a dichotomous perspective is futile. It is presented here merely as a point of departure.

READING AS A COGNITIVE PROCESS

A cognitive process is defined in Webster's as *a set of ordered stages; a set of operations that accomplish some goal.* A cognitive view implies a beginning state, an end state, and intervening transformations. In *The Psychology of Reading and Language Comprehension*, Just and Carpenter (1987) include in their definition:

- what information in the text starts the process
- how long the process takes
- what information was used during the process
- the likely sources of mistakes
- what the reader has learned when the process is finished. (p. 4)

In other words, taking a cognitive perspective means examining the reading process as an intrapersonal problem-solving task that takes place within the brain's knowledge structures. The activity taking place within the brain is the focus of research and theory in this view on the reading process.

Perhaps a few words about problem solving would be helpful at this juncture. Hayes (1989) defines "problem" as "Whenever there is a gap between where you are now and where you want to be, and you don't know how to cross that gap, you have a problem" (p. xii). Hayes (1989) adds that in order to solve the problem, one must represent the gap, "that is, understand the nature of the problem" (p. xii) and then look for a way out. In a cognitive view on reading, the conceptualization of the problem (i.e., the material to be understood) as well as the way out (i.e., processes for understanding) take place "inside the head."

A number of reading models are cognitive in nature. These models view how information from the text is processed into meaning. Figure 1.2, for example, is the LaBerge and Samuels (1974) model. It illustrates how print information is

Figure 1.2.   The LaBerge-Samuels model of human information processing.

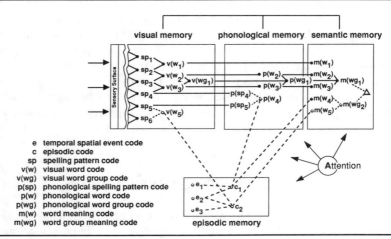

Figure 1.3.   The Just and Carpenter model of reading comprehension.

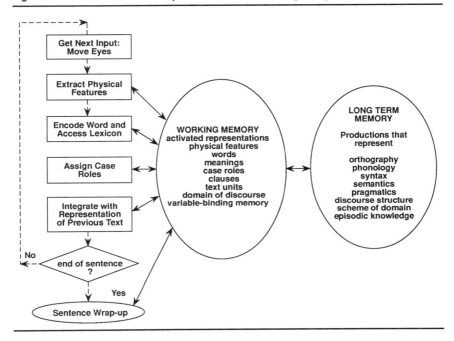

perceived by a reader and then sent to various locations in the brain for processing. This particular model is heavily text-based in nature in that it focuses on characteristics of print as the essence of the process it attempts to describe. Notable about the model is its lack of attention to ''meaning.'' In a sense, the model projects the image that perception is the key factor and that what is understood is not terribly important. In reflecting on the development of the model, however, Samuels (1987, personal communication) explains that the model was developed ''before we believed you really could try to figure out how people understand.''

Another example of a cognitive perspective on reading is that developed by Just and Carpenter (1980) (Figure 1.3). Their model, too, views text as the most critical feature in the understanding of reading. At the same time, it is important to realize that the concept of ''text'' within the Just and Carpenter (1980) view is a much more sophisticated one when compared with the LaBerge and Samuels (1974) view. LaBerge and Samuels implicitly define texts as sets of individual words. The Just and Carpenter view reveals a view of text that includes concepts of cohesion and synthesis.

Notable within the framework of the Just and Carpenter (1980) model is that the process is defined and described as a clearly nonlinear one. In other words, individual readers are active in their selection of portions of the text for processing. This action on their part may take the form of former portions of the text informing latter ones and latter portions of the text informing former ones through feedback.

The critical element in any cognitive view of reading is that it is an individual act. This individual act consists of processing steps that are separate and measurable, although interdependent. Such a view generally implies that the sum of these individual processing steps constitutes the act of reading; furthermore, that as each reader performs in this manner, the output will be the same successful product.

Figure 1.4 is a conceptualization of a cognitive view. This view posits that able readers have processors that act on information in rule-governed ways much like a computer program. Information, in Hayes' (1989) words "the gap," is input in specific ways and the program acts on the information (according to

Figure 1.4.   Reading as a cognitive process.

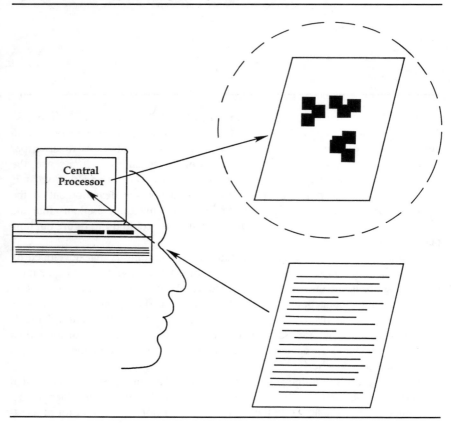

Hayes, "the way out"). The program consists of processing steps written in the usual "if . . . then" format. After the if . . . then statements are completed, the text has been "read" and "understood."

Another reference to Hayes is important at this point. Hayes notes:

> To understand a problem, then, the problem solver creates (imagines) objects and relations in his head which correspond to objects and relations in the externally presented problem. These internal objects and relations are the problem solver's *internal representation* of the problem. Different people may create different internal representations of the same problem. (p. 5)

This phenomenon is represented by the output from the central processor in Figure 1.4. In other words, the internal representation of the text is not a duplicate of the input text, but rather, an individual's intrapersonal conceptualization. The analogy implies, then, that *processing* is, to a large extent generalizable—not unique to particular readers, but that output is individual. This implication is perhaps most concretely vivified by the Carpenter and Just research program since it seeks to generate humanlike responses from "intelligent" computers.

The implications of the cognitive/problem-solving view for second language reading are many and will be discussed in the next section of this chapter. To readers who read in a second language, who try to read in a second language, and/or who teach people to read in a second language, the meaning of "the gap" and "the way out" are already realities.

READING AS A SOCIAL PROCESS

In a 1984 article entitled "Directions in the Sociolinguistic Study of Reading," Bloome and Green state:

> As a social process, reading is used to establish, structure, and maintain social relationships between and among peoples . . . a sociolinguistic perspective on reading requires exploring how reading is used to establish a social context while simultaneously exploring how the social context influences reading praxis and the communication of meaning. (pp. 395–396)

Bloome and Green (1984) include in their discussion that, within this view of the reading process, research and theory target "how reading—and literacy in general—are part of the processes of cultural transmissions, enculturation, and socialization" (p. 396). Figure 1.5 is an attempt to conceptualize this view. Reader 1 and Reader 2 interact with a text and have understandings that overlap.

This view of reading is rooted in the belief that texts are manifestations of

Figure 1.5.   Reading as a social process.

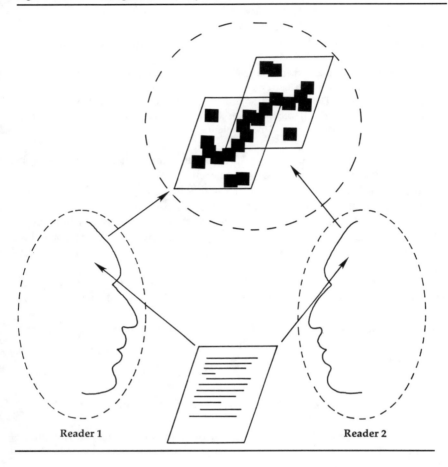

Reader 1   Reader 2

cultures. These manifestations inherently imply socially acquired frames of reference, value systems, the sociopolitical history of the writer, as well as idiosyncratic knowledges and beliefs held between the writer and the implied reader. When texts are viewed as cultural artifacts, they become fluid and open to multiple interpretations. In other words, to contrast the social view with the cognitive one above, the processing of text can be viewed only within a unique cultural context. Each cultural context will bring a different set of values into play. Therefore, each cultural context will provide a different reading of the text.

The view of reading as a social process *entails* a number of assumptions. First, it assumes that there are basically no generic or generalized readers or reading behaviors. That is, there are multiple ''readers'' within one person since each context will influence each reader; that is, a different reader will surface depending on the context. Second, it implies that there are basically no generic or generalized texts. That is, there are multiple ''texts'' within a text since each text consists of a number of implied value systems. Third, this view ultimately implies that seeking generalized principles of text processing is futile since each data collection, for example, is an artifact of place and time. Figure 1.6 is an attempt to conceptualize this view.

There is considerable research and scholarship in support of a social view of reading. Clearly, analyses of classrooms in which minority children must participate reflect that the context or social background from which the learner emerges influences his acquisition of literacy skills. Wells (1986) has documented that when a learner's home environment does not mesh with the school environment (generally the majority culture), the learner's attainment of literacy skills from the majority culture's point of view is retarded. The critical point here is that this retardation is not the result of a cognitive deficit, but rather the result of the conflict between home and school cultures; in other words, the result of a social mismatch.

But classroom settings are not the only manifestations of literacy as a social process. Another very clear example is in literary analysis or text interpretation. In that process interpreters expect that appropriate decoding has taken place. The interpretive process ensues from different perspectives such as feminism or Marxism (clearly different social points of view) or from different historical points of view such as a 20th-century interpretation of an 18th-century conflict.

Such views are widely held about literacy in general. It is widely accepted that indeed ''literacy'' entails these many facets and that these facets are fluid in nature—not strictly structured.

As mentioned briefly above, anyone who has had the experience of either reading in a second language or trying to teach others to read in a second language intuitively understands the meaning of ''reading as a social process.'' The task of the next section of the chapter is to translate some of the intuitions about both the social and the cognitive perspectives on reading into explicit hypotheses about second language reading.

IMPLICATIONS OF THE COGNITIVE AND SOCIAL VIEWS ON READING FROM A SECOND LANGUAGE PERSPECTIVE

Chapters Three and Four provide detailed analyses of the cognitive and social views of reading. These analyses are embedded in text-driven and reader-based views of the reading process and are generated from new as well as from previously published data. The function of the latter portions of this chapter is, therefore, to mention and to explore broadly some of the implications of these views so that they lead toward more principled research and instruction in second language reading.

Figure 1.6. Reading from a sociolinguistic perspective.

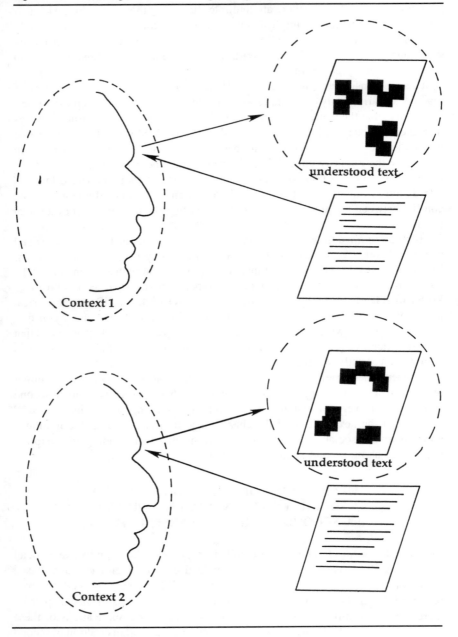

The Cognitive View

The view of reading as a cognitive process conceptualized in Figure 1.4 above posits a central processor that is set or predetermined as well as input data also established and routinized—much as numerical data must be input into a book-keeping program in a set format. The view also posits that fluent readers input information in a set fashion so that operations may be performed on them. The reason that the image of a computer is used here is because a computer is preset to receive certain kinds of information in certain ways. The preset nature in reading is determined by the nature of texts and the learned ways of dealing with such texts in the native tongue context.

A concrete example clarifies the point. The rules of English, for example, limit *which* words and *what* type of words may follow the definite article *the*. *The* introduces a noun or adjective phrase; for example, *the apple*; *the juicy, red apple*. The word *the* does not introduce verb phrases; for example, *the run too fast* is not an admissible combination in English. A native speaker of English possesses or has competence in these rules. These rules are applied during linguistic activities such as reading, enabling readers to anticipate, moment by moment, information that is being input. In fact, this anticipatory ability becomes, through the acquisition of the mother tongue, an innate cognitive ability. In other words, native speakers' cognition becomes hardwired (to use a computing term) to accommodate input information in a particular way.

In the second language situation, this preset program is already wired in cognitively. It is "English-speaking" or "Hindu-speaking" or "German-speaking," for example. The input, however, to that program in the processor is not "English-speaking" or "Hindu-speaking" or "German-speaking." That input is characterized by another language that may be radically different from the processor language. To go back to the previous example with the definite article *the*: If that same English-speaking reader applied the English-speaking rules of *the* introducing noun and adjective phrases, she may encounter success in reading German on any number of occasions; for example, *der Apfel*; *der rote, saftige Apfel*. However, when she encounters *der von dem Baum fallende Apfel* (the from the tree falling apple), her processor program (which is English-speaking) fails since it is not equipped with anticipatory rules that accommodate a prepositional phrase after a definite article. While this is just one simple example it serves to highlight the potential complications and cognitive restructuring involved in reading second language texts.

The Social View

A social view on reading posits that reading performs a socializing function. In other words, it enculturates its readers and makes them belong to a group. This view also posits that texts are social and cultural artifacts reflecting group values and norms. A social view on reading attempts to account for many of the "interpretive" dimensions of definitions of reading.

Concrete examples are helpful at this juncture. If the *National Enquirer* is mentioned, Americans react in any number of ways. Some respond with embarrassed laughter, others with pompous indignation; some react with "what inquiring minds want to know," others with "oh, that supermarket trash." Whatever the response, each expresses social values. Rarely do the responses refer explicitly to the linguistic content of the *National Enquirer* but allude somehow to its general nature and, perhaps more importantly, to the general nature of its readers. Certainly no educated person or person implying such education would quote from the *National Enquirer* for serious information. Similar things might be said about *People Magazine* or *Us*. In like manner, a political conservative would not quickly turn to *The Atlantic Monthly* for information to buttress his arguments on the economy nor would a political liberal quote *The National Review* freely. These magazines all communicate certain social values that the reader needs to at least perceive in order to attempt an interpretation. It is important to note here, that in order to understand the previous paragraph, one must have knowledge of U.S. publications over and above linguistic skills in the English language. In like manner, if *Saturday Night* had been used as an example, perhaps a Canadian reader would have gained greater understanding of the paragraph.

In the second language situation, however, a second language reader is rarely equipped with the knowledge to perceive in a culturally authentic, culturally specific way. In other words, a text is a text is a text. A second language reader frequently has very clear linguistic skills. Rarely does a second language reader have finely honed sociocultural skills. The end result—comprehension—is based on *linguistic* data.

Another example serves to illustrate the social view of reading. If a second language reader reads "Mike is a manic-depressive," he may interpret this utterance as "a man by the name of Mike has a mental disease that causes him to experience drastic shifts in mood and attitude that are characterized by swings of extreme elation to utter despair." Depending on the reader, he or she may respond neutrally in a clinical sense (as if reading the sentence in a medical casebook) or may respond affectively if he or she has some personal experience with the disease. The second language reader may not be able to respond on a sociocultural level: That level that would call the statement into question if it appeared in a weekly tabloid under the picture of a prize fighter by the name of Tyson. In other words, a social view argues that words and sentences are not enough. It argues that a second language reader, in order to be successful, must somehow gain access to implicit information possessed by members of the social group for which the text was intended.

TOWARD A SYNTHESIS: A SOCIOCOGNITIVE VIEW
OF SECOND LANGUAGE READING

Viewing second language literacy from its cognitive and then from its social perspective is meant neither to dichotomize nor to oversimplify the process of second language reading. Rather it is meant to organize and to provide a lens for observing learners and conducting research. If the objective is to provide easier pathways toward principled language instruction, teachers and researchers will need an integration of the perspectives into a holistic view.

The model in Figure 1.7 is an attempt toward such an integration. The process as illustrated includes a different concept of text. Text is no longer characterized simply by its linguistic elements (semantics and syntax), but also by its structure, its pragmatic nature, its intentionality, its content, and its topic. These sets of features interact with the reader in process. The model also posits that readers are not static entities, but are individuals who change and react differentially—in other words, are different readers at different times. The character of these interactions yields a selection of differential features for the processing of the text. Simply put, certain readers ''see'' different things in texts. They make individual decisions about what is important in texts and make sense of it or ''reconstruct'' it according to those decisions. As a result, the input text and the output text are, in this integrated view, different entities.

This perspective on understanding is not a new one. It has not been fully explored nor substantiated, however, within a second language framework.

Figure 1.7.   Comprehension: A reader-based perspective.

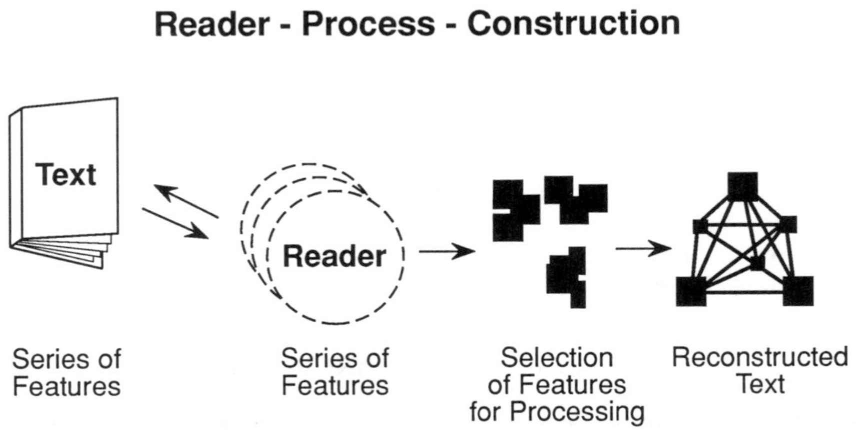

Reader - Process - Construction

Series of	Series of	Selection	Reconstructed
Features	Features	of Features	Text
		for Processing	

Critical within the second language framework is that readers and the texts they encounter represent separate and distinct social entities. Second language readers approach a text from their first language framework. This framework is not the framework from which the intended audience for the text interprets. Hence, before second language readers even reach a text, an inherent conflict exists. This conflict exists from microlevel features of text (e.g., orthography) through grammatical structures (is adverb placement similar in the two languages?) to the social nature of access to literacy (I am female; am I supposed to be reading this? or What is meant by *supermarket tabloid*?).

It is important at this juncture to consider research for a moment and the philosophy of science. The process under discussion is literacy, which seems to be both social and cognitive in nature. Therefore, to represent it appropriately models must be built that are both social and cognitive in nature. In addition, any interpretation of research must be made within that context. In other words, if research is conducted from only *one* view, findings are automatically skewed. Concretely expressed: If a cognitive question is asked such as *Are there any differences between native and nonnative highly proficient processing strategies on a technical text?* and native and nonnative readers are used without considering social background, what can the research actually say? Or if a social question is posed, such as *Are certain ethnic groups able to succeed at literacy acquisition better than others?*, without acknowledging very real cognitive differences in text processing depending upon L1 literacy background, what enlightenment does the research provide? There are a number of studies that generically lump L2 readers and collect "cognitive" data without considering L2 social background. Concomitantly, there are studies that look at social interactions between and among children, for example, and fail to acknowledge that some of the children or subjects have word recognition problems, or are not as intelligent, or come from less compatible literacy backgrounds. The point is that when intending to understand a process, researchers try to simplify it—to get to its essence. But to simplify should not imply making a process *simplistic*. No language comprehension process is *simplistic*.

The themes of information processing, problem solving, cognitive, social, and sociocognitive used in this chapter will appear again and again throughout the pages that follow. Clarifying the nature of second language reading so that it leads to both principled research and principled instruction lies in understanding each perspective as thoroughly as possible and then in integrating each into a coherent and consistent view.

ASSUMPTIONS AND RESEARCH METHODS

The theory and integrated perspective posited in this book are based on a number of assumptions. The first assumption is that learner-generated data are critical. While this assumption seems rather obvious, it is clear that many books in second language instruction have been published that are based on few, if any, data in the empirical sense. The second assumption is that reading development and reading proficiency exist. That is, that there are various stages and competencies through which learners progress. Assumption three is that thinking through issues in theory and research—either at the individual teacher level or at the profession-as-a-whole level—leads to more principled language instruction. The fourth assumption is the most salient: Research and theory must lead to practical implications and applications because what is most important is effective and efficient student learning.

These assumptions imply a number of research tools. The first and principal research tool used in developing the arguments in these pages is learner-generated immediate recall to operationalize comprehension. Immediate recall in contrast to traditional questioning techniques, provides the more sensitive measure of reading comprehension because it is continuous rather than discrete (Kamil, 1988, personal communication). In other words, recall provides a picture of learner processes. Another research tool used is the observation of learner processing strategies via eye movement. These learner-generated data illustrate microlevel strategies used by individual readers *during* reading. A third tool for developing insight into the nature of second language reading is self-report. Self-report data are also used in this book to provide a reality check, particularly in terms of classroom behaviors.

2

The Data Base in Second Language Reading

INTRODUCTION

This book aims toward the development of more principled teaching and research in the area of reading in a second language. The previous chapter provided the sociocognitive backdrop against which the arguments in this book are set forth. This chapter also provides a backdrop; that is, the backdrop of empirical research that has been conducted since the mid-1970s—the onset of concepts of communicative language teaching.

The stage setting has a number of dimensions. The first is the nature of the theory of reading and literacy held by second language researchers. The second dimension is the nature of the variables considered to be important in the second language reading process and the ways in which these variables have been investigated. The third is the nature of the commonalities and consistencies between and among research studies. All of these dimensions must be explored in order to provide a fairly comprehensive view of the data base in second language reading as well as to provide a base from which to evaluate the ideas, theory, and research in this book. At the outset, it is important, however, to define the term "data base." A data base is constituted by systematically documented evidence. It is also inclusive. In other words, it contains all attempts to collect evidence about a phenomenon—not just those efforts to support a particular view on or explication of a phenomenon.

Evidence of the reading process can only be found by probing *readers*. While this comment may seem rather obvious, the research area of second language has been plagued by books and articles arguing the nature of language processes, yet providing no evidence for those processes. Hence, the first step in understanding the data base in second language reading is to locate it. This is the task of the first part of this chapter: to differentiate between research reports and clinical/ reflective reports on second language reading.

In addition to defining the term "data base," an examination of the context in which research has been generated is critical. Indeed, the catchword of the latter years of the 20th century seems to be *context*. Context is used to explain, to make excuses for, and to clarify. Cognitive psychologists, sociologists, educators, and theorists in other academic areas seem to agree that knowledge does not exist in a vacuum, but is generated and interpreted through theoretical views. Understanding any research area, then, entails understanding the fundamental views that the instigator of a research study holds. This view is certainly not a revolutionary one. In fact, second language educators, Richterich and Chancerel (1980), argue the matter this way with regard to data collection:

> Methods of collection . . . are simply channels of communication introduced for the purpose of causing the information to emerge so that it can be made use of. As a result, they make it figurable: a questionnaire can explore only what the questions explore . . . (p. 54)

In like manner they add that:

> A questionnaire may be used for any objective collection of data. However, the manner in which the question is put influences the answer. (p. 61)

In other words, if a question always implies an answer, then it is important to understand the genesis of the question.

The genesis of a research question lies in the theoretical framework of the researcher. Put in concrete terms, the intellectual root of a research study is found in the review of the literature. Hence, in order to make generalized statements about the research base in second language reading, an analysis of reviews of literature is appropriate. This analysis constitutes the next section of this chapter.

The principal goal of this chapter is not, however, simply to focus on theoretical frameworks. The principal goal is to make the data base in second language reading visible and accessible. Hence, the major portion of the chapter reviews the set of publications published within scholarly journals and books since 1974 that can be considered to be contributions to "evidence" of the second language reading process. Each of these studies has been categorized according to its major thrust. These categories are: (a) word recognition; (b) background knowledge; (c) text-structure analyses; (d) oral-aural factors; (e) syntactic factors; (f) cross-lingual processing strategies; (g) metacognitive strategies (h) testing methods; and (i) instruction. The third section of this chapter highlights difficulties in synthesizing these studies. It points out that the wide array of subject groups studied, experimental tasks, and methodologies employed makes such a synthesis extremely difficult.

THE NATURE OF THE DATA BASE

In order to begin the investigation, a version of a methodology used by Guthrie, Seifert, and Mosberg in a 1983 *Reading Research Quarterly* article was used. *First*, the following second language (L2) journals were isolated for perusal: *Applied Linguistics, Canadian Modern Language Review, English Language Teaching Journal, Foreign Language Annals, French Review, Hispania, International Review of Applied Linguistics in Language Teaching, Language Learning, Language Testing, Modern Language Journal, Reading in a Foreign Language, RELC Journal, System, Studies in Second Language Acquisition, TESOL Quarterly, Unterrichtspraxis, Working Papers in Linguistics and Language Teaching, ON TESOL* volumes, as well as the following native language (L1) journals: *Applied Psycholinguistics, Canadian Journal of Psychology, Journal of Reading, Journal of Reading Behavior, Reading Research Quarterly, The Reading Teacher,* and the *Yearbooks of the National Reading Conference.* These publications were selected because they are of greatest interest to and accessed by teachers and researchers in the area of second language learning in the United States, Canada, and English-speaking Europe and Asia. Several European journals were discounted from the review due to their general inaccessibility in North America. *Second,* the ERIC system was searched for listings of publications not included in the above journals in order to locate any books and collections of essays published on the topic of reading in a foreign language. This search uncovered authored and edited books by: Alderson and Urquhart (1984), Barnitz (1985), Berger and Haider (1981), Bruder and Henderson (1986), Carrell, Devine, and Eskey (1988), Cates and Swaffar (1979), Devine, Carrell, and Eskey (1987), Dubin, Eskey, and Grabe (1986), Hudelson (1981), Kellerman (1981), Mackey, Barkman, and Jordan (1979), Nuttall (1982), Pugh and Ulijn (1984), Twyford, Diehl, and Feathers (1981), Ulijn and Pugh (1985), and Wallace (1986). In addition, three edited volumes of general second language acquisition contained chapters on reading. In summary, these publications provided the resources for data collection. In other words, they are the subject pool for this discussion.

"Models of the Reading Process" (Samuels & Kamil, 1984) provided the independent variables, that is, the theoretical frameworks, for the study: Gough (1972), Goodman (1968), Smith (1971), Just and Carpenter (1980), Kintsch (1974), LaBerge and Samuels (1974), Rumelhart (1977), Stanovich (1980), and Van Dijk (1979). An article by Massaro (1984), "Building and Testing Models of Reading Processes," provided an additional theory based on the research of McConkie and Rayner (1975). In summary, the work of 12 theoreticians comprised the independent variables.

The data were collected by conducting citation counts within the reference sections of all articles and books in the pool. These counts were developed from the *total* number of articles found within the *general* topic of reading in a second language and included breakdowns according to the number of references to authors of the L1 models or theories. Next, the number of research articles was determined. A research article within the context of this chapter is defined as one in which the authors collected, reported, analyzed, and inferred from data on the *reading* process from subjects reading in a nonnative language.

Table 2.1 notes the total number of articles that deal explicitly with second language reading within selected journals from 1974 to 1988. It also includes the number of research articles, the total number of citations, and lists the number of references to all authors of L1 models and/or theories.

An examination of Table 2.1 indicates that the psycholinguistic model (Goodman, 1968; Smith, 1971) has been the overwhelming conceptual framework within second language reading for this period. In fact, of the L1 citations ($N = 562$), 66.4 percent of them refer to either Goodman or Smith ($N = 373$), more than all of the citations on the other models combined ($N = 189$). The most frequently cited Goodman works are "Analysis of oral reading miscues: Applied psycholinguistics" (1969); *The psycholinguistic nature of the reading process* (1968); and "Reading: A psycholinguistic guessing game" (1967). Other Goodman citations are scattered across articles from 1967 through 1979. The overwhelming majority of Smith citations are from *Understanding Reading* (1971).

An awareness of word recognition or text based models such as those advanced by Gough (1972) and LaBerge and Samuels (1974) ($N = 34$) or of interactive models such as those advanced by Just and Carpenter (1980) and Stanovich (1980) ($N = 26$) is essentially nonexistent within the second language research base. The appearance of Carrell, Devine, and Eskey (1988) indicates a shift, however, in this theoretical direction. The only other models recognized with any frequency are the following: (a) Rumelhart (1977) ($N = 66$) in a relatively broad representation of journals in the subject pool; and (b) Kintsch (1974) ($N = 39$) principally, in *TESOL Quarterly* and in *Applied Linguistics*.

Finally, and perhaps most importantly, Table 2.1 indicates that approximately 34 percent ($N = 121$) of the total articles ($N = 352$) in the pool fit the definition of *research*.

One of the major findings in this examination of the literature is the dominance of the psycholinguistic model exemplified by the writings of Goodman (1968) and Smith (1971). It is remarkable that an area of disciplined inquiry such as reading in a second language could be so dominated by one conceptual framework. There may be two explanations for this phenomenon. It may be that academicians in this field have agreed that the psycholinguistic framework provides the most viable explanation of reading a second language. Another is that there is a basic lack of awareness and perception of the capabilities of models other than those of Goodman (1968) and Smith (1971) to explain second language reading phenomena. Since unanimity is rare in any academic area, the latter explanation is more convincing.

The dominance of the psycholinguistic framework à la Goodman (1968) and Smith (1971) in second language reading is slightly disturbing for a number of reasons. First, it is not a dominant model in L1 reading research. Publications by Goodman and Smith do not appear in the top 41 most frequently cited articles devoted to the reading process in L1 (Guthrie et al., 1983). In fact, as Kamil (1984) comments:

> It is difficult to know what to say about Frank Smith's (1971) seminal work describing reading as a psycholinguistic process. It is not so much a model of reading as it is a description of the linguistic and cognitive processes that any decent model of reading will need to take into account . . . But to call it a model of reading would misrepresent Smith's aim. (p. 187)

In another publication, Kamil (1986) remarks:

> the generality of the [Goodman] model has also made it difficult to verify in a scientific sense. (p. 74)

Of greater irony is that models essentially ignored in L2, as illustrated by the data in Table 2.1, appear with great frequency in L1 research (Guthrie et al., 1983). Table 2.1 indicates that the Rumelhart (1977) and Kintsch (1974) models are cited generally either by researchers in English as a Second Language (ESL) or by researchers in Europe. In other words, awareness of these models by traditional foreign language educators in North America seems to be minimal.

The data base in second language reading research is certainly meager. In contrast to L1 where literally thousands of research studies have been conducted, the present analysis as of 1986 found only 121 such data collections to have been conducted in L2 in a little over a decade.

THE DATA BASE

After the basic descriptive data indicated in Table 2.1 were collected and analyzed, the list of empirically based studies was separated from the clinical pieces. Each one of the studies was then examined in terms of its generalized intent stated *explicitly* by the author. Researchers' central concerns grouped into nine categories: word recognition; background knowledge factors; text-structure analyses; oral-aural factors; syntactic features; cross-lingual processing strategies; metacognitive strategies; testing methods; and instruction. Tables 2.2 through 2.10 outline major components and findings in each of the 121 research studies.

Table 2.1. Total Articles Devoted to the Topic of Second Language Reading, 1974–1988, with a Breakdown according to Number of Research Articles and Citations of Reading Models.

Journals	Total Articles	Research Articles	Total Citations	Carpenter	Goodman	Gough	Just	Kintsch	LaBerge	McConkie	Rayner	Rumelhart	Samuels	Smith	Stanovich	Van Dijk
Foreign Language Annals	21	2	243	0	14	0	0	1	0	0	0	1	1	8	0	0
TESOL Quarterly	22	10	294	0	17	0	0	5	0	0	0	8	0	10	0	4
Language Learning	16	15	313	0	23	2	0	0	2	0	0	2	0	10	0	4
English Language Teaching Journal	21	5	136	0	5	0	0	0	0	0	0	0	0	5	0	1
Reading in a Foreign Language	16	3	233	1	7	0	0	1	0	0	0	4	0	0	0	0
Modern Language Journal	18	8	404	0	12	1	1	1	1	0	0	3	1	3	0	2
System	15	6	409	0	9	1	0	0	0	1	0	1	0	7	0	0
Canadian Modern Language Review	18	3	157	0	10	0	0	2	0	0	0	0	1	2	0	0
Applied Linguistics	4	0	71	1	1	0	0	11	1	0	0	2	0	0	0	0
Int'l Review of Appl. Linguistics	4	1	34	1	1	0	0	0	0	0	0	0	0	0	0	0
Others	3	3	84	0	3	0	0	0	0	0	0	0	0	4	1	0
Applied Psycholinguistics	1	1	21	0	0	0	0	1	0	0	1	0	0	0	0	0
Language Testing	1	1	9	0	0	0	0	0	0	0	0	0	0	0	0	0
Unterrichtspraxis	10	1	130	0	3	0	0	1	0	0	0	1	0	1	0	1
Hispania	3	0	27	0	4	0	0	0	0	0	0	1	0	4	0	0
French Review	1	0	0	0	0	0	0	1	0	0	0	0	0	0	0	0
RELC Journal	6	5	77	0	8	0	0	0	0	0	0	1	0	1	0	1
Studies in Second Language Acq.	1	1	12	0	0	0	0	0	0	0	0	0	0	0	0	0
J. of Verbal Learning/Behavior	0	0	0	0	0	0	0	0	0	0	0	0	0	0	0	0
Canadian Journal of Psychology	1	1	18	0	0	0	0	0	0	0	1	0	0	0	0	6
Reading Teacher	17	3	233	0	3	0	0	0	0	0	0	1	1	1	0	0
Journal of Reading	4	2	72	0	1	0	0	1	0	0	0	0	0	0	0	0
Reading Research Quarterly	2	2	57	0	0	0	0	0	0	0	0	1	0	0	0	0
Journal of Reading Behavior	3	1	35	0	2	0	0	0	0	0	0	0	0	0	0	0

On TESOL Volumes	14	7	207	0	11	0	0	0	1	0	0	0	0	5	0	0
NRC Yearbook	4	4	67	0	0	0	0	1	0	0	0	2	0	0	0	1
BOOKS (authored and edited)																
Devine, Carrell, & Eskey	12	5	377	0	9	2	2	2	2	0	0	8	1	5	1	1
Bruder & Henderson	N/A	N/A	34	0	3	0	0	0	0	0	1	1	0	2	0	0
Barnitz	N/A	N/A	218	0	5	0	0	1	0	0	0	1	0	1	0	0
Carrell, Devine, & Eskey	17	6	607	0	24	3	1	1	3	0	0	18	4	7	9	0
Cates & Swaffar	N/A	N/A	58	1	1	0	0	0	0	0	0	0	0	1	0	0
Alderson & Urquhart	14	6	316	0	4	0	1	1	0	1	1	3	0	2	0	1
Pugh & Ulijn (1984)	22	5	405	0	2	0	3	2	0	1	0	1	0	3	1	1
Kellerman	N/A	N/A	39	0	1	0	0	0	0	0	0	0	0	1	0	0
Mackey, Barkman, & Jordan	13	1	176	0	8	1	0	0	0	0	0	0	0	3	0	0
Berger & Haider	11	1	265	0	10	0	0	1	1	0	0	0	0	6	0	0
Hudelson	10	7	115	0	18	0	0	0	0	0	0	0	0	3	0	0
Twyford, Diehl, & Feathers	7	1	131	0	16	0	0	0	1	0	0	1	0	9	0	0
Ulijn & Pugh (1985)	20	4	336	0	8	0	0	4	0	0	0	2	0	5	0	0
Dubin, Eskey, & Grabe	N/A	N/A	283	0	3	1	0	0	0	0	0	3	3	6	3	1
Wallace	N/A	N/A	99	0	4	0	0	0	0	0	0	0	0	4	0	0
Nuttall	N/A	N/A	67	0	1	0	0	0	0	0	0	0	0	2	0	0
Total	352	121	6869	3	251	10	8	39	12	3	4	66	12	122	15	17

Table 2.2. Word Recognition.

Investigators	Subjects	Independent Variable	Dependent Variable	Findings
Brown & Haynes, 1985	62 adult ESL learners (Japanese, Spanish, and Arabic speakers)	1. pretests on component skills 2. visual, discrimination of abstract figures 3. word, pseudo-word, nonsense string identification	1. reaction times 2. error rates	differences in visual and orthographic processing based on literacy background
Favreau & Segalowitz, 1982	30 Francophone and 30 Anglophone fluent bilingual adults	variable dominance of French or English or equal reading rates in L1 & L2	1. optimal reading rate: reading rate in wpm and M-C scores 2. optimal listening rate: self-determined pace in wpm and M-C scores	1. Bilinguals exhibiting language dominance listened at slower rates in L2 2. Nonlanguage dominant bilinguals read and listen at equivalent rates in L1 & L2 3. Reading and listening specific factors do not appear to be independent 4. Real processing differences may exist
Favreau, Komoda, & Segalowitz, 1980				
Study One	12 English-French bilinguals	1. words 2. anagrams 3. letters with single letter stimuli	number of errors	no word superiority effect with L2 stimuli; however, an effect was found with L1 stimuli
Study Two	9 English-French speakers	words as stimuli	number of errors	additional processing time required to demonstrate a word superiority effect

Hatch, et al., 1974

	Subjects	Procedure	Measure	Results
Study One	40 adult native speakers of English; 40 advanced ESL learners	4 passages of differential syntactic and semantic complexity	scores on crossing letters out of words	1. both ESL and NS groups attended more to content words than to function words 2. overall rate of cancellation remained constant as passage difficulty increased for NSs, but decreased for ESL Ss as passage difficulty increased 3. ratio of function words to content words cancelled was not influenced by passage difficulty
Study Two	12 elementary ESL students; 12 intermediate ESL students; 12 speakers of English	2 passages; one focused on "e", one on "c" (alone and in digraph)	percentage of correct crossouts	1. all Ss cancelled more letters in content than in function words; significant interactions obtained between subject groups and word type 2. "c/e" letter variable was significant
Study Three	18 elementary ESL students; 18 intermediate ESL students	2 passages; one focused on "a", one on "o" in stressed and unstressed syllables	percentage of correct crossouts	1. ESL groups marked more unstressed vowels than did NSs 2. more "o's" than "a's" were marked
Hayes, 1988 Study One	17 native readers of Chinese; 17 nonnative readers of Chinese	1. proficiency level (native or nonnative) 2. processing strategies (phonological, graphic, semantic)	word (character) recognition test	1. phonological encoding was the primary strategy for native readers 2. nonnative readers used a mixed strategy of phonological and graphic encoding
Study Two	"	"	word (character) recognition test disguised within a sentence validity test	1. native readers used a mix of graphic and semantic strategies 2. nonnative readers used primarily a graphic strategy

Table 2.2. Word Recognition (cont.).

Investigators	Subjects	Independent Variable	Dependent Variable	Findings
Haynes, 1981	63 adult ESL students (speakers of Japanese, Spanish, French, and Arabic)	2 passages of parallel story structure and syntax containing 2 nonsense words	guessing success for unknown words in a text	1. all groups profited more from local context clues than from global clues 2. graphemic features may override syntax 3. ESL readers attend to word structure
Koda, 1987	26 Japanese university students	silent reading decoding strategies: phonological vs. logographic word decoding	recognition of nonsense words matched to memorized pictures	reading strategies specific to L1 orthography are transferred to L2 reading with a different orthography
Meara, 1984	native speakers of English; nonnative speakers of English	1. word length 2. word frequency 3. morphological complexity	1. percentage of words correctly identified 2. scores on letter cancellation task	1. certain types of words caused disproportionate difficulty for nonnative speakers 2. Spanish speakers recognize words more slowly in L1 than do English speakers in L1 3. English speakers rely more heavily on beginnings and endings of words; Spanish speakers show no effect
Walker, 1983	100 ESL speakers of Spanish	10 reading strategies, of which 7 were statistically significant	frequency	1. pronouncing strategy used most frequently 2. ignoring strategy used least frequently

Word Recognition

Nine studies comprise the data base in second language word recognition investigations: Brown and Haynes (1985), Favreau and Segalowitz (1982), Favreau, Komoda, and Segalowitz (1980), Hatch, Polin, and Part (1974), Hayes (1988), Haynes (1981), Koda (1987), Meara (1984), and Walker (1983). They are outlined in Table 2.2. Both Favreau et al. studies employed English/French bilingual populations. The Hatch et al. study investigated English as a Second Language readers at a number of proficiency levels as did Walker's. Haynes and Brown also used an ESL adult population, but did isolate the language backgrounds of subjects. Two of the subject groups in both of Haynes' studies stemmed from non-Roman orthographic backgrounds, namely, Arabic and Japanese; Koda used Japanese readers, while Hayes investigated Chinese readers.

Findings from these studies are fairly consistent. The Favreau studies as well as Brown and Haynes basically examined processing times and error rates in the identification of words across languages. They found processing speeds dependent upon fluency as well as familiarity with orthography. The remainder of the studies, Hayes, Haynes, Hatch et al., Koda, and Walker found evidence supporting phonological factors in word recognition. Second language readers attended to graphemic features which frequently overrode an attention to meaning or syntax.

Clearly, few studies have been conducted that have concerned themselves with the processes second language readers employ in order to recognize words. In a research area which has been heavily dependent upon the first language reading base, this finding is rather surprising. First-language reading research has a considerable volume of word recognition studies. One of the reasons for the dearth of such studies in second language reading has been perhaps the belief in the Universals Hypothesis—in other words, that all learners regardless of language background use the same cognitive processes to come to know words. Yet, this assumption has come into question recently (see Cross-lingual Processing Strategies below).

Interestingly, these word recognition studies do lend themselves to generalizability to the extent that they employed similar research designs and data collection techniques—principally reaction time measures and error rate analyses. However, these studies lose generalizability to the extent that they do not describe the proficiency levels of their subjects, use both single word stimuli as well as full text stimuli, and for the most part, define subject groups *generically* rather than explicitly stating the word recognition behaviors exhibited by individual language background subjects.

Background Knowledge

A considerable number of recent studies have revealed the importance of background knowledge within the comprehension process in a second language. This finding is hardly surprising since a preponderance of first language studies have

Table 2.3. Background Knowledge.

Investigators	Subjects	Independent Variable	Dependent Variable	Findings
Adams, 1982	124 learners of French; 174 psychology students	presence or absence of a script activator	target word recognition in a variety of contexts	the presence of a script activator yielded a higher comprehension score
Alderson & Urquhart, 1988				
Study One	groups of students in: finance (15), engineering (11), math/physics (6), and the humanities (5)	variable text comprehension in areas of specialization vs. nonspecialization	cloze scores on five texts: two in engineering, two in economics, and one "general"	subjects tested better in their own fields
Study Two	students in: finance (24), engineering (20), science and math (30) (a broader group than in Study One), and liberal arts (19)	same as for Study One	cloze testing and short-answer responses to text comprehension questions on the same texts as in Study One	1. specialists outperformed nonspecialists in their fields 2. high correlation between scores and specialization 3. overall linguistic proficiency not a predictor
Campbell, 1981	1 native speaker (low achiever); 1 ESL learner	1. cloze test 2. explanation for choice	scores on a cloze test and self report	1. the major difference between the learners lies in the contextual area of reading 2. absorbing the language and culture of the society in which s/he lives gave the native speaker a definite advantage in reading English texts 3. when the contextual framework is largely supplied within the school situation and the language of the text is literal, the ESL learner coped adequately, although not perhaps as well as his/her oral reading suggested

Study	Sample	Variables	Measures	Findings
Carrell, 1983	48 native speakers of English; 66 advanced ESL; 42 intermediate ESL	different background contexts based on the presence or absence of: 1. a title and picture 2. concrete lexical items 3. familiarity with content area	percentage of idea units recalled in English	nonnative readers show no significant effects from different background contexts
Carrell & Wallace, 1983	36 native English speakers; 50 advanced ESL learners; 26 high intermediate ESL learners	1. proficiency levels 2. context vs. no context 3. three degrees of familiarity	1. comprehension ratings 2. recall scores	1. natives used context more profitably than nonnatives 2. nonnatives not sensitive to passage difficulty
Carrell, 1987	28 ESL learners of Muslim background; 24 ESL learners of Catholic Spanish-speaking background	1. cultural background 2. familiar/unfamiliar organizational frame	1. scores on M-C tests 2. recall scores 3. debriefing questionnaires	content knowledge more significant in comprehension than knowledge of text structure
Connor, 1984	10 speakers of English; 11 Japanese ESL learners; 10 Spanish ESL learners	nationality	recall scores on superordinate and subordinate propositions	1. no relationship between language background and recall of subordinate ideas 2. native speakers recalled more ideas 3. native speakers recalled more propositions than ESL speakers
Hudson, 1982	93 ESL learners at 3 proficiency levels	3 methods of intervention: prereading activities: 1. visuals and questions 2. vocabulary 3. read-test/read-test	test scores	1. advanced level students are better able to use nonvisual information than beginners 2. type of treatment has a greater effect at the beginning and intermediate levels than at advanced levels

Table 2.3. Background Knowledge (cont.).

Investigators	Subjects	Independent Variable	Dependent Variable	Findings
Johnson, 1982	72 advanced ESL students of 23 nationalities	4 types of vocabulary availability on familiar vs. unfamiliar passages	recall	1. familiarity with topic predicted recall 2. vocabulary treatments had no effect on recall
Johnson, 1981	46 Iranian ESL adult learners; 19 native English speakers	adapted and unadapted stories from Iranian and American folklore	recall	1. cultural origin of text had more of an impact on comprehension than syntactic or semantic complexity for ESL students 2. topic and linguistic complexity affected native English readers
Lee, 1986	320 adult learners of Spanish	3 components of background knowledge: 1. context 2. transparency 3. familiarity [replication of Carrell, 1983]	recall in native language	1. all 3 components of background knowledge affect comprehension 2. no one component affects comprehension uniformly across the other components 3. the interaction among these 3 components is complex 4. Carrell's findings dubious since comprehension was assessed in the target language
Mohammed & Swales, 1984	12 adult ESL speakers; native speakers of English	proficiency and levels within several scientific fields	speed of completion of a mechanical task	field familiarity is a better predictor of comprehension than language proficiency
Nunan, 1985	100 ESL students at 2 proficiency levels	familiar vs. unfamiliar topics	cloze scores	topic familiarity aids the use of cohesive ties
Olah, 1984	ESP students	general vs. topic knowledge for specific text	translation success	grammatical difficulties may prevent the understanding of a sentence or text; their absence, however, is not a guarantee of full understanding

Study	Subjects	Variables	Measures	Findings
Omaggio, 1979	664 learners of French	1. 6 levels of pictorial content 2. 3 levels of textual materials	1. resumé 2. 20-item test of recognition knowledge	pictures facilitated comprehension
Parry, 1987	20 seminary students from 12 African tribes learning ESL as first literate language	activation of correct schemata during reading	1. supplying synonyms/definitions of words in context 2. comprehension questions	incorrect schemata activated by misinterpreted context as shown by incorrect word definitions
Perkins & Angelis, 1985	33 advanced ESL learners of 9 western and non-western language backgrounds	graphic concept stimuli	M-C reading comprehension test	no differences between the Spanish and Arabic language groups in concept formation
Steffenson et al., 1979	19 Indian adults; 20 U.S. adults	2 passages: one of U.S. and one of Indian content	1. reading time 2. written recall 3. recall of important vs. unimportant information 4. modifications of text in recall	1. text corresponding with speakers' native background knowledge was read more quickly 2. native speakers supplied appropriate elaborations for native passages 3. distortions were produced for nonnative passage 4. recall higher for native passage
Zuck & Zuck, 1984	6 native and nonnative English speaking biology specialists; 10 native and nonnative English speaking ESL teachers	texts about biology or botany	1. perception of the difficulty of the text; 2. key words and phrases essential to the understanding of the passage 3. choice of comprehension questions	there may be systematic variation between specialists and non-specialists in requests for definitions, recognition of certainty of claim, local vs. global questions, implicit vs. explicit information, and explicit use of rhetorical information to simplify

yielded parallel results. The background knowledge studies outlined in Table 2.3 may be subdivided for discussion into several categories. First, there are those studies that have examined "cultural background" and have blocked subjects within experimental designs according to ethnic background. Second, there are studies that have examined "topic knowledge" background, generally blocking on that particular variable along with proficiency level. Third, a number of training studies have investigated the manner and type of "background knowledge" that might be given to readers in order to increase comprehension.

The seminal study that examined the impact of cultural background knowledge in the reading comprehension process is Steffenson, Joag-Dev, and Anderson (1979). This particular study examined the comprehension of U.S. adults and Indian adults reading passages that described either an American wedding or an Indian wedding. Steffenson et al. found that comprehension was higher on the passage that most closely matched the cultural background of the reader whereas readers tended to distort in recall the passage that was not from their own cultural background in order to more closely align it with their cultural background. Since that time, a number of studies have generated similar findings. Johnson (1981) and Campbell (1981) examining adults and children, respectively, found that direct cultural experience was a greater predictor of comprehension than linguistic proficiency. In parallel, Carrell (1987) found that content knowledge and experience were greater predictors of understanding than knowledge of text structure. Connor (1984) and Perkins and Angelis (1985) investigated the impact of language background on two comprehension skills: recall of propositional type and concept formation, respectively. Neither study indicated a difference on the basis of language background. A final study in this group (Parry, 1987) finds evidence for the constructivist model of L2 text comprehension. Parry found that individual vocabulary words—out of context—were misinterpreted when an understanding of a text was askew.

The second group of studies has examined the background knowledge component of topic. Alderson and Urquhart (1988), Johnson (1982), Mohammed and Swales (1984), Nunan (1985), Olah (1984), and Zuck and Zuck (1984) all found that topic familiarity is most often a greater predictor of comprehension ability than are text-based linguistic factors such as syntactic ease or explicit vocabulary knowledge. One study in this particular group, however, Carrell and Wallace (1983), presents findings that are not wholly consistent with the other studies. This study concludes that nonnatives tend to be insensitive to content difficulty.

The third group of studies has manipulated different types of mechanisms for providing background knowledge. The four studies in this group, Adams (1982), Carrell (1983), Hudson (1982), and Omaggio (1979) all used pictorial support to provide background knowledge. Both Omaggio and Adams found that the presence of a picture facilitated comprehension in a second language. Carrell found no impact on the recall scores of second language readers whether they had pictorial support or not. Hudson found differential impacts of such support;

pictorial support was more efficacious for beginning and intermediate learners but a read/reread strategy was the most profitable for advanced students.

There are, however, a number of problematic areas within this set of studies. The first is the reliability of many of the findings considering Lee (1986a). Lee replicated Carrell (1983) and found a different pattern of recall depending on the language of recall— either native or second. All studies involving ESL readers have to this point asked these readers to recall in English. Lee's data suggest that the findings of these studies are inherently biased against the actual comprehension abilities of the subjects and are skewed by their writing abilities. A second problematic feature concerns the cultural compatability of the pictures used in several of the studies and the readers' understanding of the pictorial representations. The pictures used in the studies were Western in nature and, consequently, place an added cultural burden on the comprehenders. Finally, and rather characteristically, the studies generically group nonnative readers of English into proficiency levels without considering their orthographic or cultural background variables. With these caveats in mind, however, the studies reveal a remarkable consistency in the impact of prior knowledge on the scores generated in the studies.

Text Structure

Nine studies investigate the manner in which texts are configured and the impact of that configuration on second language readers' comprehension. One study, in contrast, (Perkins, 1987) looked at the converse: whether L2 readers could mentally configure a structure in the texts they were reading. The outlined studies are in Table 2.4. Carrell (1984), Davis, Samuels, and Lange (1988), Stanley (1984), and Urquhart (1984) examined particular types of text structure. In another perspective, Cohen, Glasman, Rosenbaum-Cohen, Ferrar, and Fine (1979), Davies (1984), Flick and Anderson (1980), and Steffenson (1988) examined microlevel text features.

Particular types of texts examined include time-ordered, cause and effect, as well as problem solving. The four studies in this group (Carrell, 1984a; Davis, Lange & Samuels, 1988; Stanley, 1984; Urquhart, 1984) all indicate that when readers have specific knowledge of particular kinds of text structures, comprehension increases. The studies examining microlevel text features such as cohesive devices, syntactic difficulties, and implicit rather than explicit statements (Cohen et al., 1979; Davies, 1984; Flick & Anderson, 1980; Steffenson, 1988), indicate that second language readers have difficulty with cohesive devices, improve comprehension with simplified rather than authentic texts, and increase understanding with textually explicit rather than implicit statements. Perkins (1987), taking a different perspective on structure, found that those readers who were able to conceptualize their own structure had higher multiple choice scores.

Table 2.4. Text Structure.

Investigators	Subjects	Independent Variable	Dependent Variable	Findings
Carrell, 1984a	40 intermediate ESL learners	2 versions of 3 stories: standard and interleaved	delayed recall of story nodes	1. comprehension increased when story structure conformed to readers' anticipated story structure 2. readers of interleaved version tended to re-establish normal sequence
Cohen et al., 1979	12 Hebrew-speaking students from 4 different subject matter backgrounds	subject matter background	interview questions	1. long noun phrases performing a single grammatical function were difficult for the learners to perceive as such 2. regardless of background, learners had difficulty with cohesive devices and nontechnical texts 3. nontechnical terms created more of a problem than technical terms; synonymous lexical items caused difficulty as did specialized nontechnical lexis
Davies, 1984	experienced Japanese teachers of English	original vs. simplified text	scores on cloze test	simplified text produced better comprehension
Davis, Lange, & Samuels, 1988	40 English-speaking readers of French	1. instruction in structure of experimental reports 2. no instruction 3. scrambled order	total number of idea units recalled	training in text structure helpful when text is in its normal order

Study	Subjects	Variables	Measure	Findings
Flick & Anderson, 1980	67 EFL learners; 36 native English speakers	1. implicit and explicit texts 2. level of proficiency: native vs. nonnative	scores on a comprehension test	implicit difficulty levels constant across both groups
Perkins, 1987	22 advanced adult ESL learners	1. ability (high/low) to form nonverbal schemas 2. reading comprehension	M-C comprehension test	an ability to identify and categorize patterns, as in story grammars, transfers to an ability to comprehend by establishing schemata
Stanley, 1984	4 native speakers of English; 5 nonnative speakers of English	4 different summaries for 2 engineering texts: 1. original problem/ solution structure 2. 3 distorted versions of the original structure	interviews in which order of preference of the 4 summaries and reasons for choice were elicited	no difference between subjects in identifying problem-solving text structures
Steffenson, 1988	20 East Indians; 20 North Americans	recognition of text cohesion devices	evidence of cohesive ties in reading recalls of culturally familiar and unfamiliar texts	no significant differences between native and nonnative recalls, in terms of cohesion
Urquhart, 1984	22 L1 readers; 23 Japanese speakers; 21 speakers Arabic or Turkish	time ordered vs. nontime ordered text	free recall test	time-ordered text produced higher comprehension

Two facets of these studies serve as caveats. The first key factor in considering these studies as a whole is the constructed nature of the passages used in the studies. Few of the studies used naturally occurring texts. Rather, the studies manipulated texts in order to test the impact of the manipulations on understanding. Hence, the role of text structure in naturalistic settings remains relatively unclear. Second, since so little is known about text patterns across cultures, a real understanding of the impact of different texts within these different subject groups is equally opaque.

Oral-Aural Factors

A number of studies have investigated the relationship between second language learner competencies in reading and listening as well as learner sensitivity to the phonological system of the second language. These studies listed in Table 2.5 fall into three categories. The first concerns the relationship between oral reading ability and comprehension characterized by Bernhardt (1983), Connor (1981), Devine (1987), Grosse and Hameyer (1979), Hodes (1981), Romatowski (1981), and Tatlonghari (1984). The second examines the facilitation of reading comprehension through listening comprehension. Studies within this group include Nehr (1984), Neville and Pugh (1975), and Reeds, Winitz, and Garcia (1977). The third group of studies probes the necessity of a phonological base for reading comprehension to occur. These studies are Devine (1988), Ewoldt (1981), and Muchisky (1983).

The relationship between oral reading ability and reading comprehension in a second language is problematic. Three studies, Devine (1981), Romatowski (1981), and Tatlonghari (1984), indicate that second language readers produce oral reading errors of rates and qualities similar to those of native language readers. Connor (1981), however, finds patterns dissimilar to these studies and, in contrast to Grosse and Hameyer (1979), finds that variations in oral reading are not predictable on the basis of language background. Finally, in this series is Bernhardt (1983) that indicates that oral reading consistently impedes comprehension for second language readers in general. This study casts doubt on the appropriateness of using oral reading for any investigation of the comprehension process as well as on the findings of the former studies.

Inconsistent results are found in the studies investigating the relationship between reading and listening. Nehr (1984) found that a firm phonological base did not improve comprehension rates. Neville and Pugh (1975), however, suggest that aural input is facilitative of reading comprehension. Moreover, Reeds, Winitz, and Garcia (1977) argue with conviction that training in listening comprehension increases reading comprehension.

The third set of studies investigates the impact of phonological capacity on reading comprehension. Ewoldt (1981) found that deaf children relied exclusively on features of texts and did not use the phonological base they had been

Table 2.5. Oral-Aural Factors.

Investigators	Subjects	Independent Variable	Dependent Variable	Findings
Bernhardt, 1983	14 intermediate German learners at 2 proficiency levels	1. ability group (good or poor) 2. reading modes (oral or silent)	recall (repeated measures)	1. students with good grammatical ability had higher comprehension than those with poor grammatical ability 2. comprehension of passages read silently was higher than that of passages read orally 3. comprehension improved from the first reading to the second to the third reading 4. all 3 factors proved to be significant
Connor, 1981	7 ESL students of 4 different language backgrounds: Vietnamese, Spanish, Farsi, and Arabic	1 of 3 stories	1. oral reading miscues 2. story retelling 3. probe questions	1. variations in miscues not predictable by language background 2. differences between individuals within groups greater than differences between groups 3. subjects did not self-correct 4. only some miscues cause meaning change 5. synonymous with comprehension
Devine, 1981	20 beginning ESL students	oral reading proficiency	1. accuracy of supplied definitions 2. correlation of miscue analysis and language proficiency	
Devine, 1984	2 ESL adults	internal models of reading processes: 1. phonological decoding vs. 2. lexical decoding	oral reading interviews (percentage of miscues made in retelling of text)	phonologically-oriented reader had more miscues in retelling than the meaning-centered reader

(Continued)

Table 2.5. Oral-Aural Factors.

Investigators	Subjects	Independent Variable	Dependent Variable	Findings
Ewoldt, 1981	3 deaf children	text difficulty	proficiency in signing and retelling	1. the more difficult text produced smaller percentages of grammatical and meaningful syntactic structures 2. more attention is paid to print on the more difficult text
Grosse & Hameyer, 1979	beginning learners of German	dialect groups (southern vs. northern)	scores on a production and perception task	mother-tongue dialect influences second language reading ability
Hodes, 1981	6 bilingual speakers of Yiddish and English	texts in English and Yiddish	oral reading errors	1. the RMI coding sheet yielded high correlation for a foreign language 2. no increase in efficiency detected by alphabet or direction 3. oral reading accuracy does not predict reading proficiency 4. prior knowledge influences comprehension
Muchisky, 1983				
Study One	11 ESL students	simple visual presentation of word pairs vs. visual presentation of word pairs accompanied by an oral repetition task	reaction time (MRT)	L2 students' reaction times decreased (speeded up) in the shadowing condition
Study Two	35 ESL students	simple visual presentation of word pairs vs. visual presentation of word pairs accompanied by an oral repetition task	reaction time (MRT)	1. second language students in non-shadowing condition showed phonological interference from their native language 2. the shadowing task involving the oral production of English curtailed the interference, thereby, improving the time

Study	Subjects	Conditions	Measures	Findings
Nehr, 1984	108 German native speakers with no command or knowledge of the foreign language	audio-lingual vs. no audio-lingual component in learning Serbo-Croation, Serbo-Cyrillic, or Japanese "alphabet"	1. test scores on grapho-morphological and morphosyntactic competencies 2. translation ability 3. total scores	in all test sections and on the total score, groups with no audio-lingual component had significantly better results
Neville & Pugh, 1975	7 overseas students	passages under silent reading and aural input conditions	comprehension scores	the technique of variable pacing of silent reading could be useful with nonnative speakers of English
Reeds, Winitz, & Garcia, 1977	38 English speakers	training sessions in listening comprehension	scores on picture/sentence matching task	reading transfers from listening comprehension
Romatowki, 1981	Polish-speaking learners of English	English language vs. Polish language story	oral reading errors	1. 39.8% of the miscues in English story and 55.9% of the miscues in Polish story were of high graphic similarity 2. 20.9% of the miscues in the English story, but only 11.5% in the Polish story were of low graphic similarity 3. few miscues created major syntactic or semantic changes 4. the fewer the miscues, the lower the comprehension score
Tatlonghari, 1984	20 fourth-grade ESL learners		miscue scores	ESL readers exhibit substitution, omission insertion, and reversal oral reading errors

provided in order to become proficient readers. Muchisky (1983), on the other hand, found that by increasing the second language aural input, reading proficiency increases. Devine (1984) found that a meaning-centered reader has fewer miscues in retelling than a phonologically oriented one.

The inconsistent and problematic results in these studies reflect a much debated, unresolved issue in first language reading. Some researchers argue from evidence that phonological concepts are necessary for the development of reading skills (for example, Gough, 1972). Others argue, however, also from evidence, that it is the act of reading itself that facilitates the development of phonological awareness (Goodman, 1968). Clearly, the second language studies provide data on both sides of this issue. One resolution to the dilemma may be that some phonological awareness is indeed necessary, *but*, that in order for comprehension to occur phonological awareness may not have to be an accurate approximation of the second language's sound system—merely an approximation of *some* sound system.

Syntactic Factors

Relatively few second language reading studies have investigated the impact of syntactic knowledge on the ability to understand text. This lack of data is surprising on two counts. First, second language classrooms tend to expend a significant amount of time in the instruction and practice of syntactic structures. Second, materials are developed principally according to readability formulae (Bernhardt, 1986) that are clearly measures of syntactic complexity.

The area of syntax seems to be characterized by three strands of research. These are found in Table 2.6. The first strand, characterized by Bean, Potter, and Clark (1980), and Robbins (1983), examines reference in text. Bean et al. found that young learners were indeed sensitive to pronoun usage in text. Robbins, who investigated adult subjects' accuracy in the understanding of reference, found little relationship between the ability to understand a referent's use in a passage and the ability to understand the passage. The second strand investigates syntax at the sentence level and beyond. Barnett (1986) found that increases in syntactic knowledge impact differentially on comprehension as general language proficiency increases. The Guarino and Perkins (1986) study provide compatible data. Bhatia (1984) and Blau (1982) provide data parallel to a considerable portion of L1 data (Pearson, 1975; Bormuth, Carr, Manning, & Pearson, 1970). These investigators found that syntactic complexity of text can actually aid comprehension even for lower proficiency learners. In other words, simple syntax does not necessarily mean simple meaning. Olshtain (1982) provides consistent findings in this regard. In analyzing compound word usage, she found that second language readers draw upon a multitude of linguistic skills in order to resolve words for which they may or may not be fully equipped syntactically. In a similar vein, Strother and Ulijn (1987) indicate that syntactic complexity does not affect comprehension significantly. They argue that knowledge of vocabulary is much more important. In a third line of research, Jarvis and Jensen (1982) provide evidence that parallel translations can aid in the acquisition of syntactic patterns.

The types of experimental tasks used in these studies and the variety of methodologies employed make the comparison and contrast of findings rather difficult for a number of reasons. First, the limitations of multiple choice tests in respect to passage dependence vs. passage independence as well as their tendency to "lead" the reader toward an answer rather than providing an actual measure of understanding are well known. Second, recent findings regarding cloze cast doubt on the findings of studies that use it as a measure. Third, the different nature of the subject groups further compounds the difficulty in the development of research generalizations regarding syntax. Fourth, the investigators tended not to discuss issues of comparative syntax. Subject groups from different language backgrounds may have generated different patterns of findings and yet these patterns are masked by the generic subject groupings. Finally, the topic of the texts and subjects' knowledge of the topics used is rarely noted. Hence, it is frequently unclear whether syntax is the key variable or whether syntax is confounded with topic knowledge.

Cross-lingual Processing Strategies

A large number of second language reading studies compares and contrasts reading strategies within particular second languages, that is, intralingually, while others compare and contrast strategies across the native and target languages; that is, interlingually. Studies examining intralingual processing behaviors are Barrera, Valdes, and Cardenes (1986), Bernhardt (1986), Block (1986), Carrell (1984b), Cziko (1980), Devine (1981), Kendall, Lajeunesse, Chmilar, Shapson, and Shapson (1987), McLeod and McLaughlin (1986), Padron and Waxman (1988), Perkins (1983), and Rigg (1978). Studies characterized as interlingual in nature generally compare first language processing behaviors with second language behaviors. These studies are Clarke (1979, 1980), Cziko (1978), Dank and McEachern (1979), Douglas (1981), Elley (1984), Groebel (1980), Irujo (1986), MacLean and d'Anglejan (1986), McDougall and Bruck (1976), Roller (1988), de Suarez (1985), Sarig (1987), and Wagner, Spratt, and Ezzaki (1989). All of these studies are outlined in Table 2.7.

The intralingual processing studies have generally indicated that second language reading skill acquisition is developmental. Barrera et al. (1986), Cziko (1980), Devine (1981), Kendall et al. (1987), McLeod and McLaughlin (1986), and Rigg (1978) all employed oral reading analyses to indicate that processing strategies change and evolve according to increases in proficiency. Bernhardt (1986a) noted similar findings using an eye-movement methodology. Highly

Table 2.6. Syntactic Factors.

Investigators	Subjects	Independent Variable	Dependent Variable	Findings
Barnett, 1986	131 adults studying French	1. syntactic complexity 2. vocabulary density	1. scores on: M-C tests and rational deletion cloze test 2. recall scores	1. comprehension increases in relation to vocabulary knowledge and syntactic proficiency 2. these increases are differential in upper proficiency levels
Bean, Potter, & Clark, 1980	45 fourth- and fifth-grade students reading in English and Spanish	3 story conditions with pronoun variations	probed recall	1. a significant difference in comprehension for the 3 story conditions 2. no difference in the pronoun rewrite and the original conditions 3. significant differences for the story structure/pronoun rewrite condition
Bhatia, 1984	15 fairly advanced second language learners of English from various countries	discontinuous constituents vs. no discontinuous constituents	scores on a modified cloze test	for two groups of second-language learners it was more difficult to process and understand the sentences which contained discontinuous constituents than those in which such discontinuities had been removed by syntactic reorganization
Blau, 1982	85 college and 111 junior high ESL students	3 versions of the same text with syntactic variations	scores on a M-C test	more syntactically complex, unedited texts yielded higher comprehension for both groups

Guarino & Perkins, 1986	35 intermediate and advanced ESL adults	proficiency levels	recognition of linguistic structures	1. awareness of form class and reading comprehension are significantly related 2. morphological competence is but one dimension of reading comprehension 3. other knowledge may be equally or more robust in explaining the reading comprehension variance as form class awareness
Jarvis & Jensen, 1982	39 beginning and 18 advanced Russian students	4 different types of parallel translations	two 7-item M-C tests	parallel translations seem to be of some value for the acquisition of syntax
Olshtain, 1982	56 Hebrew speakers; 11 English speakers	isolated vs. contexted compounds	test scores	readers use linguistic, textual, and pragmatic information
Robbins, 1983	speakers of Spanish and English	proficiency level	scores on referent task	partial language proficiency not a hindrance to comprehension
Strother & Ulijn, 1987	24 computer science majors, native English speakers; 24 humanities majors, native English speakers; 46 computer majors, ESL students (24 Dutch, 22 Chinese); 69 humanities majors, ESL students (widely mixed background)	effect of syntactic complexity on reading comprehension	true/false comprehension questions	1. syntactic complexity does not affect comprehension 2. vocabulary is more important than syntax

Table 2.7. Cross-Lingual Processing Strategies.

Investigators	Subjects	Independent Variable	Dependent Variable	Findings
Barrera, Valdes, & Cardenas, 1986	30 third-grade students	10 Spanish-English bilinguals reading Spanish as a first language, 10 English-Spanish bilinguals reading ESL, 10 English monolinguals reading English as a first language	oral reading analysis and recall	1. no significant differences among the 3 groups of readers for the recall variables studied 2. significant difference among the 3 groups of readers for in-process comprehension behavior
Bernhardt, 1986a	14 adult beginning and advanced learners of German; 7 native readers of German	3 different text types repetition	eye-movement indices	1. advanced and native readers demonstrated equivalent cognitive processing strategies 2. beginning readers demonstrated strategies characteristic of readers of English
Block, 1986	3 native speakers of Spanish; 3 native speakers of Chinese; 3 black native speakers of American English	language background: Spanish, Chinese, American English	retellings: 1. think-aloud protocol 2. recall, and M-C	native speakers and nonnative speakers did not differ in their patterns of strategy use
Carrell, 1984b	43 ESL learners; 17 speakers of English	1. types of inferences 2. proficiency level	scores on true/false judgments about each premise-conclusion pair	ESL learners are in the process of acquiring pragmatic ability in English

Clarke, 1980				
Study One	21 low-level ESL students (native Spanish speakers)	good L2 readers vs. poor L1 readers	scores on cloze tests in Spanish and English	1. in their native language, the good readers seemed to rely on semantic rather than syntactic cues 2. in English (L2) the use of syntactic cues by both good and poor readers was equal
Study Two	1 good L1 reader; 1 poor L1 reader (native Spanish speakers)	good L1 reader vs. poor L1 reader	oral reading errors in Spanish and English	1. good readers produced fewer miscues than did the poor readers both in L1 and L2 2. in Spanish, good readers produced a much higher percentage of semantically acceptable miscues 3. poor readers produced the same percentage of syntactically acceptable miscues but did not produce as many semantically acceptable miscues
Clarke, 1979	2 ESL readers	proficiency level of the two subjects	1. miscues per hundred words (MPHW) 2. comprehension score 3. residual MPHW 4. comprehension ranking 5. syntactic acceptability 6. semantic acceptability	good L1 readers are good L2 readers

(Continued)

Table 2.7. Cross-Lingual Processing Strategies (cont.).

Investigators	Subjects	Independent Variable	Dependent Variable	Findings
Cziko, 1980	English speaking students with intermediate and advanced competence in French as a second language; native speakers of French	2 texts	oral reading	1. intermediate students made a significantly lower proportion of deletion and insertion errors than did the advanced and native speaker students 2. advanced learners made significantly higher proportion of substitution errors that graphically resembled the text than did the native speakers 3. the intermediate students made a significantly higher proportion of errors that did not conform to the syntactic, semantic, or discourse constraints of the text than did the advanced and native students
Cziko, 1978				
Study One	English and French speaking students	passage formats (oral vs. silent modes)	reading speed	1. all 4 groups were able to make use of the syntactic constraints present in the anomalous texts 2. only the 2 groups most proficient in French were able to take advantage of the semantic constraints present in the meaningful text
Study Two	English and French speaking students	passages in 3 different cloze formats	scores on the cloze tests	a relatively high level of competence in a language is a prerequisite to the ability to use discourse constraints

Study	Subjects	Materials	Measures	Results
Dank & McEachern, 1979	French immersion students; traditional English language students	French immersion vs. traditional group	oral reading errors	French immersion group demonstrated that their use of graphic and sound cues were slightly more effective than those used by their counterparts in the traditional English language group
Devine, 1981	14 Spanish-speaking ESL learners	2 short stories	oral reading miscues	confirmatory of Goodman's findings (1971) on native readers of English
Douglas, 1981	34 speakers of Japanese; speakers of English	cloze tests in English and Japanese	two cloze-generated scores	1. 2 scores correlate 2. cloze discriminates between native and non-native groups
Elley, 1984	Fijians; Indians; ESL students; native speakers		score on: 1. cloze test 2. M-C test 3. reading tests correlation	1. similarity in the reactions of L2 and L1 users to different reading tests 2. similarity in the pattern of their errors 3. similarity in their attitudes and in their language development as a result of reading programs derived from first language settings
Groebel, 1980	454 ESL students	reading abilities measured by standardized tests	scores	significant correlations between L1 and L2 reading scores
Irujo, 1986	12 advanced ESL learners (native Spanish speakers)	3 different idiom types	scores on: 1. M-C 2. definition 3. translation 4. completion tests	1. similar idioms showed interference from Spanish 2. different idioms were difficult to comprehend; showed no interference

Table 2.7. Cross-Lingual Processing Strategies (*cont.*).

Investigators	Subjects	Independent Variable	Dependent Variable	Findings
Kendall et al., 1987	46 French immersion students; 47 English language instruction students	1. program type 2. subtests	1. scores on letter and word reading test 2. scores on oral reading and comprehension test	1. no differences in scores at the kindergarten level 2. English instruction students in other grades scored higher
MacLean & d'Anglejan, 1986	21 advanced ESL students (native speakers of French)	L1 and L2 texts of 2 difficulty levels	cloze test scores	1. subjects use across-sentence information more effectively in L1 than L2 2. text difficulty was not a factor
McDougall & Bruck, 1976	French immersion students	time of introduction to reading in English	1. scores on Spache Diagnostic Scales	stage at which English reading was first taught was found not to affect reading grade levels
McLeod & McLaughlin, 1986	20 adult native speakers of English; 44 adult foreign students	2 passages	scores on: 1. reading passages 2. oral cloze test scores	ESL reading has at least 2 modes of learning—achieved by the gradual accretion of automaticity and that achieved by restructuring
Padron & Waxman, 1987	82 Hispanic students		1. scores on Stanford Diagnostic Reading Test 2. scores on reading strategy questionnaire	perceptions of cognitive strategies can predict test scores

Study	Subjects	Variables	Measures	Findings
Perkins, 1983	43 adult ESL learners	3 different proficiency levels	scores on a semantic determinant task	1. a difference in the magnitude of misrecognitions across proficiency levels 2. ESL students exhibit semantic constructivity similar to L1 children and adults; they use their knowledge of the world and contribute to information found in the text
Rigg, 1978	Arabic, Navajo, Samoan, and Spanish children	proficiency level	oral reading scores	ability to understand not related to L1
Roller, 1988	approximately 300 native Shona speaking ESL readers	1. language 2. text type 3. grade level	vocabulary measure	1. first language literacy level a significant factor 2. advisable to delay the introduction of L2 reading
Sarig, 1987	10 female high school senior ESL students (native speakers of Hebrew)	similarity of reading processes in L1 and L2	choice of reading strategy ("reading moves")	1. reading processes transfer cross-lingually 2. readers use unique strategies in both L1 and L2
de Suarez, 1985	1st year Spanish speaking students	translation vs. summary task	individual performance on tasks	1. no differences between the responses of each group 2. great difficulty in retrieving information from TL and expressing it in NL 3. choices in translation were guided by structural features of TL, not contextual constraints or appropriation of meaning
Wagner et al., 1989	approximately 150 elementary school children (mother tongue of Arabic or Berber)	1. native language 2. preschool literacy experience	1. scores on Arabic reading tests 2. French tests 3. several cognitive tasks	1. no significant influence of mother tongue literacy on second language reading scores 2. children taught exclusively in the L2 ultimately achieve at the same rate as monolingual peers

proficient nonnatives employed processing strategies more akin to native strategies than the less proficient readers who employed first language processing strategies. Block (1986) using story retellings; Carrell (1984b) using true/false judgments to probe inferencing strategies; Cziko (1978) using cloze testing; and Padron and Waxman (1988) using standardized tests came to similar conclusions.

The second group of studies analyzes behaviors in the first language and compares them with those in the second language. Clarke (1979, 1980), Elley (1984), Groebel (1980), Roller (1988), Sarig (1987), and Wagner et al. (1989), all find that good native language strategies *transfer* to the second. Clarke (1979, 1980) based his conclusions on cloze testing and oral reading; Elley (1984) and Groebel (1980) on correlations between standardized test scores in the two languages; and Roller (1988) on a vocabulary measure. Another set of interlingual studies finds first language *interference*. Irujo (1986) found that when figures of speech were similar but not identical in two languages, the first language meaning interfered with the development of the second. Parallelly, de Suarez (1985) found that translation tasks were guided by first language syntax rather than by meaning. A third set of interlingual studies indicates that first language processing behaviors tend to *dominate* throughout the development of proficiency in a second language. MacLean and d'Anglejan (1986) found that strategies for using intratextual information did not transfer consistently to the second language, while Douglas (1981) found consistently higher cloze test scores in first language than in second language reading. Dank and McEachern (1979) concluded that second language instruction facilitated first language reading skill acquisition; McDougall and Bruck (1976) provide parallel data.

This area of second language research provides complementary as well as contradictory evidence. Developmental data parallel a well-established research tradition and data base in first language. Transfer and interference data parallel a long-running debate in second language acquisition research in general. The extent to which first language strategies facilitate acquisition and the extent to which they impede acquisition—in this case, of second language reading skills—remains unclear.

Unfortunately, however, a synthesis of this research area, too, is extremely troublesome. Many of the studies, for example, employed either oral reading or cloze methodologies. The doubtful nature of oral reading was discussed above. Moreover, the dubious nature of cloze testing (see Chapter Seven) for revealing data about the comprehension process makes further generalizations even more suspect. Perhaps most problematic, though, in any attempt to compare and contrast, is the variability in texts, in language background—both culturally and orthographically—and in proficiency levels of subjects.

Metacognitive and Affective Factors

Table 2.8 lists studies involving metacognition and affect. Hosenfeld (1977) and Neville (1979) have focused on metacognition or the conscious awareness of

Table 2.8. Metacognitive and Affective Factors.

Investigators	Subjects	Independent Variable	Dependent Variable	Findings
Fransson, 1984	university students	1. level of anxiety 2. level of intrinsic motivation	1. recall 2. short-item test 3. interview	1. motivation for reading influences strategy use 2. anxiety may be debilitating
Hosenfeld, 1977	40 students of French, Spanish, and German		interview	1. good readers keep the meaning in mind 2. they read in word groups 3. they skip words they don't view as important 4. they think positively
Neville, 1979	adult learners of Spanish in a natural setting		introspection	oral-aural command of the second language is critical

cognitive processes. Hosenfeld found that good readers attend to meaning, read in phrases, and persevere through texts. Using a slightly different methodology, a single-subject case study, Neville concluded that an oral command of a language was requisite for second language reading comprehension. Such studies have had a considerable impact on understandings of learners' behaviors. Problematic is the very limited number of subjects within the studies. Fransson (1984) is the only second language study that has focused on affective variables and finds positive affect facilitative of reading comprehension.

Testing

The testing literature consists of a number of thrusts. It is listed in Table 2.9. The first thrust involves the use of first language school-based standardized tests for second language readers. This thrust is characterized by Baldauf, Dawson, Prior, and Propst (1980), by Propst and Baldauf (1979), and by Brown (1985). A second strand investigates the efficacy of the cloze procedure and miscue analysis as assessment devices. Investigations of cloze as an appropriate assessment device include Kamil, Smith-Burke, and Rodriguez-Brown (1986); Markham (1985); and Mustapha, Nelson, and Thomas (1985). Mott (1981) investigated the use of miscue analysis as an assessment measure. A third group views test reliability, focusing on the language of response and question type. In this group are Bensoussan and Ramraz (1984b); Hock and Poh (1979), Lee (1986b), Shohamy (1984), Perkins (1984), Perkins and Brutten (1988), and Sim and Bensoussan (1979). A fourth strand investigates relationships between reading subtasks and overall test scores. These studies are Bensoussan, Sim, and Weiss (1984), Henning (1975), and Homburg and Spaan (1982). A final strand of testing research has focused on the efficacy of the ACTFL Guidelines for Reading as an assessment measure. The studies for this group include Allen, Bernhardt, Berry, Demel (1988) and Lee and Musumeci (1988).

The studies that focus on standardized test measurements indicate that such measurements tend to be biased against second language readers. Better predictors of achievement seem to be cloze test results (Mustapha et al., 1985). Interestingly, however, the studies focused specifically on cloze testing seriously question the validity of the cloze procedure as a reading assessment device. Both Kamil et al. (1986) and Markham (1985) indicate no significant difference between and among subject cloze test performance whether the text is random, anomolous, or normal. In other words, cloze testing does not seem to measure a construct directly related to an ability to comprehend. The miscue studies conducted by Mott (1981) and Hodes (1981) (see Oral-Aural Factors above) provide parallel data. While Mott (1981) finds an increase in the quality of oral reading errors as readers progress through a text, Hodes (1981) finds no relationship between the oral reading errors and comprehension.

The third group of testing studies focuses on reliability. Bensoussan and

Ramraz (1984b) examined the relationships between subtests and found them highly related to each other. Hock and Poh (1979), Lee (1986b), and Shohamy (1984) all found that the language of response—either native or target—differentially impacted on subjects' test performance. Perkins (1984) came to a similar conclusion—knowledge of text topic affected the reliability of reading tests. Finally, Sim and Bensoussan (1979) looked at different question types for assessing comprehension and found no difference in performance between content questions focused on form and content questions focused on content.

In a fourth strand of test research, Bensoussan, Sim, and Weiss (1984) found no difference between and among subjects regarding the type and frequency of dictionary usage. Henning (1975) found no relationship between grammar subtests and comprehension. In contrast, Homburg and Spaan (1982) did find a relationship between word building strategies and comprehension test scores. This area is probably the most important area of second language reading research presently. Until reliable and valid measures of second language comprehension abilities are developed, the entire area of second language reading research will remain dubious. Tables 2.2 through 2.10 underline the importance of the testing issue: there are 15 instances of the use of cloze testing; 12 instances of the use of oral reading and miscue analysis; and 15 instances of the use of recall many of which do not indicate the language of recall or the manner in which recall was scored. In summary, almost 50 percent of the second language reading research base needs to be used with the utmost caution considering studies that question their data collection and analysis procedures. This, of course, is not to argue that the remainder of the studies employed appropriate data collection procedures. The validity of their data collection devices has simply not been investigated.

A final strand of testing research investigated the use of the ACTFL Guidelines as an assessment measure of reading proficiency. These studies have found the Guidelines to be a wholly inappropriate framework for L2 reading assessment. Allen et al. (1988) revealed that there is no evidence for a heirarchy of reading proficiency based on text genre. Similarily, Lee and Musumeci (1988) found that reader performance on different text types was not consistent with the ACTFL text heirarchy. These findings seriously question the use of the Guidelines as a valid measure of reading proficiency.

Instruction

Second language reading studies grouped under the general heading of instruction and listed in Table 2.10 focus on one of two aspects. One group discusses and provides data on course designs that facilitate reading achievement. This group includes studies by Barnett (1988), Bensoussan and Ramraz (1984a), Bernhardt and Berkemeyer (1988), Cooper (1984), Cowan and Sarmad (1976), Elley and Mangubhai (1983), Feldman (1978), Groebel (1979), Hill (1981),

Table 2.9. Testing.

Investigators	Subjects	Independent Variable	Dependent Variable	Findings
Allen, Bernhardt, Berry, & Demel, 1988	105 high school learners (35 subjects per language and 7 subjects per level)	1. foreign language (German, French and Spanish) 2. level or year (1, 2, 3, 4, 5) 3. text type (friendly letter, general interest article, business letter, and newspaper article)	Percentage of text propositions recalled	1. students can cope with authentic texts; all texts on average were comprehended to the same degree 2. there is no evidence for a hierarchy of reading proficiency based on text genre 3. 5 years of language exposure yielded 3 levels of language development
Baldauf, Dawson, Prior, & Propst, 1980				
Study One	28 Australian ESL students	1. rank orders of students by teachers 2. 7 language tests; 5 types of cloze tests, 2 standardized reading tests (PATV and GURT-RI)	test scores	1. matching cloze procedure, at least as measured by MEAT 4, provided as good or better validity estimates of Aboriginal pupils' reading performance, using teachers' rating as the criterion, than did other types of cloze or standardized reading procedures 2. the cloze-based procedures provided more reliable estimates of pupils' performance than did the standardized tests
Study Two	62 8th-grade male ESL students	1. 2 teacher-made cloze tests: (Cloze M5 and M6) 2. 30-item reading tests (MTEA) 3. school grades in English	test scores	1. reconfirmed the validity of the matching cloze procedure as a measure of secondary school ESL performance 2. passages varying in difficulty should be combined to make a single 50-item teacher-made matching cloze test 3. structure words may be retained in matching cloze tests for ESL students without reducing test difficulty

	Subjects	Treatment	Measures	Results
Bensoussan & Ramraz, 1984				
Study One	435 advanced learners	1. fill-in test 2. 3 M-C cloze tests	scores on test types	1. differences in scores among the texts suggested that topic may be more important than test format 2. M-C cloze format produced higher scores than the fill-in test
Study Two	1487 adults	same texts as in Study One, different formats		
Bensoussan, Sim, & Weiss, 1984				
Study One	9 intact classes totaling 91 ESL students	3 different dictionary treatments: 1. without a dictionary 2. with a monolingual dictionary 3. with a bilingual dictionary	comprehension scores	test scores were not affected by use or nonuse of dictionaries
Study Two	670 ESL adults			
Study Three	740 ESL adults			1. more than half chose to use bilingual dictionaries; whereas approximately 20% used monolingual dictionaries and 21% did not use any dictionary 2. when given the choice, students preferred to use bilingual dictionaries, but no significant difference on the test whether a student used a bilingual dictionary, or a monolingual dictionary, or no dictionary at all 3. no significant relation between the dictionary used (or not used) and the time needed to complete the test

Table 2.9. Testing (cont.).

Investigators	Subjects	Independent Variable	Dependent Variable	Findings
Brown, 1985	university graduate students: 29 American native speakers of English in engineering, 29 Chinese nonnatives in engineering	reading comprehension test for engineering English	scores on reading comprehension test	1. both groups of Americans had higher means than both groups of Chinese 2. engineers performed higher than corresponding TESL/TEFL trainees of the same nationality 3. methodology of test construction that includes criterion referencing is useful in testing foreign students' abilities
Henning, 1975	27 Iranian college ESL students	test difficulty and test type	scores on tests	1. intermediate difficulty synonym–antonym selection and M-C sentence selection exhibited the highest correlations with reading comprehension 2. synonym–antonym selection with low difficulty material is an invalid predictor of reading comprehension 3. student grammar performance should not be taken into account in the scoring of reading comprehension
Hock & Poh, 1979	39 Malaysian ESL learners	English or mother-tongue questions	scores on comprehension tests	comprehension performance in English improved when test questions were given in Malay

Study	Subjects	Variables	Measures	Results
Homburg & Spaan, 1982	39 advanced ESL subjects	proficiency level	1. main idea test 2. grammar classification 3. identification of synonyms 4. knowledge of nonsense words 5. word-solving strategies 6. written summary	1. word-solving strategies predict comprehension 2. word solving not related to proficiency level 3. understanding the main idea occurred with equal frequency at both high and low proficiency levels
Kamil, Smith-Burke, & Rodriguez-Brown, 1986	16 Spanish bilingual graduate students and professors	1. passage language (Spanish or English) 2. sentence order (normal or randomized)	cloze scores	1. no difference between cloze scores on Spanish normal and Spanish randomized passages 2. no significant differences for the same comparison between English passages 3. no difference between English normal and Spanish normal passage nor between randomized versions 4. cloze shown to be insensitive to intersentential integration of information
Lee, 1986b	320 learners of Spanish in 4 levels	1. first or second language recall 2. task directions or no directions	recall scores	1. native language recall increases comprehension scores 2. task orientations had differential impacts

Table 2.9. Testing (cont.).

Investigators	Subjects	Independent Variable	Dependent Variable	Findings
Lee & Musumeci, 1988	73 college readers of Italian (26 first semester, 28 second semester, 5 third semester, 14 fourth semester subjects)	1. semester level (1st, 2nd, 3rd, 4th) 2. text type (characteristic of 5 different levels of reading proficiency) 3. reading skills (characteristic of the different levels of reading proficiency as stated in the ACTFL Guidelines)	scores on questions in English designed to tap the different reading skills	1. reader performance on different text types is not consistent with the ACTFL hierarchy of text types 2. reader performance on reading skills is also not consistent with the hierarchy of reading skills characterizing the different levels of reading proficiency 3. reader performance is not consistent with notion of cross-sectioning parallel hierarchies of text types and reading skills
Markham, 1985	84 college learners of German at 3 proficiency levels	normal, sequential, and scrambled passage cloze tests	scores on the tests	1. no significant performance differences between sequential and scrambled tests with mechanical or rational deletion 2. the means associated with rational deletion (sequential or scrambled) were generally lower than the means associated with mechanical deletion
Mott, 1981	7 German ESL learners	2 English and 2 German short stories	1. oral reading errors 2. retellings	1. twice as many miscues made in the second language as in the first 2. miscues increased over the 2nd half of texts 3. quality of miscues improved as second language readers progressed through texts
Mustapha et al., 1985	20 ESL students of earth science	1. type of classroom 2. type of exercises	scores on 3 cloze passages	1. pretest and posttest cloze scores were significantly different at the .005 alpha level using a t-test 2. correlation was .608 between cloze tests and end of term grades

Study	Subjects	Variables	Measure	Findings
Perkins, 1984	19 Egyptian adult ESL learners	4 test-item types	item discrimination	1. tests exhibited differential reliability estimates 2. reliability dependent upon how "readable" the subjects found the passage 3. M-C and true/false items discriminate better than do missing letters and grammar paraphrase items
Perkins & Brutten, 1988	113 nonnative speakers of English at three proficiency levels	1. proficiency level of subjects 2. type of exam	estimates of personal ability on test items	1. higher the ability per proficiency level, the more able to uncover micro-propositions in texts 2. higher proficiency students able to infer better 3. all subjects integrated information
Propst & Baldauf, 1979	third-, fourth-, and fifth-grade students; nonnative speakers of English	1. three reading achievement tests using cloze 2. Gates-MacGinitie Reading Test	test scores	1. standardized achievement tests in reading are inappropriate measures for nonnative ESL students acquiring English-speaking context 2. locally constructed cloze test more accurately depicted the range of individual differences than did the Gates-MacGinitie
Shohamy, 1984	655 12th-grade ESL students at 3 proficiency levels	1. testing methods 2. text difficulty 3. language (L1 & L2)	scores on multiple-choice (M-C) and open-ended (OE) questions	1. each testing method produced different degrees of difficulty for the test takers 2. each of the variables (methods, text, and language) had a significant impact on students' scores in reading comprehension 3. effects were strongest for low-level students
Sim & Bensoussan, 1979	187 undergraduate ESL students	questions testing function words and questions testing content words	number of items correct	function-word questions appear to be as difficult as content-word questions

Table 2.10. Instruction.

Investigators	Subjects	Independent Variable	Dependent Variable	Findings
Barnett, 1988	approximately 200 students of French	specially designed exercises and materials	scores on reading achievement tests	1. no difference between experimental and control groups 2. positive affect engendered
Bensoussan & Ramraz, 1984a	349 students	different proficiency levels	three parallel versions of M-C tests	special courses help
Bernhardt & Berkemeyer, 1988	254 high school German learners in five instructional levels	1. level of instruction (1, 2, 3, 4, 5) 2. text type (friendly letter, general interest article, business letter, and newspaper article	1. percentage of material recalled 2. types of errors made according to constructivist model of L2 text comprehension	1. students can cope with authentic texts at all instructional levels 2. scores differentiated between two types of expository texts: reportage and letters 3. data indicate three distinctly different reading proficiency levels; proficiency in reading implies an increase in the total number of propositions recalled from any text
Bialystok, 1983				
Study One	79 English-speaking learners of French	4 types of cues: 1. picture 2. dictionary 3. lesson 4. control	scores on: 1. short answer 2. vocabulary tests	1. short answer easier than vocabulary test 2. picture cue improved short answer scores 3. other cue improved both scores
Study Two	80 learners of French	4 types of cues: 1. picture 2. dictionary 3. lesson 4. control	scores on: 1. short answer 2. vocabulary tests	1. subjects more successful at comprehension test than vocabulary 2. picture cue better than other cues for the comprehension test 3. the lesson cue did not significantly improve vocabulary test scores

Study	Subjects	Variables	Measures	Findings
Brown, Yongpei, & Yinglong, 1984	118 Chinese-speaking ESL learners	1. different types of reading materials 2. attitudes toward the materials		1. materials caused an increase in gain scores for reading comprehension 2. students found materials motivating
Cooper, 1984	a one-third sample of all entrants to University of Malaya	unpracticed vs. practiced readers	1. general comprehension test 2. 3 passages-each with 10 traditional M-C questions	1. practiced readers are distinguished from unpracticed readers by their ability to use the whole context to decode the meaning of unfamiliar words 2. correlation of performance on syntactic features with general comprehension 3. texts which discriminated most clearly between practiced and unpracticed readers had lexical cohesion and cataphoric reference 4. practiced readers distinguished from unpracticed readers by their relatively superior lexical competence
Cowan & Sarmad, 1976	students in the first, third, and sixth grades	school type; immersion curriculum vs. split curriculum	performance in reading Persian and English as measured by: 1. comprehension test 2. vocabulary test	1. bilingual children did not perform as well as either of their monolingual peer groups 2. the difference was more striking for Persian than English
Elley & Mangubhai, 1983	614 school students	method of instruction	scores on pretest and posttest	1. pupils exposed to many stories progressed in reading and listening comprehension at twice the normal rate 2. after 20 months the gains had increased further and spread to related language skills
Feldman, 1978	54 ESL school readers	"Reading System Method"	scores on various reading achievement tests	program shown to be effective

Table 2.10. Instruction (cont.).

Investigators	Subjects	Independent Variable	Dependent Variable	Findings
Groebel, 1979	125 adult ESL learners	teacher frontal instruction vs. self-directed learning	scores on pretest and retest cloze test	1. no significant difference between the gain in the level of achievement of students taught by the traditional-frontal method and the gain in the level of achievement of students taught by the self-directed method 2. small positive tendency for the self-directed group to show a slightly higher improvement
Hill, 1981	67 Belgian ESL learners	years (1–3) of reading courses in English	1. reading speed (wpm-words per minute) 2. scores on M–C test	the students who took these courses made significant progress in handling text material in English presented and tested in the ways described
Hosenfeld, 1984	2 high school learners of French and Spanish	learning strategies	thinking aloud data	both inductive and deductive teaching strategies are appropriate techniques
Kleinmann, 1987	76 ESL readers from 12 different native languages	1. computer-assisted instruction 2. control	pre- and posttest scores	no difference between groups with and without computer-assisted instruction
Laufer-Dvorkin, 1981	1500 adult ESL learners	intensive vs. extensive method of instruction	posttest scores	statistically significant progress made by intensive method only group
Lutjeharms, 1985	learners of German	open-ended vs. M-C questions	scores on tests	correlations between class attendance and test scores are higher for open-ended questions than for M-C questions
Narayanaswamy, 1982	Arabic speaking ESL readers	particular reading program type	1. reading speed 2. comprehension	gains in reading speed and comprehension

Study	Subjects	Variables	Measures	Findings
O'Flanagan, 1985	334 engineers	20 word pairs; stimulus word being a nonsense word	time for memorizing	everyone has a reliable memory
Pederson, 1986	136 learners of French	1. passage availability 2. conceptual level of the adjunct question 3. verbal ability	recall	passage-unavailable treatment always resulted in a comparatively higher comprehension rate than occurred in counterpart passage-available treatments regardless of the level of question or level of verbal ability
Pugh, 1977	32 ESL students	book-use	1. reading comprehension 2. reading speed 3. intelligence	learners who chose an appropriate method to locate the text were not significantly more likely to obtain a correct answer from the text
Taglieber, Johnson, & Yarbrough, 1988	40 Portuguese-speaking ESL readers	1. pictorial context 2. vocabulary preteaching 3. pre-questions 4. control	1. open-ended questions 2. M-C questions	pictorial and preteaching increased M-C scores the most
Tang, 1974	106 Cantonese-speaking ESL children	translation method vs. non-translation method	1. scores on pretest and posttest 2. gain scores in science reading comprehension test	significant interaction between the method of teaching second language reading and the attitudes of learners to read their own language as well as the language to be learned
Van Parreren & Schouten-Van Parreren, 1981	113 subjects	text types	think aloud data	student self-report useful for setting up instruction

Table 2.10. Instruction (cont.).

Investigators	Subjects	Independent Variable	Dependent Variable	Findings
Williams, 1981	368 Nigerian ESL pupils	1. language environment 2. reading resources 3. attitude towards reading English 4. exposure to the mass media (English) 5. types of schools 6. sex differences 7. age	1. performance on reading comprehension (cloze procedure) 2. vocabulary knowledge (alternative choice questions) 3. rate of reading (sentence completion) 4. questionnaires administered to pupils and teachers	1. type of school and reading resources were the best predictors of scores on the reading tests 2. attitude towards reading English contributed significantly to the prediction of reading tests 3. exposure to the mass media, and age, acting in combination with other variables, accounted for some of the variation in the reading scores

Lutjeharms (1985), Narayanaswamy (1982), and Williams (1981). The other group of studies focuses specifically on instructional strategies and materials. Bialystock (1983), Brown, Yongpei, and Yinglong (1984), Hosenfeld (1984), Kleinman (1987), Laufer-Dvorkin (1981), O'Flanagan (1985), Pederson (1986), Pugh (1977), Taglieber, Johnson, and Yarbrough (1988), Tang (1974), and Van Parreren and Schouten-Van Parreren (1981) comprise this group.

The first group finds particular curricular designs facilitative of reading comprehension. Among these designs are different grouping strategies, various distributions of native and target language instruction in reading, and types of materials and exposure to reading materials available to learners. The second group finds particular instructional strategies in reading to be useful including types of comprehension cues, inductive and deductive teaching strategies, open-ended questioning strategies, instruction in intensive reading strategies, training in memorization, questioning with reading texts removed, nontranslation techniques, and training in think-aloud strategies.

These instructional-evaluative studies reflect a "what worked for our program" spirit. For the most part, they provide some insights into curricular design. As a whole, however, they do not describe contextual variables in enough depth to advise and seriously inform the field on questions of generalized curricular directions and methodologies.

THE PROBLEMATIC NATURE OF THE DATA BASE

A possible reaction to a critical look at the data base in second language reading is despair. Clearly, the next generation of work in second language reading needs to attend to a number of different areas in order to refine the research area, to help it grow as a viable scientific endeavor, and to make it a legitimate and useful base for principled decisions in instruction and curriculum development.

One area in need of attention is theory development. Future research needs to explore models of reading in general where the bulk of reading research lies. Such explorations will lead toward the development, modification, and substantiation of fundamentally sound second language specific reading models. Clearly, this book is the expression of a particular theory of reading in a second language and is meant to provide a perspective—not *the* perspective—on reading in a second language.

A second area that must be taken up as a concern of second language reading research is the specification of variables in studies. In the present data base, instrument development, reliability, validity, and scoring are rarely mentioned. The studies listed in Tables 2.2 through 2.10 frequently cite "comprehension test scores" (just as an example) without providing information about the tests. Perhaps more importantly, complete descriptions of subject groups, including native language background, age, educational level, interests, and attitudes must be provided so that legitimate comparisons can be made. For the most part at the present time, each study seems to be an N of 1 rather than a piece of a larger puzzle. By attending to these concerns, more valid views on the reading process in a second language can be developed.

Of course, these concerns are not the exclusive domain of second language reading research. In a research synthesis entitled "Models of the Reading Process" Samuels and Kamil (1984) note how difficult it is to generate research-based generalizations about reading behavior. They argue, first, that there is an extremely limited knowledge base from which to draw. Second, they note that changes in materials, readers, reading tasks, and the context of experiments alter and influence experimental findings. Within their article they remark that findings "may be an adequate description of the reading process for a particular set of conditions *but not for all conditions*" (p. 190; emphasis theirs).

These comments are clearly relevant to second language reading research. On the one hand, there is an extremely limited data base. Moreover, within that limited data base the changes from study to study are immense: Materials may be artificial or natural; readers may be children or adults, from any one of a multitude of cultures both literate and nonliterate; the reading task may range from the completion of a cloze test to 10 multiple-choice questions to recall in either the native or second language to thinking aloud while reading; and finally, the contexts in which the data are collected are almost as varied as the readers themselves, stemming from bilingual to foreign language contexts, to second language contexts, to school-based or to adult education settings.

The variability from study to study makes comparisons in reading development across readers, languages, and proficiency levels tantamount to impossible. To further aggravate the difficulties in coming to an understanding of development, the majority of second language studies are product-oriented. In other words, they generally focus on an outcome measure or on a result. While they may examine how readers *use* data from a text in order to understand the text, they rarely probe how learners *gather* those data in order to construct their understandings. Moreover, second language reading studies tend to *infer* development rather than *trace* it. They infer from data gathered across different subject groups of different proficiency levels on different text types, rather than tracing it along with the development of general language proficiency within a stable passage topic domain.

SUMMARY

This book is written with the intention of rectifying some of the ills currently extant within the area of second language reading. The following two chapters will provide an in-depth look at comprehension processes exhibited by several groups of second language readers. The discussion of these processes will take place within the contexts of text-driven elements (i.e., vocabulary, syntax, orthography) as well as reader-based factors such as topic knowledge. The goal of these discussions is to buttress and to develop a theory of second language reading.

Subsequent chapters will also call attention to other issues raised within the discussion of the data base. If research in second language reading is in a very real sense "unprincipled" and directionless, the same comment can be made regarding instruction and assessment. A similar confusion and a sense of the generic pervade instruction as they do research; a parallel inconsistency between the knowledge base and how knowledge is assessed is even more pronounced. The goal of these chapters is to provide alternative models of both teaching and assessing second language reading that are more consistent with and reflective of the phenomenon to which they are tied.

3

Text-Driven Operations in Second Language Reading

INTRODUCTION

The model posited in Chapter One (Figure 1.7) is one that has developed over several years of analyzing the reading comprehension processes and products of second language readers. It attempts to illustrate process and, at the same time, to highlight a number of seen and unseen variables critical to it. That is, the model attempts to integrate both social and cognitive perspectives in second language reading. Such an attempt is both challenging and risky. It is challenging in that the entire second language reading process seems to be so complex, individual, and idiosyncratic. It is risky in that the model posits an integrative process and yet labels elements as separate, albeit interdependent, entities.

The discussion in this and the following chapter focuses on components in the model and the ways in which various facets of the process illustrated in the model interact to yield a second language reader's understanding. Evidence generated by second language readers of different proficiency levels, under a number of different research conditions, using a variety of different text types and contents, is listed and discussed.

Books are of necessity linear and chronological. *Reading Development in a Second Language* as one such entity is also linear; hence, there is a chapter three and a chapter four. This organization is not, however, meant to imply that the factors discussed in Chapter Four *follow* those in Chapter Three; nor is it meant to support any of the dichotomies so prevalent in the educational literature. Some of these dichotomies are:

data driven	conceptually driven
text-based	reader-based
bottom-up	top-down
inside the head	outside the head
cognitive	social

explicit	implicit
visible	nonvisible
intellectual	affective
external	internal
text-based	knowledge-based

Even the briefest, most cursory analysis of second language readers yields data casting doubt on these either/or perspectives. The words of Lee Shulman are appropriate here:

> If I could speak in tongues, I would, in order to present to you a model that can be grasped in its fullest sense all at once. But, I can't. And so I will list. But the list is not meant to be an ordered list. With that said, I still know what you'll do. (Shulman, 1987)

Although Shulman was referring to a model of teacher education, his words are most relevant. The reading process is clearly multidimensional and multivariate, and it is critical, at all times, to keep that fundamental concept in mind. But since words on a page are not like notes on a music staff that denote tones happening simultaneously, discussion of multivariateness is forced into a unidimensional mode.

As in the writing of any text, judgments have been made while writing *Reading Development in a Second Language*. A major decision was whether Chapter Three should be Chapter Four and Chapter Four Chapter Three. In the dilemma encountered over chapter placement, Chapter Three ended up to be Chapter Three for several reasons. First, its topic deals with the "visible" in reading—the text as it appears on paper or screen. Second, its topic has not been very popular in discussions of second language reading. The literature review in Chapter Two reveals that researchers have been concerned with the more myste-rious components of reading such as background knowledge and with holistic rather than componential processes. Third, after several studies utilizing eye movement protocols, it became very clear that second language readers—like their first language counterparts—were indeed attending to microlevel features in texts, and that if processing were indeed interrupted at the microlevel, processing was affected at other stages. Hence, the decision was made to place Chapter Three as three and Four as four.

Specifically, Chapter Three examines the learner internal variables associated with the "seen" text, while Chapter Four examines learner internal and learner external variables associated with the "unseen" text. It is important to reiterate an argument in Chapter One: In the reading process there are both "seen" texts (those that appear in black and white) and "unseen" texts (those that are intended by the author and that carry implicit sociocultural elements). Any conceptualization of reading must account for reader interaction with both dimensions of text.

THE VISIBLE IN READING: AN ISSUES ANALYSIS

As mentioned above, it is risky to begin a discussion of reading with "words, sentences, and paragraphs," since such a beginning implies that reading is about "words, sentences, and paragraphs." Indeed, it is "about" much more, but it must also be said that without "words, sentences, and paragraphs" reading does not exist. The purpose of this chapter, then, is to examine how second language readers cope with words, sentences, and paragraphs as they read and how that coping manifests itself ultimately in comprehension.

At the outset it is important, however, to dispel a prevalent myth—it is not true that "fluent" readers glide over a page of print catching words here and there. In fact, fluent, native readers of English "see" approximately 84 percent of all content words in a text and approximately 17 percent of all function words (Carpenter & Just, 1977). Another way of saying this is that they look at most of the words on a page. Admittedly, the easier the text, the fewer words native readers need to look at directly; the harder the text, the more words they need to process. An eye movement protocol of a native reader of English serves to illustrate this phenomenon. The protocol in Figure 3.1 illustrates the eye movement patterns of a college-level reader of English. The text is taken from *Science Magazine*. The circles covering the text indicate the points of fixation (the centers of the circles) as well as the material which each reader captures in peripheral vision during reading. The point is well established within the context of the protocol that the reader has seen almost every word in the text.

Figure 3.1.   An eye-movement protocol of a native reader of English.

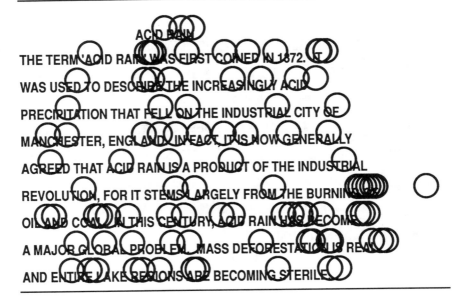

In a brief comparison, Figure 3.2 illustrates a nonnative reader of English reading in English. This eye movement protocol illustrates that a nonnative reader fixates even more densely over a fairly simple text in English than a native reader. The particular reader illustrated in Figure 3.2 is a fluent, nonnative reader; in fact, this reader is employed at a university as a professor and uses English more often than his native Japanese.

The point in these illustrations is that readers do "see" the text. While the point may seem rather obvious, it is, nevertheless true, that many researchers seem to dismiss or ignore this cognitive process of getting information from a text into the brain. Concomitantly, instructors (see Chapter Six) suggest "skimming and scanning" activities designed to get second language readers away from the text. Text features will be discussed in greater detail in a few pages; they are mentioned here merely to orient the reader toward thinking about components in a second language text.

WORDS

Word recognition

At one time, the bulk of reading research consisted of studies investigating word recognition processes on the part of beginning (child) readers and advanced (adult) readers.

Figure 3.2.   An eye-movement protocol of a nonnative reader of English.

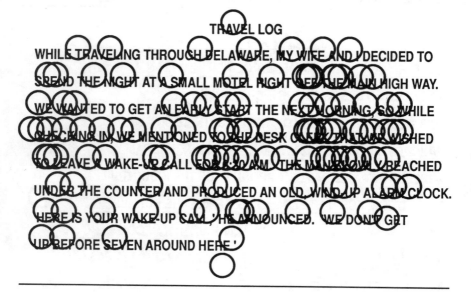

Samuels, LaBerge, and Bremer (1978), for example, compared the word processing strategies of second and fourth graders with those of skilled college readers using reaction time for word recognition as a response measure. They found that word recognition for children was often dependent on word length. Second-grade children seemed to process letter by letter, taking longer to react, for example, to h-o-r-s-e than to c-o-w. Fourth-grade readers, on the other hand, seemed to process in larger units, not taking as long as the second graders, for example, to process h-o-r-s-e. The college students demonstrated the shortest reaction time to all words, while not needing more processing time for a five-letter word than for a three-letter word. Samuels et al. concluded that readers seem to develop from "component processing to holistic processing over time" (p. 718).

Research has not concluded, however, that experienced readers process exclusively holistically. In a 1976 study, Terry, Samuels, and LaBerge, concluded that skilled readers may devote attention to whole words as well as to component parts of words depending on need. Using normal and mirror image texts with letters in their natural or "degraded" conditions, Terry et al. also measured processing time. Terry et al. found that subjects devoted the least amount of processing attention to the word "wren," for example, more processing time to degraded "wren," even more processing time to "wren" written upside down and backwards, and the largest amount of processing attention to degraded "wren" written upside down and backwards. In a theoretical follow-up to these findings, Samuels (1977) argued that readers seem to cognitively opt for holistic or component processing and that the two processes interact.

Samuels, Miller, and Eisenberg (1979) also examined word recognition latency, but included a practice variable. They found that upon first exposure, children tended toward the use of component processing—that is, they attended to single letters, to spacing, and to the sequence of letters. After repeated exposure to the same words, the children began to attend to "global features such as word length, contour, and the internal relationships" (p. 518) among letters within words. The researchers concluded from the decrease in response time to words which the children had practiced, that "processing units" increase in size as familiarity with words increases.

Patberg, Dewitz, and Samuels (1981) also found that readers were able to attend to larger processing units over time. They added a context variable to their research and found that good readers were able to use context to increase the amount of information to which they could devote attention. In other words, if the readers were told they would be identifying farm animals, good readers speeded up their processing of c-o-w versus h-o-r-s-e. Poor readers maintained the letter by letter processing regardless of context. In other words, the Patberg study found that good readers seem to utilize the "option" of component or holistic processing depending upon context, whereas "unskilled readers seemed to be locked into component processing."

In summary, these studies that measured chronometric characteristics of the process of word recognition tend to conclude that processing is dependent upon the experience of the reader, the skill of the reader, and the task that the reader must perform. The manner in which attention is allocated seems to develop over time.

Word recognition studies are generally not in vogue in reading research at the present time, because they provided as much insight as they were going to into comprehension processes. Clearly, readers who gain in proficiency gain in automaticity. Readers who do not have automatic processing are doomed to fretful decoding with little effort left over for trying to understand a message.

What relevance does a discussion of word recognition have to second language reading? Real distinctions between first and second language reading processes as well as real distinctions between and among reading in different languages begin to reveal themselves at the word level.

The distinction between first and second language reading processes appears, first, among readers who are already literate in one language and try to become literate in another. Adams (1980) notes: "[O]rthographic regularity has a strong influence on the ease with which skilled readers can encode a string of letters. . . . [H]owever, such sensitivity to orthographic regularity develops only gradually through years of reading experience" (p. 15).

It is important to consider readers who learn to read another language based on the same orthographic system—English to Spanish or German to French are examples. These languages contain a significant amount of overlapping orthographic regularity. Therefore, second language readers of these languages from particular native tongues begin the language learning process with orthographic sensitivity that they have already developed. An important study that documented the word recognition advantage that readers of English have with French is Sacco (1984). That study indicated that readers of English, even with no instruction in French, were able to detect words and nonwords in French, thus illustrating their capacity to identify spelling patterns.

Readers who must switch orthographies—from English to Arabic or from German to Korean encounter a different experience. They do not have sensitivity to orthographic regularities. In fact, they must, like child learners, first, develop a sense of the orthography. They must learn to distinguish between "d" and "b" or "П" and "Л." Only after these distinctions can be made can learners begin in their development of sensitivity to spelling patterns.

Of further importance is that some languages do not have spelling patterns per se. In other words, there are cognitive distinctions between switching orthographic systems that are principally phonetic representations (readers of German learning Russian or Arabic, for example) and switching orthographic systems that are not phonetic in nature (Spanish, written with a phonetic code, into Chinese, a character system that is only partly phonetic). If it is true as Adams (1980) argues that "sensitivity . . . develops only gradually through years of reading experience," then there is a need to differentiate between and among learners from different language backgrounds and to recognize that they are at different positions on a word recognition continuum. Succinctly said, some second language readers regardless of age must begin the second language reading process at the decoding level. Others are able to begin immediately with some type of automatic processing capacity.

This argument is not meant to suggest that having automatic processing provides positive transfer in all cases. In fact, in the case of lexical knowledge it may provide interference that a learner focused on decoding may not encounter (see below).

Consideration must be given too to phonological encoding. Words are indeed *speech* in print. Despite arguments to the contrary that contend that written texts are not wholly "speech written down" (Olson, 1981), there is, nevertheless, a phonetic component to all reading events. Even character systems that are widely believed to be exclusively "conceptual" in nature are phonologically based. DeFrancis (1984) notes that "there is much justification for considering the Chinese script to be basically—that is, more than anything else—a phonetic system of writing" (p. 111). Hence, some attention must be given to the question of a phonological base and to what extent second language readers need to acquire one. Clearly, phonological processing occurs. How second language readers cope with this processing demand needs to be understood.

A considerable amount of classroom time, for example, is spent in the act of oral reading (see Chapter Six). This instructional technique ostensibly facilitates phonological processing. Teachers argue that oral reading provides needed pronunciation practice; some researchers argue that it provides windows on the learning process. In reality, though, oral reading impedes comprehension in a second language as noted in Chapter Two.

Yet, the extent to which readers' own accents interfere with, facilitate, or have no impact on the reading process remains uninvestigated. Because of the nature of reading itself, phonological processing occurs.

Subvocalization is a standard phenomenon in reading. Evidence indicates "without any doubt, that subvocalization is . . . an involuntary stimulus input utilized by all individuals as the difficulty level of the information to be processed increases" (Hardyck, 1968, p. 20). Despite pleas to the contrary on the part of speed reading afficionados, readers do "hear" what they are reading. Admittedly, if the text is extraordinarily easy little subvocalizing occurs; for the most part, however, readers listen to themselves.

The important point is that some kind of subvocalizing *probably occurs* in second language reading. Evidence for this may be extrapolated from studies with native readers of English coping with Chinese texts. Both Hayes (1988) and Everson (1986) as mentioned previously found evidence of phonological processing on the part of both native and nonnative advanced readers of Chinese. Even those readers who have little prior knowledge for applying an appropriate phonological base nevertheless apply some phonological base. The critical point is how accurate that base needs to be. In other words, does one need to be able to pronounce *Qu'est-ce que c'est?* in order to "read" it in French and know that it says "What is that?" *or* may one read *kes ke sest* to oneself and also understand *What is that?* That is, may a second language reader simply apply *a* phonological system regardless of *which* system and accomplish as much as a second language reader with an *appropriate* phonological system? A reasonable argument may be that, at some point, any phonological system will suffice *but* as proficiency increases, the phonological system will need to match more closely to that which is encoded in the text in order to provide the reader with more appropriate tools for achieving speed and accuracy.

Lexical entries

A distinction needs to be made between word recognition and lexicon. In some sense, that distinction in a second language is clearer than it is in a first. Second language readers may well be able to "recognize" words without knowing what they "mean." Said another way, a native reader of English might be able to recognize *Sprachgefühl* as a German word (identifying the umlaut, perhaps) or Smørrebrød as a Danish word (identifying the / through the o as characteristic of Danish). Such a process denotes word recognition. A similar process occurs in a first language when a reader is able to fluently "read" *inundate* and yet have no knowledge of its meaning. A real distinction, however, is that in first language reading, reading begins with the recognition of oral vocabulary.

Lexicon refers to meaning. Second language readers have a store of words to which they attach meanings. In a real sense, these meanings are frequently unidimensional in nature—the one-word, one-meaning mentality pervading much second language teaching. When materials are presented to students, "contextually relevant" meanings are generally provided. This implies that a word such as the German *Stock* may be glossed as "floor (of a building; ex.: first floor)." The gloss does not include an alternative meaning such as *stick*, a perfectly plausible "meaning," yet irrelevant to the context.

It seems unwise to present readers with every possible "meaning" of a particular set of letters. The alternative is not any more acceptable. It implies a second language lexicon that is ultimately potentially *larger* than for a native speaker since the second language reader has to constantly re-learn individual words. A risk on the part of the nonnative is not knowing alternative meanings and getting "stuck" with encoding an appropriate meaning in an inappropriate context. This hypothesized facet of second language reading will be illustrated in the latter portion of this chapter.

SYNTAX

The second visible element in reading is word order or syntax. Adams (1980) comments:

> Syntax is the primary means by which we can specify the intended relation among words. Thus, syntax subserves communication not only by disambiguating the referents of the words, but also by defining new relations among them. It is clear that syntactic competence is an important dimension of linguistic competence in general. (p. 18)

From a second language perspective, syntax is rarely viewed in its functional sense; that is, indicating relationships between and among words. Syntax is generally dismissed as "grammar" and is kept conceptually distinct from semantics. It is rare when semantic elements of syntax—the fact that syntax carries with it the *meaning* of relationships—are perceived. Adams (1980) comments further:

> If readers cannot recognize a word, they generally know they cannot. If they cannot correctly recognize a syntactic structure, they may not even realize it. Further, at the lexical level, it is easy to distinguish between whether readers do not know a word or just cannot read it. The parallel distinction at the syntactic level may be unclear. (p. 23)

Interestingly, from a second-language perspective, Adams' caution may be even more profound. From the above discussion, first-language-literate second language-readers may be able to read a word, *but not know it* in addition to being *unable* to recognize unknown or unique syntactic structures.

In another article Adams with Huggins (1980) refer to Grice's (1975) principles of cooperation, indicating that:

> [The] obligation is to try by any means possible to interpret what is said. Consequently, children faced with a syntactic construction beyond their capacities do not discard the message as frivolous or nonsensical. Either they rely on semantics, or they try to apply known syntactic rules that work for similar constructions. [This leads toward] interesting misunderstandings. (p. 102)

The implication of these views is that second language readers—who are also syntactically constrained like first language children—use the tools that they have available to them for syntactic processing. This is especially true of literate adults who know that written texts convey messages; that is, adults employ the Gricean principle of cooperation, making any syntactic structure they may have at their disposal work for them. This second language processing leads to even more "interesting misunderstandings" than are found in first language. A discussion of such misunderstandings that can be traced to flawed syntactic processing parallel to those rooted in word recognition and lexical difficulties is found in the latter portion of this chapter.

Several additional points need to be made regarding syntactic processing in second language reading. Oller's (1979) concept of "anticipatory grammar" is very useful at this juncture. Although Oller (1979) is specifically referring to listening, his comments also apply to reading. He argues the following:

> We are practically always a jump ahead of the person we are listening to, and sometimes we even outrun our own tongues when we are speaking. It is not unusual in a speech error for a speaker to say a word several syllables ahead of what he intended to say, nor is it uncommon for a listener to take a wrong turn in his thinking and fail to understand correctly simply because he is expecting something else to be said. . . . the constraints on what may follow in a given sequence of linguistic elements go far beyond the traditionally recognized grammatical ones, and they operate in every aspect of our cognition. . . . The sequence itself may consist of highly structured elements, but there must be a sequence because the totality of even a relatively simple aspect of our universe is too complex to be taken in one gulp. In a sense we take in elements single file at a given rate . . . by treating sequences or clusters as unitary chunks, the mind constructs a rich cognitive system. (pp. 20–30)

Oller's words provide an "idealized" picture of syntactic processing that is useful for considering a theory of second language reading. Second language readers approach text processing with this model of chunking. That is, they expect to encounter certain features as they read; when these expectations are filled they proceed. Adams (1980) concurs with Oller's (1979) view and states:

> [A]s the reader proceeds through the text, each word is entered into a short-term memory buffer. After each word is entered, the reader checks to see whether or not it completes a constituent structure. If not, she or he proceeds to the next word. As soon as the reader thinks a phrase has been completed, the contents of the buffer are recoded or collapsed into a composite meaning complex. (p. 21)

These statements need to be considered in light of second language text processing. Second language readers actually have two systems from which to work: a native language syntactic processing system that signals the end of constituent elements, and an imperfectly developed knowledge of the signaling system in the second language. It is important to include that a second language reader, depending upon proficiency level, may merely have knowledge of the syntactic system, but no processing knowledge. Comparison of a native reader of German, a nonnative, yet knowledgeable reader of German, as well as a beginner illustrate the point of syntactic processing.

Figure 3.3 illustrates the behaviors of a native reader of German on an authentic passage, "Die Sprachwissenschaft." This native reader's data indicate that the reader devoted maximum attention to Line Four. The reader essentially decoded the line with a total of 24 fixations, averaging 600 milliseconds per fixation (Bernhardt, 1984).

The native reader's initial reading evinces processing strategies similar to those employed by other native German readers. First, the native reader illustrated in Figure 3.3 demonstrates an integrating behavior that tends to occur at the right of the text. Second, the native reader tends to skip copular verbs such as *waren*, *werden*, and *ist*, while directly fixating verbs such as *diskutiert*, *verwenden*, and *auseinandersetzen*. Third, the native reader directly fixates each dual function article with the exception of *der* in Line Six. Fourth, the reader directly fixates all punctuation.

Line Four serves as an important illustration of processing behaviors. The native reader remembered only the word *Formen* in the recall protocol (Bernhardt, 1984). The reader's protocol consists of "Sprachwissenschaft/Linguistik/es wird sehr viel studiert/Formen," indicating that despite the attention allotted to the text, the reader was not able to comprehend the text sufficiently to hold it in memory.

Figure 3.4 illustrates a nonnative experienced reader's behaviors. An overview of Figure 3.4 reveals several distinct differences between the strategies employed by the nonnative and the native reader. First, the nonnative experienced reader chose to devote extensive attention to Lines Two and Five and little attention to Line Four. Second, the fixation sequences on Lines Two and Five appear to be different from the native reader's. The experienced reader's fixations consist of groupings of fixations on sections of the lines. This pattern of fixations divides Line Five into three sections: *die Untersuchungen/zum Inhalt/der sprachlichen*. In summary, the nonnative experienced reader processed constituents making up the line rather than the entire line as a *gestalt*, implying a lower level processing strategy than that employed by the native reader.

Figure 3.5 illustrates the eye movement behaviors of a nonnative inexperienced reader of German as a foreign language. An overview contrasts with both the native and the experienced reader. The native reader, for example, consistently fixated initially at least 15 characters into the line and ultimately devoted processing time to the right of the text. The experienced reader, employing a different strategy, spanned the entire text line by line with fixations. In contrast to the experienced readers, the inexperienced reader illustrated in Figure 3.5 relied on information on the left section of the text, demonstrating integrative processing strategies on the left rather than on the right. An overview reveals, in addition, that fixations were not nearly so dense; the inexperienced reader used slightly fewer fixations than the experienced reader. Third, fixations are denser on Line Five than on the other lines in the text. Fourth, similar to the experienced

Figure 3.3. An eye-movement protocol of a native reader of German.

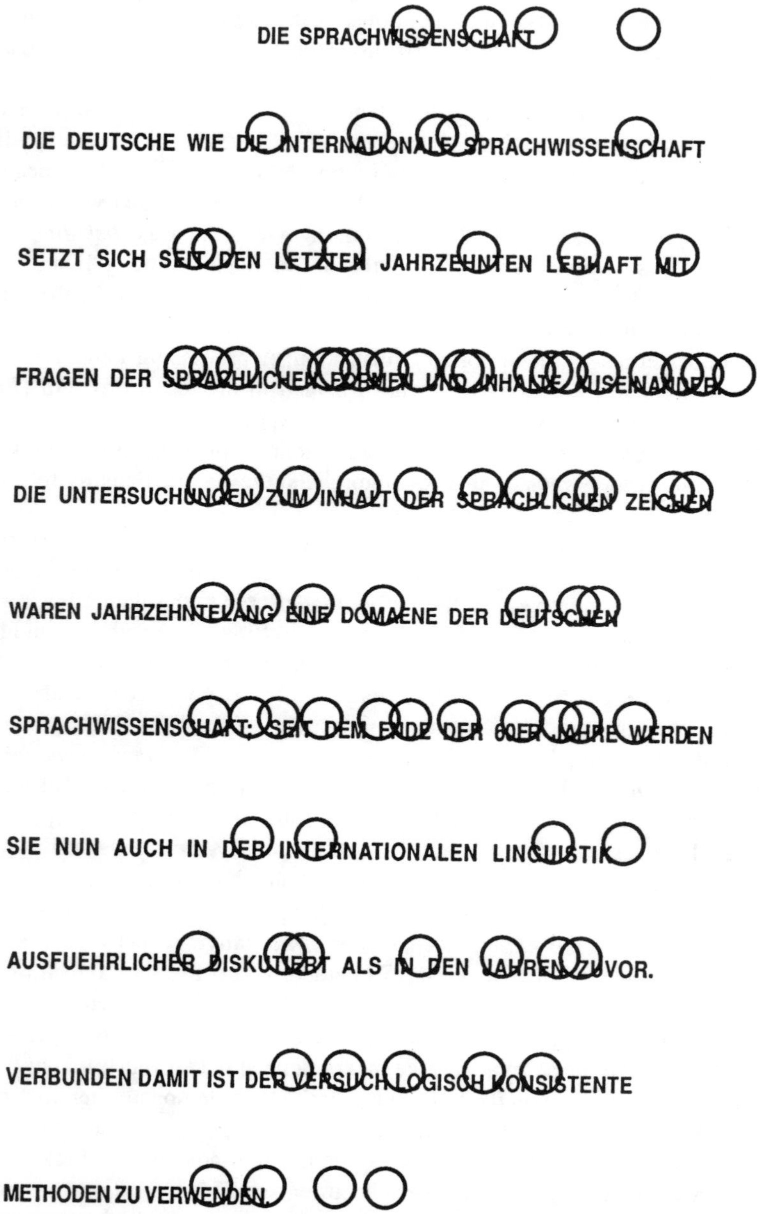

DIE SPRACHWISSENSCHAFT

DIE DEUTSCHE WIE DIE INTERNATIONALE SPRACHWISSENSCHAFT

SETZT SICH SEIT DEN LETZTEN JAHRZEHNTEN LEBHAFT MIT

FRAGEN DER SPRACHLICHEN FORMEN UND INHALTE AUSEINANDER

DIE UNTERSUCHUNGEN ZUM INHALT DER SPRACHLICHEN ZEICHEN

WAREN JAHRZEHNTELANG EINE DOMAENE DER DEUTSCHEN

SPRACHWISSENSCHAFT; SEIT DEM ENDE DER 60ER JAHRE WERDEN

SIE NUN AUCH IN DER INTERNATIONALEN LINGUISTIK

AUSFUEHRLICHER DISKUTIERT ALS IN DEN JAHREN ZUVOR.

VERBUNDEN DAMIT IST DER VERSUCH LOGISCH KONSISTENTE

METHODEN ZU VERWENDEN.

Figure 3.4. An eye-movement protocol of a nonnative experienced reader of German.

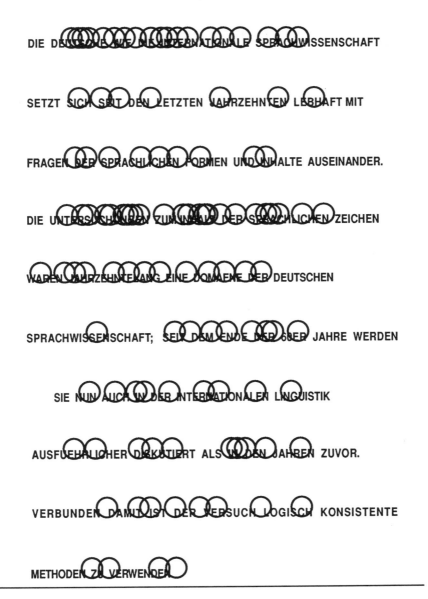

Figure 3.5. An eye-movement protocol of a nonnative inexperienced reader of German.

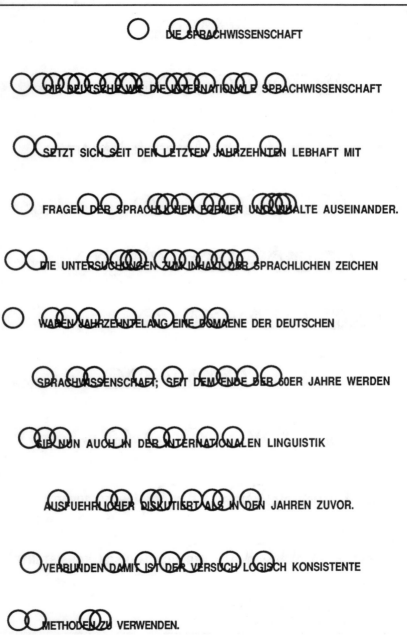

DIE SPRACHWISSENSCHAFT

DER DEUTSCHEN WAR DIE INTERNATIONALE SPRACHWISSENSCHAFT

SETZT SICH SEIT DEN LETZTEN JAHRZEHNTEN LEBHAFT MIT

FRAGEN DER SPRACHLICHEN FORMEN UND INHALTE AUSEINANDER.

DIE UNTERSUCHUNGEN ZUM INHALT DER SPRACHLICHEN ZEICHEN

WAREN JAHRZEHNTELANG EINE DOMAENE DER DEUTSCHEN

SPRACHWISSENSCHAFT; SEIT DEM ENDE DER 60ER JAHRE WERDEN

SIE NUN AUCH IN DER INTERNATIONALEN LINGUISTIK

AUSFUEHRLICHER DISKUTIERT ALS IN DEN JAHREN ZUVOR.

VERBUNDEN DAMIT IST DER VERSUCH LOGISCH KONSISTENTE

METHODEN ZU VERWENDEN.

reader, the inexperienced reader does not demonstrate a consistent fixation pattern across the line, concentrating, rather, within words.

The inexperienced reader's recall protocol after the first reading consists of the following elements: "The German Sprachwissenschaft/ Sprachwissenschaft was formerly the domain of/after the 60s/more constant/international Linguistik/ zu verwenden." These phrases were scattered across the protocol paper, deliberately placed, indicating that as the subject encoded the information, the subject retained memory for the position of the phrase as it appeared on the screen.

The Structure of Texts

The third component of the "visible" important for consideration in the development of a principled view of second language reading is the structure of texts. The term "structure of texts" is used rather than text structure. Specifically, "text structure" refers to the rhetorical organization of texts; namely, features such as a comparison-contrast argument structure or the five paragraph essay (introduction, body, and conclusion). Indeed, text structure is an important issue for discussion. But the concept "the structure of texts" also includes typography or the manner in which texts are physically displayed. Both components— rhetorical organization and graphic display—are variables of importance for any second language reader.

Of the "seen" variables in second language reading, text structure is the one that has received the most attention. A considerable amount of research has been conducted focusing on the variable of text structure for second language readers. Chapter Two highlighted text structure components in reading. Most studies investigating text structure present readers with various rhetorical structures and then measure readers' comprehension relative to the structures. As noted in Chapter Two most of these studies utilize specially structured and constructed texts for investigating the variable of text structure and tend not to investigate naturally occurring text structures under naturalistic conditions.

In contrast to text structure, the graphic dimensions of texts have not been investigated. It is important to understand that print size, type face, punctuation, the use of color, for example, are culturally loaded. They are chosen by authors and editors to facilitate the comprehension process. This facilitation may be in the role of providing emphasis, signalling topic shifts, or communicating the very nature of the discourse.

This dimension of texts was alluded to already in Chapter One. The interpretation of "Mike is a manic depressive" may also be made simply in terms of the *typeface* in which it is printed. A medical journal tends to use a serif typeface; the *National Enquirer*, a sans-serif typeface. Just as beginning readers tend to ignore punctuation when reading aloud and tend to overload on concepts leading to a breakdown in comprehension, second language readers may fail to see or understand the typesetting cues. They, too, can overload or begin to build a fallacious interpretation.

Another aspect of anticipating the messages sent by graphic set-up is applying the culturally determined rules for typesetting in an inappropriate situation. Once again the dilemma becomes one of either having no knowledge of the cuing system or applying culturally inappropriate knowledge of cuing systems. Waller (1987) notes that "very young readers may not have reached the level of development needed to make decisions about the relevance of printed material to particular tasks" (p. 82). A parallel argument may be made about second language readers: they do not perhaps have the experience to make relevant decisions about the typographic make-up of texts.

According to Waller (1987), typography is "macropunctuation at the discourse level." He adds: "Like sentence-level punctuation, macropunctuation has the dual function of directing the reader's strategy and explaining the structure of a document" (p. 91). Waller's statement is reminiscent of Oller's conceptualization of syntax as sequence. Waller defers to de Beaugrande's argument, stating:

> De Beaugrande (1984) emphasizes the[se] similarities between sentence structure and paragraph structure through his theory of linear action which, he suggests, accounts for the way writers and readers are able to manage the transition between complex multidimensional "cognitive space" and linear linguistic sequences. (p. 92)

Ultimately, Waller (1987) notes that "the general knowledge and cultural attitudes that we bring to texts can lead to quite definite expectations about the content and design of different types of text" (p. 99). In other words, an "expectancy grammar" seems to exist at the textual level. This is just another level of expectancy that a second language reader must acquire.

THE VISIBLE IN READING: A DATA ANALYSIS

Throughout the previous pages, issues were raised regarding word recognition, lexical accessing, phonological elements, syntactic processing, and text configuration and display within the context of second language reading. The intent of these next pages is to place the issues raised in the previous pages in the context of specific texts and readers. A similar format will be used in the following chapter focused on conceptually driven elements in reading. In fact, data drawn from the same second language texts and readers will be explored.

This final portion of the chapter relies on data from three separate studies. The first study, Allen, Bernhardt, Berry, and Demel (1988), challenged the concept of proficiency guidelines developed from the Foreign Service Institute framework for proficiency assessment. Arguing that the framework emphasized text-based components such as words, syntax, and text structure and that it essentially ignored the reader, the study set out to determine if indeed there were a text hierarchy for second language readers. The next set of two studies, Fry (1988) and Beltran, Cabrera, and Coombe (1989) are replications of Allen et al. (1988). All three studies, quantitatively oriented, indicate that a perspective on second language reading that is text-oriented neither clarifies nor predicts the nature of the second language reading process.

ALLEN, BERNHARDT, BERRY, AND DEMEL (1988)

The intent of the Allen et al. study was to examine the following research questions: (a) Do students perform differentially according to text type? (b) Does there seem to be a hierarchy of reading proficiency based on (1) text genre; (2) linguistic features of texts; or (3) topic of text? These questions were posed within the theoretical framework outlined in previous pages.

Participants in the study were students in the ninth through twelfth grades enrolled in first- through fifth-year courses in French, German, and Spanish in two upper middle-class suburban school districts. Texts for the study were chosen from a variety of sources: newspapers, magazines, and various types of correspondence. The texts were representative of the text genres mentioned for different proficiency levels as outlined in the *ACTFL Proficiency Guidelines*.

Testing occurred during regularly scheduled foreign language class periods. Each class was given four texts to read. As a test of comprehension students wrote recall protocols in English about the content of each of the experimental passages. They were told to write down as much as they could possibly remember from each text.

The students' recall protocols were scored using Meyer's (1985) recall protocol scoring system (see Chapter Six). This system identifies the structural characteristics as well as lexical units of a passage. As is true for L1 protocol scoring, any reasonable paraphrasing of lexical units was judged as present in the protocol and awarded a point. Interrater reliability for the scoring averaged .93.

Data were analyzed using a repeated measures Analysis of Variance. The total N for data analysis in the study was 105 learners, 35 subjects per language, 7 per level. The dependent measure was percentage of text propositions recalled.

The following figures illustrate the basic findings of the study.

The data do not indicate a textual hierarchy (Figure 3.6). Average comprehension scores across all of the subjects ranged from 23.7 percent to 21.3 percent—a range signifying no statistically significant differences. In fact, different text types were found to be more or less difficult by various learners in different levels. Figure 3.7 clearly portrays the complex interactions that occurred in the study. The friendly letter was easiest for the French students, while the German

Figure 3.6.   Average comprehension scores according to text type.

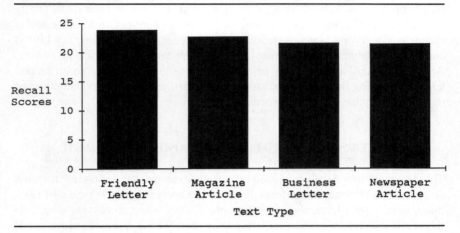

and the Spanish students found the magazine article to be easiest for them. In contrast, the French students found the parallel French magazine article to be the most difficult. These phenonema led to the complex of statistically significant interactions. In summary, text characteristics, that is, genres consisting of different grammatical features, are not very good predictors of reading performance. The study did indicate, however, a clear progression of development across years of language instruction. That development is illustrated in Figure 3.8. Figure 3.8 illustrates the statistical development of the first and second years, to the third year, to the fourth and fifth years of instruction.

Figure 3.7.   Average comprehension scores according to language and text type.

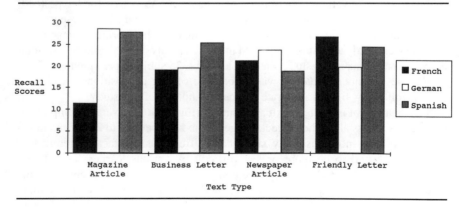

Figure 3.8.   Progression of reading development across years of language instruction.

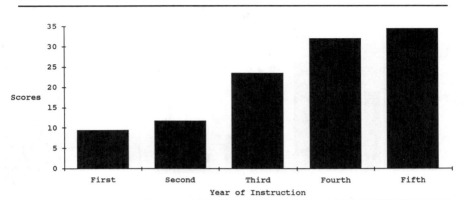

These findings formed the backdrop for two subsequent replications, analyzing the performance of college-level language learners on the same texts used in the study with high school students. The intent of the further analysis was to explore whether findings generated by a very different group of language learners would be parallel. If findings were parallel, then reading research could begin to assume that first-year students are first-year students, for example, regardless of their maturity, life experience, and so on. In other words, *exposure* to the foreign language would seem to be the principal variable of concern within any generalizations about foreign language reading rather than textual features.

Interestingly, a study appearing simultaneously with the Allen et al. (1988) study, Lee and Musumeci (1988), provides replication of the findings. Lee and Musumeci, using a more complicated schema including reading ''strategies,'' found no hierarchy of texts or strategies among college level learners of Italian. In fact, they found interactions parallel to the ones in Allen, et al. In contrast to that study, however, Lee and Musumeci found no indication of reading development. All subjects in their study scored at basically the same level regardless of level of instruction.

FRY (1988) AND BELTRAN, CABRERA, AND COOMBE (1989)

The replication took place at the Ohio State University in the French and Spanish Departments. One hundred twelve subjects participated in the French replication (Fry, 1988); 160 in the Spanish replication (Beltran et al., 1989); all subjects read the same four texts used in the previous study under similar conditions. Protocols were collected and scored in like manner.

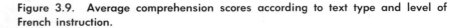

Figure 3.9. Average comprehension scores according to text type and level of French instruction.

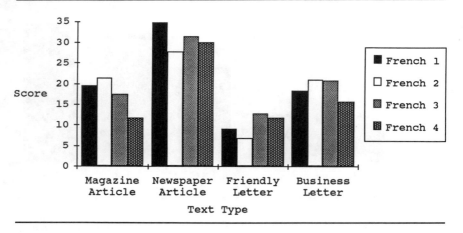

The data reveal that there was no statistical difference between and among the four levels of French. Interestingly, while this finding is different from that in the high school level study, it is exactly parallel to that of Lee and Musumeci (1988) with a college level group of Italian learners.

The data from the Spanish replication do, however, indicate a statistical difference between and among the levels of Spanish. In fact, in the four quarters of Spanish there are three distinct levels: one, two and three, and four. Figure 3.9

Figure 3.10. Average comprehension scores according to text type and level of Spanish instruction.

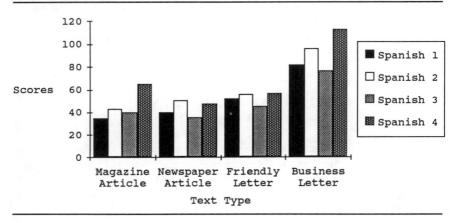

illustrates the interactions of text type and level in the French data; Figure 3.10 illustrates the interactions in the Spanish data.

In contrast to Allen et al. yet parallel to Lee and Musumeci are the statistical differences between and among the texts in both the French and Spanish data. Notably, these differences are not those, however, predicted by the typology of texts behind the *ACTFL Proficiency Guidelines*. The graphs also reveal statistically significant interactions of text type and level of instruction. That is, the data indicate some texts were relatively more or less difficult for learners of different levels. In summary, neither a textual hierarchy nor a strict level of instruction hierarchy is indicated by any of the data.

SUMMARY

This chapter places second language reading research in a conundrum. On the one hand, text-driven operations are of critical importance in understanding the second language reading process. Words, sentences, paragraph structure, print, punctuation, and the interrelationships between and among them are key variables. On the other hand, however, text variables, specifically grammatical features as well as text types, provide little if any insight toward understanding either second language reading or second language readers. The pages that follow direct attention away from textual aspects toward reader-based dimensions.

4

Knowledge-Driven Operations in Second Language Reading

INTRODUCTION

The term knowledge-driven refers to the "unseen" in texts. Knowledge can be defined as that information held by the writer and assumed to be known to the reader. Or knowledge can be defined idiosyncratically as that information held uniquely by an individual reader. The former is held implicitly in the text and is assumed to be shared; the latter is held by the reader and possesses varying degrees of relevance for the processing of any given text.

The theory and research presented in Chapter Three indicates that text-driven processes play a significant role in second language reading. Because of the imperfect knowledge of text features brought to a text by a second language reader, this imperfect knowledge of the "way the language works" (to use the words of many an experienced language teacher) inevitably plays a role in ultimate understanding. Yet as Adams (1980) notes, word recognition and grammatical ability are not the only actors in the process:

> In order to understand a written text, the reader must . . . be able to recognize the words and to analyze the syntax. But she or he must be able to access and organize the appropriate conceptual knowledge. (p. 24)

Spiro, Vispoel, Schmitz, Samarapungavan, and Boerger (1987) continue:

> A fundamental tenet of all recent theories of comprehension, problem solving, and decision making is that success in such cognitive arenas depends on the activation and appropriate application of relevant pre-existing knowledge. Despite the substantial agreement on this general claim, we know very little about the organization of background knowledge and the method of its application to the understanding of new situations when, because of a combination of the breadth, complexity, and irregularity of a content domain, formulating knowledge in that domain to explicitly prescribe its full range of uses is impossible. (p. 177)

One of the ways in which researchers have been investigating the whole area of knowledge application and activation is through the concept of *script*. According to Yekovich and Walker (1987):

> A script represents a person's prototypical knowledge of a routine activity, such as PAINTING A ROOM or GOING TO A RESTAURANT. Scripted knowledge has two features that make it useful for studying knowledge-based contributions to reading. First, a script, by definition, is culturally uniform and represents "expert" knowledge about human behavior in a routine situation. . . . Second, scripts generally have well-defined goal structures and predictable temporal properties. (p. 147)

Graesser, Haberlandt, and Koizumi (1987) provide a parallel image. They state:

> Knowledge-based inferences are inherited from the reader's knowledge about physical, social, cognitive, and emotional phenomena. We assume that this world knowledge is embodied in a large set of *generic knowledge structures* (GKSs) and *specific knowledge structures* stored in long-term memory. . . . We assume that the knowledge-based inferences generated during text comprehension are furnished by the GKSs and specific knowledge structures that are relevant to the text . . . (p. 218)

These processes of knowledge acquisition, storage, and inference generation are indeed complex. Simultaneously, it is clear from the above quotations that knowledge-driven operations in reading are culture-dependent; Yekovich and Walker (1987) as well as Graesser et al. (1987) speak to this issue explicitly. An understanding of the implications of knowledge-driven operations for cross-cultural/cross-linguistic comprehension is critical for the development of principled research and instruction in second language reading. The goal of this chapter, therefore, is to contribute to the development of such an understanding.

It is important to reiterate here that this chapter is separate from Chapter Three only for organizational purposes. It serves to complete the theory and research on which this book is based. In doing so it draws on theory from cognitive psychology as well as sociolinguistics and will present data from recent studies of second language reading. The following chapter—Chapter Five—synthesizes the knowledge-driven processes described in this chapter as well as the text-driven ones outlined and discussed in the previous chapter. Chapter Five provides a coherent and integrated view of the process of second language reading.

THE NONVISIBLE IN READING: AN ISSUES ANALYSIS

The introduction to Chapter Three highlighted some of the terms attached to the nonvisible (non-words-on-the-page) facet of reading. Among these terms are conceptually driven, implicit, internal, reader-based, and knowledge-based. All of them imply the existence of information critical to the reading process that does not appear explicitly as part of a written text.

As stated in Chapter Two, a considerable portion of second language reading research has been devoted to these factors; that is, factors related to the topic or the cultural implications of particular reading passages and particular second language readers. The intention of these initial pages is to lay out issues involved in conceptual matters in second language text processing, to discuss the extent to which the present research base has explicated these issues, and to draw attention to recent research in cognitive processes in reading.

KNOWLEDGE

The term background knowledge has evolved into an educational buzzword. While on the one hand it has been finally seen to be a variable that contributes to both race and gender discrimination in educational settings, it has also been used to dismiss learning phenomena without thorough analysis. This lack of analysis is nowhere more obvious than in second language reading research. Chapter Two alluded to this superficiality. Second language learners have been generically grouped according to background knowledge variables. Grouping 50 subjects according to background knowledge has led researchers to juxtapose "50 Catholic Spanish-speaking learners of English" with "50 Islamic Arabic-speaking learners of English" just as one example. While on the one hand one might argue that indeed there are real background differences in these two groups, there is actually no real measure of *knowledge* differences. In fact, the groups may consist of some experts in religions of the world or the groups may consist of learners who have spent considerable time in Spanish or Arabic speaking countries. Simply put, assuming "knowledge" or lack thereof on the basis of ethnic heritage is a rather naive view of "knowledge."

Local-Level Knowledge

There are many types of "knowledge." There is highly idiosyncratic knowledge that individuals carry with them such as where they keep their checkbooks or in which drawer in the kitchen the scissors are supposed to be. This type of knowledge enables intimates to communicate without words or with vague references such as "Well, you know where the checkbook is. Get it out." There is also idiosyncratic knowledge that individual groups carry with them and use for communicative purposes. On a local level, the term "Buckeye Donuts" evokes very specific knowledge on the part of certain people who work in a particular area of the City of Columbus, Ohio; on a less local level, the term may evoke less specific, yet relevant knowledge, on the part of individuals who know that Ohio is the Buckeye State, that the Ohio State teams are known as "the

Buckeyes'' and, who are able to infer, therefore, that Buckeye Donuts may be a place to get donuts somewhere in Ohio and so forth. It is clear that these examples draw on the concept of ''culture'' in its sense as the implicit knowledge particular groups have.

At a wider level, larger groups also carry implicit knowledge. It is a rare North American who does not have knowledge of McDonald's restaurants (what they look like, under what circumstances one gets a tray, how one orders, what the food will look like, what kinds of tables and chairs there will be, etc.). They also carry knowledge of income tax forms, or knowledge of rules of driving. Yet within each one of these overriding ''knowledges'' there is considerable variation depending upon individual familiarity.

Domain-Specific Knowledge

Another kind of knowledge is domain-specific knowledge. In a sense, schools provide generalized domain-specific knowledge. Schooling—at least through the high school level in North America—is to provide some knowledge of history, social science, natural science, art, music, and language. In fact, that very act of handing down the knowledge base provides the keys to socialization—that is, those facets of knowledge that separate Americans from British or Canadians from French, for example. Each cultural group provides its unique ''versions'' of history and science; these ''versions'' become defining characteristics of people schooled in those versions. Such statements can only be made at the most general level, however. For it is eminently clear that the variation in domain knowledge gathered from schooling is enormous and that some students ''catch on'' that the material presented can be analyzed and interpreted from a variety of perspectives.

Indeed, domain-specific knowledge is acquired in many ways. For some people, additional schooling provides deeper domain-specific knowledge. While general schooling gives information about the War of 1812, specific courses in early American history provide even more knowledge. Yet, additional knowledge does not have to be gained from formal schooling. Mere interest in the area that leads a person to read another history book on his own fosters additional ''knowledge.'' The point is that domain-specific knowledge can be gained in many ways. While it is possible to make the assumption that if someone declares that he has domain-specific knowledge of a particular area (since he or she happens to be a history professor with specialization in Post-Revolutionary War American-British relations), it does not necessarily mean that a person who does *not* make such a declaration does not have similar knowledge. The latter person may have made a hobby of American-British relations and have dilettante-knowledge rather than professional knowledge of the domain. Nevertheless, both may have high-level domain knowledge, albeit that knowledge is more visible in the former than in the latter.

Other domain-specific knowledge examples would include knowledge of the rules of soccer, of electrochemistry, of cooking, of how airplanes are put together and how they function, of how computers work, or of how to analyze a literary text. This argument is not meant to imply that domain-specific knowledge is in some way explicitly distinct from the other knowledges mentioned above. Obviously, there is overlap. The amount of overlap probably varies from individual to individual. The point is merely to explore facets of knowledge that any individual may draw upon in order to understand and to interpret.

Culture-Specific Knowledge

Another facet of "knowledge" is culture-specific knowledge. Culture-specific knowledge includes ritualistic knowledge as well as cultural-historic knowledge. Rituals include events such as weddings, funerals, and national holidays as well as invited dinner parties or how one lines up at a bus stop. Members of specific cultures implicitly "know" what will occur in these events—to use Oller's (1979) terms they have an "anticipatory grammar" for them. Yet, critically, this grammar per se is not written down (with the obvious exception of *Miss Manners*). It consists, fundamentally, of knowledge transmitted from generation to generation. Culture-specific knowledge also includes that information defined by the culture as having aesthetic value and as reflecting the values, the intellectual development, or the "best" of what that culture as a culture has to offer.

This discussion of issues surrounding the concept of knowledge is not meant to be exhaustive nor all-inclusive. It is meant to underline how complex and virtually inscrutable "knowledge" is. That readers need knowledge for comprehension seems to be clear. What knowledge second language readers have, how they acquire culturally appropriate new knowledge, and how they apply the knowledge they have to second language texts are intriguing questions for the development of a principled theory, principled research, and principled language instruction.

A STUDY OF KNOWLEDGE USE BY BEGINNING SPANISH STUDENTS

The data generated in previous studies as well as delineated in Chapter Three imply that a priori descriptions about the act of reading in a foreign language are not genuinely descriptive of the readers in those studies. Clearly, more careful and less contrived methods of inquiring into the foreign language reading process are necessitated that focus particularly on the knowledge that second language readers bring with them. This study focuses on the concept of inventory.

The term inventory implies that data are collected from a variety of texts rather than from one text. In traditional reading inventories, readers are permitted to choose five texts to read based on their interests and knowledge. Within this study, readers were not given options, but rather had the opportunity to provide information regarding their interests and knowledge.

As mentioned in Chapter Two, many recent studies of second language reading have indicated that background knowledge is a critical and highly influential variable in the comprehension process. Frequently, it is difficult to know whether readers are reading from language or reading from their knowledge of the world. In like manner, it is equally difficult to know whether lack of linguistic knowledge is the principal component in comprehension failures or whether it is a lack of appropriate cultural knowledge or a combination of both. What follows is an attempt to try to discern whether a reader can demonstrate background knowledge so that the "linguistic" variable in reading comprehension can become clearer.

The Free Association Measure

A number of studies on junior high school and high school subjects have been conducted using a free association measure to categorize prior knowledge (Langer, 1980; Langer & Nicolich, 1981; Hare, 1982). Three levels of prior knowledge are assigned to the associations: much prior knowledge, a score of three (3) means that the reader is able to provide "superordinate concepts, definitions, analogies, and linking;" some prior knowledge (2) means that readers are able to provide "examples, attributes, and defining characteristics;" little prior knowledge (1) means that a reader makes association with morphemes, sound-alikes, and first hand experiences" (Langer, 1980, p. 29). These scores are found to correlate moderately highly with top-level information in texts. Similar procedures were followed in this study. Level-One Spanish students at Iowa State University were asked over a 10-day period to free associate on the following topics:

> military bases in Spain
> grapes
> Olympic games
> the Shuttle program
> basketball
> viticulture
> nuclear weapons in Europe
> Chilean politics
> democracy in Latin America
> aerospace

Readers were given one minute to free associate in English by writing down everything they knew about the topic. Prior to this free association task the students were told that it was relevant to the reading study in which they would be participating.

All free associations were scored on the three-point scale noted above. In the end, each subject had two background knowledge scores on the general topics of the *U.S. presence in Spain*, on *viticulture*, on *Latin American politics*, on *Olympic basketball*, and on the *U.S. Space Program*. Figure 4.1 illustrates the total number of background knowledge scores in the collapsed categories. The students knew the least about the *U.S. presence in Spain* and the most about the *U.S. Space Program*.

In actuality, the use of the term *viticulture* appeared to skew the data a bit. The general term *grapes* actually ranked as the topic about which the students had the greatest knowledge, but few of them knew the meaning of the word *viticulture*. Hence, it seems to be in reality that the ranking of topics from highest to lowest knowledge is *U.S. Space Program*, *Olympic basketball*, *viticulture*, *Latin American politics*, and the *U.S. military presence in Spain*—a sequence of U.S. cultural issues to Hispanic cultural issues.

The Reading Task

Approximately two weeks after the administration of the free association task the students were asked to read five different texts: "U.S. Defeats Brazil in Basketball," "Back to the Future," about the U.S. Space Program, "The U.S. is Unhappy with Spanish Agreement Regarding Nuclear Arms," "The Grape," and "Pinochet." These articles had appeared recently in *Novedades* (Mexico), *El Pais* (Madrid), *Cambio 16* (Madrid), and *Hola* (Madrid). The originals and translations appear in Figure 4.2.

These texts were administered over a two day period. On the first day, the

Figure 4.1. Background knowledge scores according to topic.

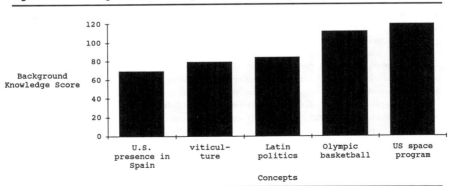

Figure 4.2.   Original and translated versions of the Spanish texts.

El País
Madrid
19 de septiembre, 1988

Estados Unidos Retrasa la Firma del Convenio Hasta
Obtener Ventajas Respecto a las Armas Nucleares

Estados Unidos desconfía de la fórmula escogida por España para prohibir la "introducción" de armas nucleares en territorio español y retrasará la firma del convenio bilateral en un intento de lograr una fórmula que garantice mejor sus intereses, dijeron a EL PAIS fuentes gubernamentales en Washington. "Sin cambios en este punto y en los de jurisdicción y contratación en las bases no hay posibilidad de que se firmen los acuerdos este mes", añadieron dichas fuentes, que agregaron que el contencioso está ya "al más alto nivel de la decisión política, incluso fuera de los negociadores del convenio."

El embajador norteamericano en Madrid, Reginald Bartholomew, ha viajado estos días a Washington, llamado por el secretario de Estado, George Shultz, para tratar del bloqueo del convenio con España, que también tropieza con dificultades en dos cuestiones no políticas, menos vistosas, pero importantes: la jurisdicción sobre los presos norteamericanos de las bases y la contratación de obras y de personal.

Fuentes españolas aseguran que Estados Unidos está presionando en lo nuclear, exagerando su importancia real, para lograr concesiones españolas en los otros dos puntos.

El próximo día 28 existe una última posibilidad, dentro del presente mes, para salvar el punto muerto de la negociación en la reunión que George Shultz y el ministro español de Asuntos Exteriores, Francisco Fernández Ordóñez, mantendrán en Nueva York. "Esperamos que la fórmula que ofrece España no sea la única posible", declaró un funcionario norteamericano.

HOLA
Madrid
10 de septiembre, 1988

La Uva
Características y Curiosidades

La uva es el fruto de la vid, de la familia de las vitáceas, con tronco retorcido, vástagos muy largos, flexibles y nudosos, con hojas alternas grandes, pecioladas y partidas.

Es una baya que nace apiñada de un vástago común, formando racimos. Cada grano contiene en su hollejo una pulpa delicada y jugosa, de la que se extrae el mosto, teniendo en su interior dos o tres pequeños granillos duros que son la simiente. De hecho, su origen no es muy seguro por los datos históricos que poseemos, confundiéndose en ocasiones la historia con la leyenda o el mito, por lo que son innumerables las referencias hechas a este fruto en toda la literatura universal, la religión y las tradiciones.

En Asia Menor se han encontrado restos que se remontan a cuatro mil años antes de la Era Cristiana, e igualmente se han hallado fósiles en el Neolítico de la Italia septentrional.

Es importante hacer notar que existen multitud de variedades, que se diferencian claramente en dos grandes grupos; las de vino y las de mesa, que son las que nos ocupan y a las que nos estamos refiriendo. De éstas, las variedades de mayor producción son las Moscatel, Rosetti, Italia y Aledo.

Europa es productora del 70 por 100 del total mundial, siendo Francia, Italia, Y España los principales países productores. Las provincias donde se obtienen mayores cosechas son Alicante, Valencia y Almería, siendo la producción anual de 550.000 toneladas y la superficie total cultivada de unas 85.000 hectáreas.

Cambio 16
Madrid
3 de octubre, 1988

Pinochet al filo de las Urnas

"Y se abrirán las grandes alamedas para que pasen hombres libres", (último discurso de Salvador Allende). A medida que se acerca el 5 de octubre, fecha prevista para el plebiscito que decidirá si el dictador chileno gobernará o no hasta fin de siglo, el clima opositor se hace cada vez más visible y contagioso en Santiago.

Cada vez son más numerosos los que exhiben en la solapa la insignia del "No" al candidato dictador. Paradójicamente, pocos creen que el plebiscito acabe con el poder de este general que hace 15 años gobierna Chile como un cuartel y consiguió que el miedo y la inmovilidad política maniataran a la mayoría de los chilenos, al punto de hacerles dudar del poder de los votos.

Con el recuerdo de las protestas de 1983 y 1984, abortadas brutalmente por el régimen, muchos temen que Pinochet aplique nuevamente su estrategia militar. Fernando Reyes Matta, de la "Comisión Sudamericana de Paz", advierte que, por primera vez "la oposición le ha desbaratado la estrategia a Pinochet: hay una unidad política más desarrollada, y personalidades carismáticas como Ricardo Lagos, una figura que irrita a los militares".

Podrá haber sorpresas, pero el régimen es tan cerrado y personalista que la política se explica en los humores y la personalidad del dictador candidato. En la calle, la oposición hace más ruido, pero nadie se atreve a predecir cuál será el resultado. Las encuestas anticipan una elección pareja con el triunfo de la oposición en Santiago, la capital del país, compensado por el apoyo que Pinochet tiene en el campo.

Cambio 16
Madrid
3 de octubre, 1988

Regreso al futuro

La recta y ondulada carretera SR-407 ha dejado atrás Orlando, el mágico reino de las Vacaciones de Disney World, el futurista Epcot Center, el espectacular Sea World, una hora más tarde, los carteles al borde de las tierras anegadas y bosques entre los que pueden verse edificios de compañías como Grumman, McDonnell Douglas, United Technologies o Astrotech, anuncian al visitante que se está acercando al Space Port USA del Kennedy Space Center de la NASA.

Es lo mejor que la Florida le ofrece al turista, según la publicidad de la agencia de viajes de la NASA. Es otra atracción más de la Costa del Espacio del condado de Brevard. Aquí todo hace referencia a lo espacial, desde las urbanizaciones a la orquesta filarmónica Florida Space Coast, pasando por el Space Coast Art Festival o el Space Coast Science Center.

Y mientras en el Centro Galaxy, donde se proyecta la película El Sueño Sigue Vivo, la voz del famoso presentador norteamericano Walter Cronkite narra cómo se entrenan los astronautas y sus peripecias en el espacio. Es el ave heráldica de Estados Unidos y esto recuerda al águila de la insignia de la misión Apolo II, la que en julio de 1969 llevó los primeros hombres a la Luna.

Eran otros tiempos, los de la ventaja norteamericana sobre los soviéticos. Ahora, mientras en la pantalla gigante cada 37 minutos la película acaba con la espectacular detonación de un lanzamiento hacia la inmensidad, los hombres de la Administración Nacional del Espacio sufren cada 90 minutos una pequeña humillación, el paso por encima de Estados Unidos de la plataforma espacial soviética habitada Mir (paz, en ruso).

Novedades
México, D.F.
21 de septiembre, 1988

Figure 4.2.   Original and translated versions of the Spanish texts. (*cont.*)

*Estados Unidos Arrolló 102-87
a Brasil en Básquetbol Olímpico*

Seúl, A.P.–Estados Unidos apoyado sobre Herman Reid, Danny Manning y Daniel Majerie venció a Brasil por 102-87 (63-55) en partido del Grupo B del básquetbol masculino de los Juegos Olímpicos.

Los brasileños, a pesar del calibre de su astro Oscar Schmidt, que anotó 31 tantos, no pudieron con el arrollador estilo de los norteamericanos de Reid que anotó 16 tantos, Majerie 12 y Manning 12. Mientras que las mejores anotaciones de los brasileros fueron de Israel Andrade con 15 puntos y Marcel Souza con 11.

Estados Unidos encabeza invicto el Grupo B con 6 puntos con 3 triunfos y Brasil está segundo con 2 victorias y una derota por 5 puntos, seguido por China y España de 1-1 con 3 puntos cada uno y Canadá y Egipto no han visto victoria en dos salidas.

Seúl, A.P.–Puerto Rico venció a Corea del Sur por 79-74 para su primera victoria del torneo de básquetbol masculino de los juegos Olímpicos.

Los mejores, encestadores por Puerto Rico fueron José Ortiz Rijos, con 14 puntos, y Ramón Ramos con 12. Por Corea, Lee Choong-Hee anotó 23 puntos.

Seúl, A.P.–El equipo de España de básquetbol masculino derrotó al de Egipto 113 a 70, en un encuentro del Grupo B del torneo olímpico que se disputa en Seúl.

Seúl, A.P.–Canadá venció a Egipto por 117-64 (61-32) en partido preliminar del Grupo B del básquetbol olímpico.

El grupo está encabezado por Estados Unidos con 6 puntos, seguido por Brasil con 5 puntos. Canadá tiene 4 puntos, China y España con 3 puntos; Egipto tiene tres derrotas.

*Estados Unidos Retrasa la Firma del Convenio Hasta Obtener
Ventajas Respecto a las Armas Nucleares*

The U.S. is unhappy with the formula chosen by Spain to prohibit the "introduction" of nuclear weapons in Spanish territory and they will delay the signing of the bilateral treaty with the intent of establishing a way that would guarantee their interests in a more substantial manner. This was told to *El País* by some governmental sources in Washington. "Without changes on this point and in those of jurisdiction and trade on the bases there is not the possibility that they will sign the agreements this month," added the aforementioned sources. They collectively agreed that the disputed point is already "at the highest level of the political decision making process, it is really out of the hands of the treaty's negotiators."

The North American ambassador in Madrid, Reginald Bartholomew, has traveled recently to Washington, called by the Secretary of State, George Shultz, to try to back the treaty with Spain. This treaty also has problems with questions that are not political in intent, less showy, but as important: the jurisdiction over North American base prisoners, construction contracts, and other personnel matters.

Spanish sources assured that the U.S. is pressuring the nuclear point, exaggerating its real importance in order to gain Spanish concessions on the other points.

On the 28th exists the last possibility, within this month (September, 1988) of saving this dead point in the negotiations at the meeting George Shultz and the Spanish exterior minister, Francisco Fernández Ordóñez, will have in New York. "We hope that the formula that Spain offers will not be the only one possible," declared a North American functionary.

La Uva Características y Curiosidades

The grape is the fruit of the vine from the vitacae [grape family], with a twisted trunk, very long, flexible, and knotty stems, and leaves that alternate being long stalked and divided.

It is a small berry that is formed on a common stem, forming bunches. Each berry has within its skin a pulp that is delicate and juicy; it is from that pulp, that one extracts the *must* (new wine). It has within its interior two or three small hard germ seeds. In fact, its origin is not very certain from the historical data that we possess. Often one confuses history with legend or myth, because of what seems innumerable references made about this fruit in all of universal literature, religion and traditions.

In Asia Minor they have found some remains (of grapes) that could be traced to four thousand years before the Christian epoch, and likewise they have found fossils in Northern Italy from the Neolithic period.

It is important to make note that they (referring to grapes) exist in a multitude of varieties, in that they are clearly divided into two large groups; those for wine and those for the table. It is the latter that we shall be concerned with and those that we shall be referring to. Of these, the varieties that are most widely produced are Muscatel, Rosetti, Italian and Aledo.

Europe produces 70% of the worldwide production, having France, Italy, and Spain as the principal producing countries. The provinces (of Spain) where they grow the majority of crops are Alicante, Valencia and Almería, having the annual production of 555,000 tons and some 85,000 hectares of land under cultivation.

Pinochet al filo de las Urnas
Cambio 16 Madrid October 3, 1988

"And the great avenues will open themselves so that free men shall pass", (from the last speech of Salvador Allende). It is the halfway point before October 5th, the date selected for the plebiscite which will decide whether or not the Chilean dictator will govern or not until the end of the century. The climate of opposition is becoming more and more visible and contagious in Santiago.

Each day there are more people wearing on their lapels the button (or sign) of "No" to the dictator candidate. Paradoxically, very few think that the plebiscite will terminate the power of this general who for 15 years has governed Chile like a military barracks and used fear and political inactivity to cause the Chileans to doubt the power of their vote.

With the memory of the protests of 1983 and 1984, brutally terminated by the regime, many fear that Pinochet will apply again his military force. Fernando Reyes Matta, of the "South American Peace Commission", warns that, for the first time, "the opposition has defeated Pinochet's strategy: there is a greater developed sense of political unity, and charismatic personalities such as Ricardo Lagos, a figure that irritates the military types."

There could be surprises, but the regime is so closed and well connected that the politics can only be explained by the whims and the personality of the dictator candidate. In the street, the opposition makes more noise, but no one dares predict what will be the result. Those that analyze anticipate an election split with the opposition winning in Santiago, the capital of the country, and support for Pinochet coming from the rural areas.

Regreso al futuro

The straight and undulating highway SR-407 takes one through Orlando, the magic kingdom of vacations of Disney World, the futuristic Epcot Center, the spectacular Sea World; an hour later, the signs on the borders of the water-logged lands and forests. Between them one can see the buildings of such companies as Grumman, McDonnell Douglas, United Technologies or Astrotech. They announce to the visitor that they are coming close to Space Port USA of the Kennedy Space Center of NASA.

This is the best that Florida offers the tourist, according to the publicity from the NASA travel agency. There is yet another attraction on the Florida Space Coast in Brevard County. Here everything has a reference to Space, from the suburbs to the philharmonic orchestra, including the Space Coast Art Festival or the Space Coast Science Center.

Figure 4.2.   Original and translated versions of the Spanish texts. (cont.)

And meanwhile in the Center Galaxy, where they show the film *The Dream Still Lives* the voice of the famous North American commentator Walter Cronkite narrates how astronauts are trained and how their weightlessness affects them in space. There is the heraldic, symbolic bird of the United States and this reminds one of the eagle, the insignia of the Apollo II mission, that in July, 1969 brought the first men to the moon.

It was other times, those of the domination of North America over the Soviet Union. Now, while on giant screen every 37 minutes the picture finishes with the spectacular explosion and launching towards infinity, the men of NASA every 90 minutes suffer a small humiliation: the passing over the USA of a Soviet Space platform called Mir (peace in Russian).

Estados Unidos Arroló 102-87
a Brasil en Basquetbol Olímpico

Seoul, A.P.

The United States helped by Herman Reid, Danny Manning and Daniel Majerie beat Brazil by 102-87 (63-55) in a game of Group B of Men's Olympic basketball.

The Brazilians, even with the caliber of their star, Oscar Schmidt, who earned 31 points, couldn't compete with the rolling style of the North Americans such as Reid who earned 16 points, Majerie 12 and Manning 12. Meanwhile the best the Brazilians could do was Israel Andrade with 15 points and Marcel Souza with 11.

The U.S. tops the teams in Group B with 6 points with 3 wins and Brazil is 2nd with 2 wins and a loss for 5 points, followed by China and Spain with 1-1 with 3 points each and Canada and Egypt who have not seen a victory in two starts.

Seoul, A.P.

Puerto Rico beat South Korea 79-74 for their first victory of the Men's basketball tournament of the Olympic Games.

The better players for Puerto Rico were José Ortiz Rijos with 14 points and Ramon Ramós with 12. For Korea, Lee Choong-Hee earned 23 points.

Seoul, A.P.

The Men's Spanish basketball team beat Egypt 113-70 in a Group B game that was played in Seoul.

Seoul, A.P.

Canada beat Egypt 117-64 in the first game of Group B Olympic Men's basketball.

The Group is lead by the USA with 6 points, followed by Brazil with 5, Canada has 4 points, China and Spain 3 points; Egypt has 3 losses.

students had 40 minutes in which to read and recall three texts. Since they were used to the immediate recall procedure, they understood that they had to pace themselves and that when they were ready to recall they would be asked to surrender the text. In this manner, the immediate recall protocol procedure is not a translation task, but rather a reconstruction task.

A total of 63 students participated in various phases of the project. However, only 23 participated in all phases and, therefore, constitute the entire sample for the study for the inventory phase of this project. All protocols were scored using a weighted propositional system (see Chapter Seven).

Means and standard deviations of the data indicate that the texts on the U.S. Space Program and on Olympic basketball were the most simple with means of 18.98 and 19.8, respectively. "Pinochet," "The Grape," and "Nuclear Arms in Europe" follow, with means of 13.88, 14.11, and 12.62 percent, respectively. The findings are represented graphically in Figure 4.3.

A repeated measures analysis of variance was then conducted to determine whether there were statistically significant differences between the texts. The means indicate that there were two groups of texts: The easiest texts being the U.S. Space Program ("Regreso al futuro") and Olympic basketball, and the most difficult being the latter three texts.

Interestingly, these text groupings match the groupings on the background knowledge text illustrated in Figure 4.1. In order to test this relationship, however, a correlation between each subject's average background knowledge score and the recall protocol score on the topic was calculated and found to be a weak to moderate correlation of .27, $p < .05$.

To probe the data further, the scores on all texts were intercorrelated with each other. Table 4.1 provides the correlation matrix. These correlations rank from .11 to .59 all moderate correlations at best.

No single text performance seems to predict the readers' performance on any other text. On the one hand, it can be argued that the texts are of similar difficulty since they stem from similar if not the same journalistic style. In other words, they are similar in terms of their text-based readability. Yet, these characteristics seem to have no predictive power. On the other hand, the two texts with possibly the least relationship (either topically or stylistically), "Back to the Future" and

Figure 4.3. Average comprehension scores according to texts (recorded as percents).

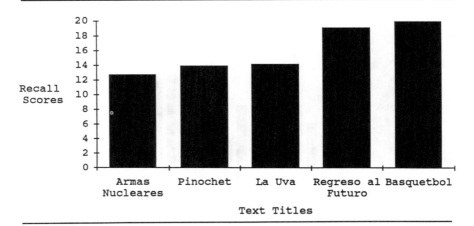

Table 4.1.   Correlation matrix of comprehension scores for the five Spanish texts.

	Regreso	Basquetbol	Pinochet	La Uva	Arms Nucleares
Regreso al Futuro	1	.59437	.44749	.31428	.19289
Basquetbol	.59437	1	.11243	.30802	.22533
Pinochet	.44749	.11243	1	.40691	.28005
La Uva	.31428	.30802	.40691	1	.23265
Armas Nucleares	.19289	.22533	.28005	.23265	1

"U.S. Beats Brazil in Basketball," have the greatest predictive power. In fact, "Back to the Future" has the greatest predictive power over all the other texts with the exception of "Nuclear Arms in Spain." Ironically, these two texts stem from Spanish magazines.

Further Quantitative Probing

A final exploration was conducted on the subjects' performances. The scores on each text were plotted and sorted. The intention of this procedure is to note whether there is any consistency in high versus medium versus low performance across all the texts. Figures 4.4 through 4.13 illustrate the performances as well as sorted performances.

A scan across each text reveals different performances among the subjects for each text. In other words, few subjects are reasonably consistent in performance. Subject Number One, for example, produces the worst performance, on "Regreso al futuro" (Figure 4.5), but moves into the middle of the pack for the

Figure 4.4.   Subject performance on Regreso al futuro.

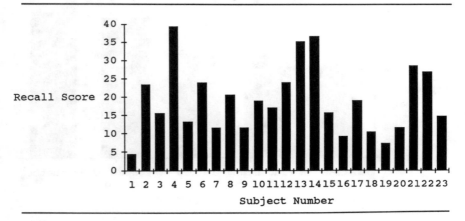

Figure 4.5.   Sorted subject performance on Regreso al futuro.

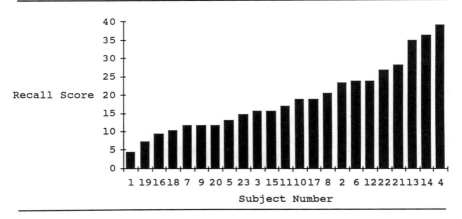

remainder of the texts. Subject 18, for example, is a relatively weak scorer across all the texts with the exception of "La Uva" (Figure 4.7) in which the subject moves into the top third of subjects. Subject 23, as a third example, is consistently in the upper third of subjects with the exception of performance on the text, "Regreso al futuro" (Figure 4.5). The critical point here is that any individual text may positively or negatively skew assessed performance, portraying some students as more competent than others, and vice versa.

A final exploration was conducted in order to analyze the actual rankings of the readers across the texts. In order to conduct this exploration, subjects were

Figure 4.6.   Subject performance on La Uva.

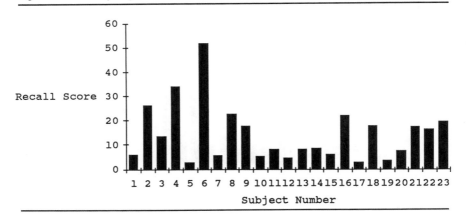

Figure 4.7.   Sorted subject performance on La Uva.

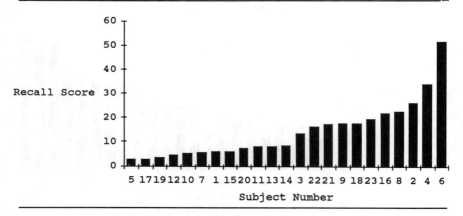

assigned rankings on each text. A *1* indicates performance in the upper third, a *2* performance in the middle third, and a *3* performance in the bottom third. These rank scores were added together and sorted from highest (meaning lowest performance) to lowest (meaning highest rank performance; that is, consistent *1*s and *2*s). This procedure ranks Student 6 as the best overall student and Readers 1, 3, 5, and 18 as having had the poorest performance. Figure 4.14 presents the graphical distribution.

   An interesting comparison should be drawn between the sorted mean performance of the subjects (Figure 4.15) and the sorted ranked performance of the

Figure 4.8.   Subject performance on Armas Nucleares.

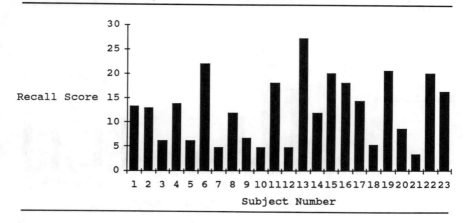

Figure 4.9. Sorted subject performance on Armas Nucleares.

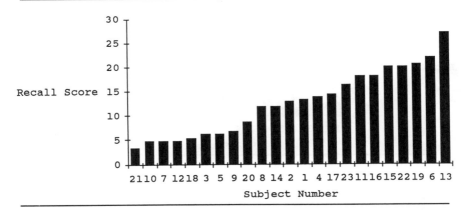

Figure 4.10. Subject performance on Pinochet.

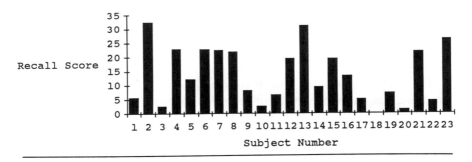

Figure 4.11. Sorted subject performance on Pinochet.

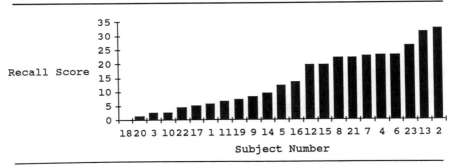

Figure 4.12. Subject performance on Basquetbol.

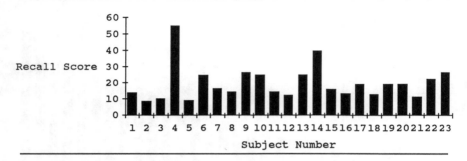

subjects. Because there is not 100 percent overlap, even mean performance does not provide an adequate picture of student performance.

Qualitative Probing

Clearly, a background knowledge measure such as a free association task rated on a 3-point scale is not sensitive enough to predict performance. Yet "knowledge" remains a significant variable. In order to continue probing the knowledge variable a content analysis on the free association task in relation to the student recalls was conducted.

The quantitative findings provide perplexing research interpretations. On the one hand, a considerable amount of second language reading research has been based on the concept of prior knowledge. Indeed, the group data presented lend themselves to the interpretation that background knowledge is a viable predictor of comprehension scores. Yet, on the other hand, individual scores linked with individual background knowledge measures are not even slightly good predictors

Figure 4.13. Sorted subject performance on Basquetbol.

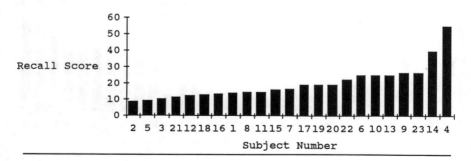

Figure 4.14.   Sorted rank performance for all texts.

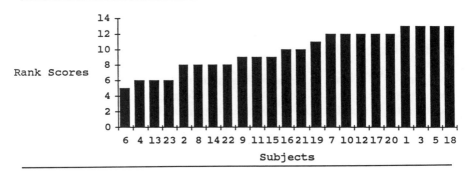

of each other. There are several possible explanations for this phenomenon: two mathematical and one qualitative. First, background knowledge was measured by means of a free association task rated on a 3-point scale. In reality, the ratings generated were very similar. That is, the scale itself had little variance. When a scale without much variance is used to predict a scale with variance, the prediction is not very good; hence, the low correlation. Second, a 3-point scale may be too coarse a measure to differentiate knowledge. It is not that differences in knowledge do not exist, but that such a scale cannot detect them. The third reason may be the most compelling: a number may not be able to sufficiently describe content. It is, perhaps, only the *content* of the free association task *in relation to* student recalls that provides a clue to "knowledge" as a variable in second language comprehension.

Figures 4.16 through 4.21 display the background knowledge probes of several subjects related to the texts, "Pinochet," "Armas Nucleares," "Regreso al futuro," and "La Uva." Figure 4.16 illustrates subject data on the

Figure 4.15.   Sorted mean performance for all texts.

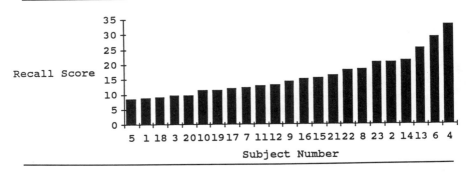

Spanish texts concerning United States military bases in Spain. The subject indicates in both free associations that he/she has a reasonable amount of knowledge regarding the role of the United States military in Spain. He/she certainly has more than common knowledge about missile types extant in Europe. His/her recall protocol indicates a better than average comprehension of the text.

Figure 4.17 lists the free recall measures from another student as well as his/her recall protocol from the text, "La Uva." On the general probe, "grapes," the subject provides descriptive knowledge that would be expected of practically any reader. The response to "viticulture," though, hints at a higher level knowledge about grapes. The subject defines and describes wine-making processes. The subject's recall protocol is remarkable. It follows the organization of the text as well as providing a substantial number of details.

Figure 4.18 illustrates a subject's responses to the probes about Latin American politics and the recall of the text about Pinochet. The free associations essentially communicate that the subject has no serious knowledge about politics in Chile and basically stereotypic knowledge about the topic of democracy in Latin America. The recall protocol reflects the shallowness of the knowledge and could well be a "reading" of the previous night's headlines rather than a genuine attempt at the Spanish text.

Figure 4.16. Student background knowledge and recall for the "Armas Nucleares" text.

"Estados Unidos Retrasa la Firma del
Convenio Hasta Obtener Ventajas Respecto a las Armas Nucleares"

Code #: 11-2

Background Knowledge:

Military Bases in Spain:	The U.S. has Air Force Bases in Spain. This is proven by the fact that Spain wouldn't allow U.S. FB-111's to fly over the country en route to Libya. We do have a naval port, however.
Nuclear Weapons:	We have ICBM's (intercontinental ballistic missiles) in Europe. Pres. Reagan and Gorbachev have agreed to reduce intermediate range weapons in Europe. We have peacekeeper, titans, and minuteman 3s. The minuteman 3s are an upgrade of 2s.
Student Recall Protocol:	Spain has prohibited the introduction of Nuclear Arms from the United States. In 28 days George Schultz and the Spanish ambassador in New York, will meet to discuss the use of nuclear weapons in Spain. The Spanish population thinks that the United States relies too heavily on nuclear weapons. Both the interests of the United States and the interests of Spain will be discussed.

Figure 4.17.   Student background knowledge and recall for the "La Uva" text.

"La Uva: Características y Curiosidades"

Code #: 15-12

Background Knowledge:

Grapes:

Grapes grow on vines. They can be red or green. Grapes, when ripe, should be sweet. They are juicy fruit but not necessarily a citrus fruit. (There are no grapes in grape nuts, or nuts either.) Grapes are dried out to make raisons. Grapes were fed to . . . .

Viticulture:

Viticulture is the science of wine making. It begins with the processes of growing the best grapes possible. It then moves to and includes the processes used to extract the juice from the choice grapes with the most efficiency.

Student Recall Protocol:

Grape is a fruit . . . It then describes the grape. Its stem etc. it then describes 2 or 3 small seeds (?) inside the grape. No one knows the origin of the grape, but they know its been around a long time because is in Relgious and other Literature. Grapes were around in the Christian age. And were also found in Fossils dating back to neolithic times. There are many types of grapes those for wine and those for the table (to eat). Europe produces 70 percent of the grapes used for wine. In Spain the main producing areas are Alraute along with two other places. Total production is 550,000 tons and 85,000 hectacres are used.

Figure 4.18.   Student background knowledge and recall for the "Pinochet" text.

"Pinochet al filo de las Urnas"

Code #: 11-2

Background Knowledge:

Chilean Politics:

Chile is a very interesting country. It is ruled by pheasants, a king and a queen, who roost in a castle by the sea. They have a daughter named "Birdy" who loves worms. Everyday she tries to find a suitable worm for her. It is a monarchy, of course. Actually, I know nothing about the politics in Chile. It must be cold though!

Democracy in Latin America:

Democracy in Latin America is actually a modifed form of the United States Government there are generally militaristic or oligarchys with a slight touch of Democracy. Often, a certain family rules the country, with the military playing a large role. Democracy is much different than we know it.

Student Recall Protocol:

About politics in Chile. There were protests in 1983 & 1984 because of the militaristic government. An election is coming up soon and it is expected that the dictator presently in office will be defeated.

Figure 4.19.　Student background knowledge and recall for the "Regreso al futuro" text.

"Regreso al futuro"

Code #: 11-17

Background Knowledge:

Shuttle Program:　After the crash of the Challenger, the shuttle program was put on hold. The shuttle program is done by NASA, paid for by the government. The shuttle can be shot off into space and can eventually land, like a plane on earth. The ship doesn't have to be wasted.

Aerospace:　Aerospace—Something that came to mind are NASA, the space shuttle, Apollo, John Denver, the Soviets, nuclear weaponry, the Boeing 747, the DC-10, the DSM-Des Moines, International airport. I remember the day the Challenger crashed and took a teacher with it. I know that are atmosphere is packed with satellites.

Student Recall Protocol:　This article begins by discussing a little about Florida. Florida is a tourist state with such highlights as Disney World, the Epcot Center and Sea World. Also of interest are space related corporations that people tour, such as Grumman MacDonald-Douglas, United Technologies, or Astro tech. Because of all the space related things here, Florida is very geared to space and has a space Festival and has dubbed the shore in the area of JF Kennedy Space Center "Space Coast".

The article goes on to discuss the Apollo II space flight, the first moon landing, which was made in July? of 1969 by the United States.

It then discusses the Space Shuttle disaster and the embarrassment of the Space Administration to (most embarrassingly) the Soviets.

In summary, a glance through Figures 4.16 through 4.18 as representative samples of data from the study validates the low correlations between the background knowledge measures and the comprehension scores. Some subjects had some background knowledge that they used, others had some background knowledge that they did not use, others had no demonstrable background knowledge, which concomitantly also did not appear in the recall protocols.

The text, "Regreso al futuro," further validates the perplexing nature of these findings. This text, "Back to the Future," had the highest free association scores with the probes, *Shuttle program* and *aerospace*. Yet Figures 4.19 through 4.21 signify subjects who had considerable background knowledge yet failed to use it in the text, others that demonstrated an almost insignificant amount of knowledge and generated remarkable recalls, and others who provided negligible scores both on the free association measures and on recall.

Figure 4.20.   Student background knowledge and recall for the "Regreso al futuro" text.

"Regreso al futuro"

Code #: 11-2

Background Knowledge:

Shuttle Program:	The space shuttle is a program of NASA. In January, 1986, the Challenger blew up caused by faulty O-rings in the solid rocket booster. In Sep., 1988, the Discovery was lauched successfully to put America back in space. The space shuttle consists of 3 parts, the shuttle itself, an external liquid fuel tank (hydrogen), and 2 solid rocket boosters, which are jettisoned over the ocean after.
Aerospace:	The U.S. Air Force has a wide assortment of planes: Fighters - F-15, F-16, F-4, F-5, F-104, and F-111. Reconnaisance SR-71, and U-2, Bombers - B-1, and B-52, Trainer T-37, and T-38. A plane has 4 major forces: 1) lift-upward force, 2) thrust-force of engine, 3) drag - air resistance, and 4) weight of plane. Pitch - rotation up or down. Yaw - rotation in horizontal plane. Bank - left or right. The SR-71 is the fastest plane in the world - Mach 3 + . It can fly up to 85,000 ft. (Subject included drawings of planes.)
Student Recall Protocol:	In Florida, there are many places to tour. The magical Kingdom of Disney world, sea world, and the NASA space center, which has a museum. A movie . . . was filmed there which was narrated by Walter Kronkite, the North American announcer. The Soviets are also in a race with us in space. In July, 1969, we launched the Apollo II rocket.

Figure 4.19 illustrates data from a subject who seems to have midlevel knowledge regarding space and the space program. He supplies rather disparate facts as well as some misinformation. His recall protocol, however, rather carefully follows the text, providing upper, mid, as well as detailed information from it. Figure 4.20 illustrates data from another student that provides the reverse pattern. The subject's free associations reveal significant and detailed information about the Shuttle program as well as in the general area of aerodynamics. The subject did not seem to avail himself of any of this fairly detailed information, however, when reading the "Regreso al futuro" passage. The passage is almost devoid of detail. In fact, this subject might have scored better if he had mentioned what he knew about the topic rather than focusing on the passage.

Figure 4.21 provides the data generated by a subject who could be described as "in the middle." Neither the free association measures nor the recall protocol indicate that the student was either highly knowledgeable about the topic or distinctly able to read the article with much detail. Yet, in comparison with the

Figure 4.21.   Student background knowledge and recall for the "Regreso al futuro" text.

"Regreso al futuro"

Code #: 15-15

Background Knowledge:

Shuttle program:	The space shuttle was first launched in 1982. There were several lauches until Jan 1986 when Challenger exploded killing all seven aboard. The shuttle is used for scientific research and putting satelites into orbit.
Aerospace:	Aerospace deals with aircraft and spacecraft. How they are designed and constructed. The laws of physics which affects air and spacecraft.
Student Recall Protocol:	This article appears to be about United States and the space program. The epcott center in Walt disney world was mentioned. It mentioned a movie narrated by Walter Cronkite. The film dealt with U.S. and Soviet space exploration.

---

previous student with considerable knowledge, this subject garnered the overriding information. This subject writes that the thrust of the article was about "the U.S. and the space program," while the previous student interpreted the article as an explanation of tourist sights in Florida.

SUMMARY

This chapter ends in parallel to Chapter Three. Knowledge-based inferencing, like text-based processing, leads to rather unsatisfactory interpretations of reading in a second language. Knowledge is clearly needed to provide conceptual mortar from sentence to sentence. Yet, as mentioned in the earliest pages of this chapter, knowledge is elusive. The attempt illustrated here to capture "knowledge" failed. While an attack may be lodged against the manner of "scoring" knowledge, a qualitative assessment of it was found to be equally wanting. The question remains one of what is necessary knowledge, who has it, and who can use it in appropriate circumstances. This question raises issues regarding the reality of "knowledge," its acquisition, its measurement, and its activation.

Clearly, it is beyond the pages of this book and the research on which it is based to answer these questions. Reflection on these questions is of critical importance toward making principled research and instructional decisions about reading in a second language. Answers are, of course, more critical. For the future, research must generate substantial evidence that determines whether background knowledge merely contributes to a description of second language reading or whether it is actually a causal variable. For the moment, though, understanding second language text comprehension lies in balancing the seen and the unseen in texts. A discussion of this balance is found in the following chapter.

5

A Synthesis of Perspectives

INTRODUCTION

Chapters Three and Four set forth issues and observations that must be considered in any principled approach to second language reading. The issue statements relied heavily on theory and research in reading, in cognitive psychology, in literacy acquisition, in problem solving, and in sociolinguistics. Each issue statement—either from a text-driven or from a knowledge-driven perspective—provided examples from second language readers. In addition, full-scale studies conducted from each perspective were included as evidence of the perspective. The studies that are essentially text-driven indicate that text-driven facets of reading do not predict reading proficiency very well. In like manner, the study that is essentially knowledge-driven indicates that knowledge-driven facets of reading also do not predict reading proficiency very well. The contention made here is quite simply that both perspectives, that is, both facets, are integral to the reading process. Neither is more valuable, apart neither is terribly useful.

The intention of this chapter is to provide the integrated view necessary to come toward a richer understanding of second language reading. Through this kind of understanding, more principled perspectives on language teaching (Chapter Six) as well as on language assessment (Chapter Seven) can be achieved.

INTEGRATION

Integration is a key term in this discussion. It refers to the integration of perspectives. It also refers to the integration of information to which the reader has access during reading. The theory presented in these pages indicates that input text is important. It also indicates that knowledge selection and use is critical. In other words, in fluent reading, the two systems work together influencing, supplementing, and supporting each other.

A common image for this process of influencing, supplementing, and supporting is building or growing. This image serves to underscore the notion of the dynamic nature of comprehension. Webber (1980) puts it this way: "In comprehending text, the import of each successive sentence must be determined within, and integrated into, an incrementally growing model of the discourse" (p. 141). Webber goes on to explain that particular linguistic features help in updating these "models of discourse."

Figure 5.1 attempts to illustrate this process. A reader has an initial conceptual model or knowledge base. Language is input and the conceptual model grows. More language is input and the model changes and grows, and so on. Graesser et al. (1987) comment:

> We assume that the reader constructs a structure of propositional units (called nodes) during comprehension. Some of these nodes are explicitly mentioned in the text, whereas other nodes are inferences. The comprehender needs to construct *bridging* inferences in order to establish conceptual connectivity between an incoming explicit statement and prior passage context. The reader may also generate *elaborative* inferences which embellish the text structure but are not really needed for establishing conceptual connectivity. (pp. 218–219)

Fundamentally, then, there is explicit language input and there is inferencing involved. This inferencing process helps to fill in the unstated or redundant information that is not explicitly in the text, thereby, helping the text "make sense." There is also other inferencing that merely makes the text "say" more than it does.

How does a second language reader play out this scenario on comprehension? The second language reader (as any reader) has perceptual systems working for him, in addition to phonological, lexical or word meaning, and syntactic processing systems that provide text input. At the same time, the second language reader (as any reader) has a knowledge base from which to inference so that things "make sense." It is this knowledge base that fills in the gaps in texts. The critical point is that within a second language reader, all of these systems *operate*; and, particularly if the second language reader is already literate, they operate from the beginning of the attempt to read in a second language. But most critically, although these systems operate simultaneously, they do so with varying degrees of success. Johnston (1983) comments on the risks involved in the simultaneous operation of these systems when the intended reader does not match the text:

> The qualitative mismatch between text and reader may pose a far more insidious problem—quite subtly causing the reader to build a completely inappropriate model of the text meaning without becoming aware of the problem. It is not that inferences would not be made, but that inappropriate ones would be made. This problem could be easily self-compounding. Once the reader has begun to construct

Figure 5.1. Concept of a growing discourse model.

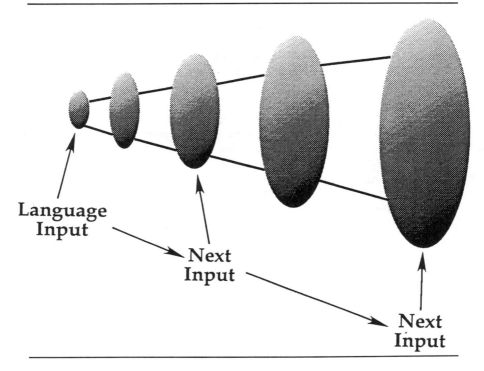

Language Input

Next Input

Next Input

an inappropriate model, inappropriate inferences would be generated by virtue of the content of the growing model itself. (p. 31)

The next pages attempt to demonstrate how processes work simultaneously and lead toward comprehension products that vary in their degree of completeness and accuracy. This variety is found not only between readers but within individual readers.

DEMONSTRATING FACTORS AT WORK

The model presented in Chapter One posits an active reader who selects text as well as nontext information in order to build a representation of the text. The model portrays the text representation as overlapping blocks (selected information) with unfilled spaces (unselected information). Chapters Three and Four outlined and discussed the nature of factors potentially involved in the selection process. The task of this chapter is to demonstrate explicitly readers' selections.

Used to demonstrate these selections, is a heuristic containing six features—three text-driven and three conceptually driven. This heuristic enables a principled and consistent analysis of recall protocol data. For the most part, the heuristic focuses on errors that lead the reader toward misunderstandings or as Johnston (1983) puts it toward "inappropriate inferences" (p. 31).

The three text-driven factors in the heuristic are *word recognition*, *phonemic/graphemic decoding*, and *syntactic feature recognition*. Word recognition involves the attachment of semantic value to a word by translation or conjecture. Errors fall into the word recognition category when subjects misinterpret the meaning of a word, for example, interpreting "Bekannten" [acquaintances] as "relatives." Phonemic/graphemic decoding involves processing whereby subjects misidentify words based on the visual or aural similarities words share with other words. An example of this process would be interpreting "Streben" [striving] as "Sterben" [death]. Moving beyond interpretations at strictly the word level, syntactic feature recognition involves the relationships between and among words. Syntactic feature processes include interpreting present tense sentences from the text as past tense or singular nouns as plural. Included also are interpretations of longer stretches of discourse, such as misinterpreting "Wenn ich einen Russen sehen will . . . ." [If I want to see a Russian] as "When he saw his first Soviet . . . ." In both instances, there is a failure to interpret the syntactic connections between the words accurately, although individual words may have been recognized correctly.

Conceptually driven factors are *intratextual perception, metacognition*, and *prior knowledge*. Intratextual perception concerns how the reader perceives and then reconciles each part of the text with the preceding and succeeding discourse context. This factor is especially important at the beginning of the recall process, because initial decisions about the text have the power to influence the reader's entire perception of the text. An example of intratextual perception is a reader who believes that a text is a personal letter from a husband to his wife, when, in actuality, it is a business letter from one colleague to another. Metacognition refers to the extent to which the reader is thinking about or reflecting on what is being read. This feature demonstrates that the reader is monitoring his/her own comprehension process. Metacognition is characterized in written recalls by question marks, parenthetical comments, vague vocabulary, or blanks that illustrate the reader's uncertainty about particular aspects of the text or demonstrate additional understanding that the text has not made explicit. An example of the first case would be "Dear Mrs ?" or "in July? 1969." An instance where a parenthetical comment is used to convey additional understanding would be "table grapes (to eat)." Vague vocabulary such as, "so and so from OSU" or "a 5 min. long something," as well as blanks, for example, "so I can discuss ——" also indicate metacognitive processes at work. Prior knowledge refers to the reader's existing knowledge of the world or of particular topics that infiltrate the reader's recall. This feature also encompasses any assumptions or expectations that readers may bring to the text based on their own experience. Readers' belief that an article is about the "summit talks" or "the arms build-up," when in actuality a text only describes an exchange of messages between the U.S. and Soviet heads of state is an example of prior knowledge influence.

These six features and their definitions provide the decision framework for qualitatively analyzing recall protocol data. This qualitative analysis provides the picture of data-driven and conceptually driven contributions to the second language reading process.

TEXT CONSTRUCTION BY READERS OF GERMAN AND SPANISH

A review of the data analysis charts in Tables 5.1–5.3 indicate that a variety of both text-based and reader-based factors operate in tandem to influence comprehension. No single component of the model, such as word recognition, can accurately account for the subject's overall comprehension of the text. In other words, no one factor dominates the comprehension process. On the contrary, the data reveal that comprehension is characterized by a complex set of interacting processes performed by the reader to construct an understanding of the text.

Figure 5.2 contains the text of a German business letter used in several previous studies (Allen et al., 1988; Bernhardt & Berkemeyer, 1988; Berkemeyer, 1989). To high school students, this text provided a significant challenge. The manner in which school students reconstructed this brief text demonstrates that readers draw from both their knowledge of the world as well as from their knowledge of German when reading. Figure 5.3 contains students' unedited recall protocols. Table 5.1 categorizes reader reconstructions according to text-based and knowledge-driven elements. A major comprehension problem for the students came in the form of false intratextual perceptions. A majority of students struggled to correctly identify the sender and the receiver of the letter. The charts in Table 5.1 reveal that the relationship between the two parties or even their respective genders was not made explicit to the readers. This situation forced the readers to turn to extratextual clues, such as the business letter format, or to decode sophisticated syntactic structures to obtain this information. The majority of students, however, were unable to identify these clues or to employ them accurately in their recalls.

In fact, a lack of prior knowledge about the standard format of a business letter apparently complicated the recall task for many students. As a result, some students interpreted the letter as a friendly letter from a husband to his wife (e.g., Subject 13 and Subject 11). Other common perceptions were that the author of the letter was writing to "a woman in Germany" (Subject 14) or that an Ohio State University professor "is writing Frau someone" (Subject 31). These misinterpretations were also not restricted to the lower levels, but infiltrated the recalls of subjects at every level.

Figure 5.2.   German business letter.

Gesamthochschule Kassel, FB 8 · Postfach 10 13 80 · 3500 Kassel

```
Prof.Dr. E. Buchter-Bernhardt
227 Arps Hall
1945 N. High Street
The Ohio State University
Columbus, OH 43210
U    S    A
```

Liebe Frau Buchter-Bernhardt,

in der Anlage finden Sie die Dinge, die ich Ihnen in Newark versprochen habe. Wenn Sie an dem einen odern andern von uns interessiert sein sollten, können wir dies gerne kopieren.

Unnötig zu sagen, daß es großen Spaß gemacht hat, Sie kennenzuler-
nen, mit Ihnen zu plaudern und gemeinsame Interessen und Bekannte
zu entdecken.

Ob Sie so nett sein könnten, mir bei Gelegenheit den Namen und die
Adresse Ihres Mitarbeiters, der jetzt in Virginia ist, mitzuteilen,
damit ich auch ihm die versprochenen Materialien schicken kann. Ich
vergaß, mir seine Adresse aufzuschreiben.

Mit den besten Grüßen und, allen guten Wünschen bin ich

Ihr

Figure 5.3.   Student unedited recall protocols for the German business letter text.

Code #11
This is a letter to Buchter-Berhardts wife from him. He is in Newark he is a professer at OSU and as soon as he gets the address where he'll be in Virginia he'll sendit.

Code #14
This is a letter to a woman in Germany. It is from a man at O.S.U. he is asking about something that is too big. He also ask for her adress when she writes.

Code #29
It's a business letter and I think it talks about sports. It mentions the names and addresses of some people.

Code #13
Letter to Dr. Butcher Barnhart at Columbus, Ohio university of Ohio State wife. Telling her of his first stop in Newark and meeting there was fun then to the one in Virginia was very intresting.

Code #17
Dear Mrs. ?

something big has just happened. I met you in Newark. You have moved to Virginia. I have forgotten your address. Best wishes.
                    Professor from OSU

Code #28
Dear Proffesor,

     Awhile ago I was speaking in Newark and thought it was very interesting. You have so much to see— I couldn't speak the language very well. Now Im in Virginia and I can speak the language much better. My best to your family
          Sincerly yours,
          [attempted signature]

Code #18
Dear Frau—

     I found out about your thing and would like to discuss it in Newark.
     Then there was something to do with a performace & people clapping, & strangers were there
     I would really like if you don't mind, if you could send me the name & adress of _____ in Virginia so I can discus _____ with them. I forgot, my address is given.
     much luck and happiness,
     [attempted signature]

Code #26
This letter is to a lady in Germany who come hear once to give speeches. The man who wrote the letter, a professor from O.S.U., wanted a copy of the speech she gave here because she spoke better than anyone else that day.

Code #30
They want to get a few people together to do something that's alot of fun, but they don't want to copy the materials until they have enough intrest. He wants her to send a letter to this guy in Virgina with his address, so the guy in Virgina can send him the materials.

Code #6
     In the envelope I have included the things that we discussed in Newark.
     It goes without saying that it was fun talking with you and discovering your interests and likes.
     I hope you wil be so kind as to contact your colleague in Virginia, so that I can send him the same things I have given you. I forgot to include his adress. I will be glad to copy these materials if necessary.

Figure 5.3.   Student unedited recall protocols for the German business letter text.
(cont.)

Code #9

Dear Mrs. Bucher-Bernhardt (spelling of name?)

I found the things that I told you about in Newark. If you are interested in one or another of them, we will gladly make copies for you.

Needless to say, it was great fun to get to know you, to talk with you and discover our similar interests and relatives.

If you would be so kind as to send me the names and addresses of your coworkers who are now in Virginia I could send them these materials as well. I forgot to write them down.

With good luck and best wishes,
yours
[attempted signature]

Code #20

Frau Bernhardt,

in this package you will find the things that I talked about in Newark. If we having anything else that should interest you, we would be glad to copy them and send them to you.

It is needless to say that I really enjoyed getting to know you and speak with you.

If you would be so kind, could you send me the name and address of your co-worker who is now in Virginia. I would like to send him the same things that I sent you.

I forgot to write down his adress.

Many greetings and regards,
yours
[attempted signature]

Code #15

Dear Mrs. Butcher Bernhardt

Here are the things you wanted to copy from Newark. If you find anything interesting, feel free to copy it.

It was a great pleasure meeting you, and finding we had so many things in common

Please send me the mames & addresses of the people you want me to send the information to, as I forgot to write them down.

Best wishes
[attempted signature]

Code #31

Professor so and so from OSU is writing Frau someone in reference to a mistake or some thing that the Frau pointed out to him. Newark is mentioned and the professor thanks the lady and tells her how nice and interesting her aquintance is. He goes on to say that he forgot to give her his adress and that it is enclosed along with an adress in Virginia where she can gain more information along the same lines.

Code #32

In the letter the man sent some materials to Bernhardt which he used in his talk in Newark. He says he can get them copied for her. He wants to talk with her and get to know her better. He wants the address of her friend in Virginia.

In trying to sort out their perceptions of the text many students relied on metacognition indicating that they were thinking about and reflecting on what they read. Their parenthetical comments and question marks reveal the students' frustration and uncertainty with the text at hand and their struggle to make sense of their interpretations. For example, Subject 17 began the recall with "Dear Mrs. ?" to indicate that the letter was addressed to a woman, but that the student could not remember her name. Likewise, Subject 31 wrote "Professor so and so from OSU," while Subject 9 remembered the woman's name but was unsure of the spelling so put "Dear Mrs. Bucher-Bernhardt (spelling of name?)." Another student showed uncertainty by prefacing the whole recall with "I think it talks about . . ." (Subject 29). Clearly, metacognitive forces were operating simultaneously with students' intratextual perceptions to impact comprehension.

Once students initiated an interpretation of the letter, they tended to adhere to that interpretation rather tenaciously, even if it meant ignoring other important textual features. This phenomenon may, at least in part, account for the multitude of problems that learners had with the complex syntax in the letter.

Serious syntactic errors permeated the recalls of students across all levels. For example, Subject 15 wrote "feel free to copy it" for a clause that actually states "we will gladly copy these" [materials]. Other students attempted to combine parts of different sentences together in an effort to cope with the difficult syntax. This strategy inevitably fueled the readers' initial misperceptions. For example, Subject 31, who believed the letter was to "Frau someone" later in the text interpreted a series of sentences as "He goes on to say that he forgot to give her his address and that it is enclosed along with an adress in Virginia." In actuality, the sentences say: "When you get the chance could you be so nice as to pass on to me the name and address of your colleague, who is now in Virginia, so that I can also send him the promised materials. I forgot to write down his address." Here the student attempted to link together words and phrases that had been understood in a way that made syntactic and semantic sense. Unfortunately, the end result scarcely resembled the author's original meaning.

In addition to major syntactic problems, the readers also encountered difficulty in trying to decipher relatively minor syntactic structures. The most common problem was misinterpreting singular nouns (i.e., den Namen und die Adresse) as plural. This problem led some students to believe that more than one person was involved in this reference; for example, Subject 29 believed that "some people" were being discussed while Subject 9 wrote "your coworkers."

Not only the difficult syntax, but also the abstract and ambiguous vocabulary in the letter complicated the students' recall task. The text includes several vague nouns used to refer to the materials, which are being sent to the receiver, such as: "die Anlage," "die Dinge," "einen oder andern," "dies," and "die Materialen." Nowhere in the text, however, are the contents of these materials ever explicitly explained to the reader. This use of ambiguous vocabulary had a profound impact on the learners' comprehension of the letter. In fact, few first

Table 5.1. Student recalls for the German business letter text according to the subject number and instructional level and categorized according to text-driven and knowledge-driven elements.

LEVEL I Student Code	Word Recognition	Phonemic/Graphemic Features	Syntactic Feature Recognition	Intratextual Perceptions	Metacognition	Prior Knowledge
11	"Frau" interpreted in the sense of "wife."		Student recognizes "schicken," "Adresse" and "Virginia" and forms these into a coherent sentence based on his/her perception of the text. Student does not seem to attend to the syntax and is overruled by his/her perception of the text.	Student assumes the letter is from husband to wife, despite the business letter format (student just ignores this). This also forces student to believe that the author is male, and this isn't explicitly stated in the text. Student recognizes Newark as a city and concludes that that must be where the author is. The letterhead obviously leads the student to believe that the sender is a professor—even though the letterhead shows only the receiver's address. Words like "as soon as" and "where he'll be" are		

			the sentence, i.e., they aren't found in the actual text.
14	It is possible that student interprets "Spaß" as "Sports" and so concludes that the letter is "about sports."	Student sees "großen" and thinks the sender is asking about something that is "too big"—not really clear from where student gets the idea of "asking." Student sees "Adresse" and also somehow links this up with ask: "He also asks for her address." "Aufzuschreiben" is then linked up with this perception to be interpreted as "when she writes."	Student thinks letter is to "a woman in Germany" despite the letterhead. Student misreads this as the sender rather than the receiver: "It is from a man at OSU." This perception pervades his/her interpretation of the text. Everything in the recall seems to be interpreted based upon the student's limited perception of the text.
29	Student recognizes "die Namen und die Adresse" but interprets them as plural and can only say that they are of "some people" rather than to identify exactly whose name and address it is.		Student begins by noting that it is "a business letter."	Student prefaces his/her statement "I think it talks about . . ." to show a measure of uncertainty here about his/her interpretation. Use of "some people" also shows student's use of metacognition (knows it is someone but just can't say who).

(Continued)

129

LEVEL II

Student Code	Word Recognition	Phonemic/Graphemic Features	Syntactic Feature Recognition	Intratextual Perceptions	Metacognition	Prior Knowledge
13	"Frau" interpreted in the sense of "wife." Student thinks it's a letter to the professor's wife.		"Spaß" is seen in reference to the travels so student thinks "meeting [in Newark] was fun." "Interessen" (a noun) is misinterpreted as "was very interesting" (an adjective).	Student perceives text as a letter to his wife about his travels, e.g., "first stop in Newark: . . . then to the one in Va."		"Frau" interpreted as "wife" is perhaps a prior knowledge interference in that not enough professors are women and so student believes a professor must be a man. Any possible prior knowledge of business letter format is ignored to account for this perception of the text.
17	"Frau" interpreted as "Mrs."	Misinterpretation of what "Dinge" actually refers to.	Perhaps a misunderstanding of who is being referred to in ". . . der jetzt in Virginia ist."	Somehow, perhaps from the format of the letter, the student believes that "something big has just happened." There doesn't seem to be any vocabulary to support this view of the text. Student does correctly perceive that the writer and the receiver met in Newark—but the mention of Virginia erroneously leads stu-	Student starts letter by saying "Dear Mrs. ?" indicating that s/he knows the letter was addressed to a woman but can't remember her name. Student maintains original format of the letter—business letter format. Student closes letter with "Professor from OSU"—probably be-	Closing with "Professor from OSU" also indicates a misunderstanding of the letterhead address—probably due to a lack of prior knowledge about conventions of a business letter.

28

Student mistakes "versprochen" for "gesprochen" and so concludes "a while ago I was speaking in Newark." Again it seems the student is influenced by the "versprochen" past participle and writes "I couldn't speak the language very well" and "I can speak the language much better."

"Family" possibly comes from a misunderstanding of "Bekannte."

Possibly "Spaß" is interpreted as "Sprache."

Student mixes "versprochen" with Virginia and creates "Now I'm in Virginia and can speak the language much better."

"interessiert" (a verb) is interpreted as "interessant" (an adjective).

the receiver has moved there. In keeping with this perception the student misinterprets "Ich vergaß, mir seine Adresse . . ." as "I have forgotten your Address." Student simply tries to reconcile his/her perception to the actual text.

Student builds a perception of the text as the writer's explanation of a visit to Newark and what took place there. As a result student includes such things as "You have so much to see [in Newark]." Even though these statements are not at all supported by the text, they seem to fit the student's perception. It seems to be a case of the student just taking off with his/her own perception of the text and completely losing sight of what the actual content is.

Student maintains the format of a business letter.

Original signature of the letter is attempted.

Student closes letter with typical letter convention probably derived from prior knowledge. "My best to your family" is used as the translation for "Mit den besten Grüßen." Student also adds "Sincerely" to "Ihr" to get "sincerely yours," probably because this is also a known convention for business letters.

LEVEL III

Student Code	Word Recognition	Phonemic/Graphemic Features	Syntactic Feature Recognition	Intratextual Perceptions	Metacognition	Prior Knowledge
18	"Versprochen" is misrecognized as just "gesprochen" ("discuss"), even though past tense is not recognized elsewhere in the recall. (This occurs in the 1st and 3rd paragraphs). Apparently "plaudern" is seen as "klatschen"—("people clapping") and "Bekannte" is misrecognized as "Unbekannte." Perhaps "Spaß" is interpreted as "performance." "Besten Grüßen and allen guten Wünschen" is very loosely translated as "much luck and happiness."		A few words are recognized and student tries to hook these together in any logical way: "I found out about your thing and would like to discuss it in Newark." "Ob Sie so nett sein könnten" is inflated a bit to be translated as "I would really like it if you don't mind . . ." "Namen und die Adresse" are recognized as singular but student refers to the person later as "them." Student misreads syntax of "Ich vergaß, mir seine Adresse aufzuschreiben" and interprets this as "I forgot, my address is given." Apparently "mir" is recognized as "meine" and "seine" is just ignored.	Student has a hard time right from the beginning getting the gist of what is being written about.	Student maintains the actual format of the letter with salutation and closing, etc. Student can't make any sense of the second paragraph at all and just collapses this whole thought into: "Then there was something to do with a performance and people clapping and strangers were there." Student leaves two blanks one after "the name and address of ——" and after "so I can discus —— "to indicate s/he knew something was there, but just can't recall or didn't understand what it was. Student also tries to recreate the illegible signature—perhaps to show s/he knew one was there.	

26

Perhaps the "sprochen" part of "versprochen" leads the student to believe that she "spoke" and gave "speeches."

Student perceives the receiver as "a lady in Germany," probably because the letter is addressed to her and is in German. Student neglects to take careful note of the letterhead address and thinks it is the sender's rather than the receiver's address. Student perceives the "man who wrote the letter" as a "professor from OSU."

Student sees Newark and Virginia and probably assumes that this "German lady" was in the U.S., i.e., "came here."

Student sees "kopieren" and to fit his/her perception just assumes that it is "a copy of the speech she gave here." This interpretation seems to make sense to the student given everything else s/he has written.
It really seems that the

Perhaps such things as "sagen" or "sprochen" from "versprochen" and "besten" from the closing give the student some basis for the interpretation "... she spoke better than anyone else that day."

Not noticing the letterhead could be a lack of prior knowledge about business letter conventions.

"Versprochen" interpreted as "gesprochen" could be attributed to the student's prior knowledge of what professional people do, i.e., give speeches, etc.

(Continued)

LEVEL III Student Code	Word Recognition	Phonemic/Graphemic Features	Syntactic Feature Recognition	Intratextual Perceptions	Metacognition	Prior Knowledge
				student continues to further this perception by writing "because she spoke better than anyone else that day." There doesn't seem to be anything directly in the text to support this view—it just seems to be the student's individual interpretation.		
30	Student completely ignores the "Ich" subject of sentence.	Perhaps "gemeinsame" is interpreted as "genug." "Sie" (you formal) is interpreted as "she" and referred to as "her."	Student just seems to take a few known words and to link them up arbitrarily into what s/he believes is a coherent text, so "Dinge," "Spaß," "Kopieren," "Materiaien," and "interessiert" or "Interessen" as: "They want to get a few people together to do something that's a lot of fun, but they don't want to copy the materials until they have enough interest."	What student constructs is perfectly logical within his/her perception but is not text-based at all. Overall, student tries very hard to fit all of this information into a coherent whole but it is extremely difficult for him/her and student doesn't focus in on any one view of the text, e.g., s/he switches from "they" to "he" and "her," so is never even sure who		

Word Recognition	Phonemic/Graphemic Features	Syntactic Feature Recognition	Intratextual Perceptions	Metacognition	Prior Knowledge
		Student uses "schicken" to come up with "He wants her to send a letter to this guy in Virginia." Student turns around the syntax of "damit ich auch ihm die versprochenen Materialen schicken kann" to render "so the guy in Virginia can send him the materials."	the major people in the text are.		

LEVEL IV

Student Code	Word Recognition	Phonemic/Graphemic Features	Syntactic Feature Recognition	Intratextual Perceptions	Metacognition	Prior Knowledge
6	"versprochen" translated as "discussed." "gemeinsame" is overlooked and translated solely as "your." "versprochen" is ignored the second time and just assumed to imply "the same things," that the receiver got. "aufzuschreiben" is translated as "include."		Syntax of last paragraph confused student into thinking that the receiver should contact the colleague directly rather than just passing the correct address along. (Incorrect understanding of "mitzuteilen" seems to be the trouble.)			

(Continued)

135

LEVEL IV

Student Code	Word Recognition	Phonemic/Graphemic Features	Syntactic Feature Recognition	Intratextual Perceptions	Metacognition	Prior Knowledge
9	"finden" translated in past tense as "found." "versprochen" interpreted as "told you about." "können" interpreted as "will" rather than "can." "Bekannte" mistranslated as "relatives." "kann" seen as "could." "besten Grüßen" is translated as "good luck."	Interpretation of "Bekannte" as "Verwandte" possibly due to phonemic interference. Interpretation of "Grüßen" as "Glück" possibly due to phonemic interference.	Student misrecognizes the syntax and interprets "finden Sie" as "I found the things." "den Namen und die Adresse Ihres Mitarbeiters" are all rendered in the plural "the names and addresses of your coworkers." Then "ihm" is also misrepresented as "them" probably to keep the textual perception coherent. Also despite the clue from "seine Adresse" (sing.), student still writes "I forgot to write them down"—also intratextual perception operating.		By the salutation the student writes "(spelling of name?" to indicate) he's thinking about the name but can't quite remember the spelling.	
20	"Anlage" is loosely interpreted as "package," which still fits with the context.			Student adds "and to send them to you" to the part about copying the text. This isn't	Student uses conventions of a business letter and maintains first-person narrative.	

"versprochen" is interpreted as "gesprochen," which student translates as "that I talked about."

"mitzuteilen" is interpreted as "send" rather than "share," but this definitely fits into the context.

"besten Grüßen" is interpreted as "many greetings and regards," which is fine in the given context.

found in the original text but is certainly implied by the context. Really shows that student has a deep meaning of the text.

Student interprets "damit ich auch ihm die versprochenen Materialien schicken kann" as "I would like to send him the same things that I sent you." Student seems to be picking up on the fact that the receiver was "promised" ("versprochen") certain materials just as the colleague in Virginia was. Perhaps this causes him/her to make this inference about "the same things that I sent you."

LEVEL V

Student Code	Word Recognition	Phonemic/Graphemic Features	Syntactic Feature Recognition	Intratextual Perceptions	Metacognition	Prior Knowledge
15	"Mitzuteilen" interpreted as "send" probably because student believes the receiver is expected to send a letter back in return. "Den Namen und die Adresse Ihres Mitarbeiters" is translated as "the names and addresses of the people you want me to send the information to." "Namen und Adresse" are seen as plural rather than singular, possibly because they look plural or more likely because "Mitarbeiters" looks plural.		". . . die ich Ihnen in Newark versprochen habe" is interpreted as "the things you wanted to copy." Student also misunderstands "können wir dies gerne kopieren" as "feel free to copy it." It seems like student just isn't paying close enough attention to syntax. Student also misinterprets somewhat the part about "die versprochenen Materialen" as something that the receiver wants him/her to send rather than something the sender has already promised to send.	Student sees the word "kopieren" and this seems to pervade his/her interpretation of the first paragraph.	Student maintains format of a business letter—even tries to recall the address in the top corner, by adding "OSU." Student attempts to recreate the illegible signature.	
31	Student probably interprets "Anlage" as "mistake" as "Dinge" as something that has happened rather than		Student uses "gemeinsame Interessen" to modify "kennenzulernen" and so comes up with "tells her how	Student believes the OSU professor is writing the letter to a woman rather than their being one in the same	Student doesn't recall the professor's name but refers to him as "Professor so and so from OSU."	The fact that the student does not recognize that the OSU professor and the woman are the same

actual tangible things. Therefore, s/he writes that the professor "is writing in reference to a mistake or something that the Frau pointed out to him."

nice and interesting her aquaintance is." "Adresse," "Virginia," "Materialien," and "vergaß mir, seine Adresse aufzuschreiben" is all jumbled up to render "he forgot to give her his address and that it is enclosed along with an adress in Virginia where she can gain more information along the same lines." Student has real problems deciphering the syntax of this long sentence and, thus, can't determine who is really doing what—so it all gets meshed together to fit his/her original perception of a professor writing to a woman.

and the receiver of the action.

With "großen Spaß und gemeinsame Interessen" student probably just adds in "and thanks the lady" because it seems to fit this context and his/her perception of the text.

person could be due to student's lack of knowledge about the form of a business letter or could also be his/her belief that professors are more likely to be men.

Student doesn't remember the name of the lady so calls her "Frau Someone."

32   The fact that the student thinks the materials sent were from a talk given in Newark could be due to the

Student misinterprets the tense of the middle paragraph as future rather than past and so deduces that

Student presumes that the materials the writer sent were from "his talk" given "in Newark."

139

LEVEL V Student Code	Word Recognition	Phonemic/Graphemic Features	Syntactic Feature Recognition	Intratextual Perceptions	Metacognition	Prior Knowledge
	student's misunderstanding of "ver-sprochen" as "gesprochen."		"he wants to talk to her and get to know her better," when really he is saying he already enjoyed doing so.			
	"Dinge" is interpreted as "materials." Probably the final paragraph's reference to "Materialen" makes the student think these are the same things.					
	Student interprets "Mitarbeiter" as "friend," rather than colleague.					

and second year students managed to recall anything about these materials, while students in the upper levels had problems describing this aspect of the letter correctly. As a result, the students missed one of the major propositions in the letter, namely that the author had "enclosed the things that I promised in Newark." Instead, students ignored this part of the text or interpreted it as: "the things you wanted" (Subject 15), "I found out about your thing" (Subject 18), "something that is too big" (Subject 14), and "something that's a lot of fun." These misinterpretations in turn spawned additional comprehension problems.

Text-driven features, such as phonemic and graphemic elements, also influenced students' recall abilities. The similarity between the past participles "gesprochen" [spoken] and "versprochen" [promised] caused students no end of comprehension difficulties. Even among upper-level students the "ver" prefix was ignored and students attended to the "sprochen" stem. This misrecognition prompted several students to interpret the word "versprochen" and related phrases in terms of "discuss" (Subjects 18 and 6), "speeches" (Subject 26), "talk" (Subjects 20 and 32), "told" (Subject 9) and "speaking" (Subject 28). Even this one small misrecognition had a profound impact on the students perception of the letter and pervaded their overall interpretations of the text.

In general, prior knowledge did not play a very significant role in the students' recall. In fact, as noted above, a lack of prior knowledge may have accounted for more of the readers' comprehension problems. Most notable was students' lack of knowledge about business letter writing conventions, which prompted them to interpret the text as a friendly letter. In addition, students' prior knowledge that there are more men than women professors may have caused students to believe that a male OSU professor was writing to his wife (Subjects 11 and 13) or to a woman (Subjects 14 and 31). Obviously, non-specific background knowledge (e.g., knowledge of letter formats in general) or inappropriate prior knowledge (knowledge that most professors are men) can seriously impede students' comprehension processes. As a result, the assumption that "background knowledge always facilitates comprehension" is thoroughly invalid. Although the potential for prior knowledge to assist the comprehension process clearly exists, that knowledge must be specific to the comprehension task at hand. What constitutes the appropriate *specificity* is not always as clear, as these data reveal.

With the business letter text, syntactic feature recognition problems were a major source of comprehension breakdown; however, those problems were also sustained by false interpretations of the text from the onset, by the misrecognition of key, albeit vague, vocabulary items, and a lack of appropriate background knowledge about the text type. Only when all of these features are taken as a whole do they adequately account for the students' recall of the text.

Figure 5.4 reproduces a newspaper article also read by some high school readers. Figure 5.5 includes the students' unedited recalls and Table 5.2 interprets their reconstructions according to text-driven and knowledge-driven com-

Figure 5.4.   German newspaper article text.

DW Washington/Moskau

Reagan kam bei den Russen an

DW Washington/Moskau

Der 79jährige Alexander Kislakow strahlte: „Das Sowjetvolk hört mit eigenen Ohren, was der US-Präsident sagt." Der Rentner freute sich vor allem über bisher nicht zugängliche Informationen, die er durch die Neujahrsbotschaft von Ronald Reagan im sowjetischen Fernsehen erhalten hatte. Es wäre gut, fuhr er fort, wenn ein solcher Austausch öfter stattfände.

Kislakow gehörte zu denjenigen, die die Ausstrahlung der Reagan-Rede zufällig miterlebt hatten. Denn die meisten Sowjetbürger waren gar nicht über die verabredete TV-Sendung unterrichtet. Weder in der Programmvorschau der Fernsehillustrierten noch in den Tageszeitungen war das Ereignis angekündigt worden. Fußgänger im Moskauer Stadtzentrum zeigten sich sehr überrascht, als sie von westlichen Journalisten darauf angesprochen wurden.

Ein junger Mann in der sowjetischen Hauptstadt antwortete auf die Frage, wie ihm Reagan gefallen habe: „Ich halte ihn für einen fähigen Mann, der weiß, daß Friede und Zusammenarbeit die wichtigsten Dinge in der Welt sind. Ich bin sehr glücklich, daß er unser Land besuchen will." Seinen Namen wollte er jedoch nicht nennen. Ein anderer Moskauer Bürger meinte, Reagan und Gorbatschow sei es offenbar ernst mit dem Streben nach Frieden. Die Ansprache des amerikanishchen Präsidenten habe gezeigt, da er die sowjetische Ansicht teilt, es gebe keine Alternative zum Frieden".

In der Parteizeitung „Prawda" und in der Regierungszeitung „Iswestija" waren die gleichzeitig ausgestrahlten Reden der beiden mächtigsten Männer der Welt auf der Titelseite zu lesen. Die „Prawda" kritisierte aber zugleich das amerikanische SDI-Projekt, mit dem „militaristische Kreise" in den USA die Gefahr eines Krieges über die Welt brächten.

Als das Neujahrsprogramm in den Vereinigten Staaten mit dem alljährlich in Pasadena (Kalifornien) stattfindenden berühmten Rose-Bowl-Umzug für die fünfminutige Fernsehrede des sowjetischen Parteichefs Gorbatschow unterbrochen worden war, griffen einige Zuschauer erbost zum Telefon und beschwerten sich bei den Fernsehanstalten. „Wenn ich einen Russen sehen will, dann kaufe ich mir einen russischen Fernseher", sagte ein Bürger in Spartanburg im Bundesstaat South Carolina.

ponents. Here, too, the students in all levels faced an interesting array of comprehension problems in trying to interpret the newspaper article. To a greater extent than in the business letter text, students' knowledge of the topic substantially influenced text interpretation. Even upper level students blended their prior knowledge of U.S. and Soviet relations, with the actual content of the article to produce their recalls. As a result, some students believed that the text was about the ''summit meeting'' (Subject 18) or Reagan's ''visit to a base'' in the Soviet Union. In actuality, the article only described an exchange of messages between the two countries made on New Year's Day.

Other students let their prior perceptions and knowledge of political and military affairs influence their interpretations of the text. For example, Subject 17 not only wrote that the SDI Project was dangerous, as the text stated, but also added that ''he [Reagan] should not go with the SDI-Project.'' Another student recalled that ''he [Reagan] was still pushing for SDI and other space weapons.'' Yet another student stated that ''the speech from a U.S. president is a change from the usual propaganda'' (Subject 6). In all cases, the students seemed to rely heavily on their prior knowledge of the topic when recalling the text, and in so doing, strayed significantly from the content of the text itself.

Figure 5.5.   Student unedited recall protocols for the German newspaper article text.

Code #11

The paragraph was on the United States and the Soviet Union. Last year president Reagan spoke to Russia on thier network channels. And Gobeshov spoke to us on our network channel. The results of this by the public of countrys was this. The Russains listened only with one ear, but one person mentioned that did not want to mention his name, said that he expected different from Mr. Regan and is very glad that he wants to come and visit Russia. American said if he wanted to listen to the Russains he would have bought a Russain tv.

Code #14

President Reagan visited a base in Russia. Pravda and "Isweltia"? reported on it. They got quotes from a young man, a soldier and a person in S. Carolina.

Code #29

They're talking about relations between the U.S.S.R. and U.S.A. They mentioned something about the arms build up, and they talked about a 5-minute long something during the Rose Bowl.

Code #13

was about television as program news were Reagan prodcasted over to Russia The Russian asked people of what they thought about the transmission. They said they thought it was very good for U.S. television. Talked about American people in California. They ate a Burger.

Code #17

President Reagen has been on Soviet TV. He asked the Russians a question in 1979. One man, whose name was withheld, said he likes to be a Russian and will stay a Russian. 2 magazines criticized Reagen. One said he should not go on with the SDI-project. The New Year's program was also shown. They showed the Rose Bowl. A man said that if he wanted to see Russian programs, he would go buy a Russian TV.

Code #28

A 79 year old man says the Soviets are hearing what the President and American people are saying. He said this is good and we should have more communication. Soviets say they like their country but they think our TV is the best in the world. On New Year's day they all watched the Rose Bowl except for a 5 minute interruption by Gorbachev. Americans say it is bad the Soviets can see our TV. Someone from Sparton, North Carolina said when we watch Russian TV were Russian watchers.

Code #7

   This article deals with U.S. president Ronald Reagen and Soviet premier Gorbachav's summit meeting and with their exchanging of messages with each other's country over that country's television air.
   Pedestrians in Moscow's city center were very quiet when western journalists questioned them.
   One young man in the capital told how Reagen pleased him. "I take him for a fair man, the right, trying for peace and working-together and the best thing for the world." The man did not want his name to be known.
   The party newspaper Pravada criticized Reagen's proposed SDI-project and said there is a "military crisis" in the U.S. that Reagen might spread throughout the world.
   Most Americans were watching the Rose Bowl that was taking place in Pasenda, California while Gorbachev's five minute message was being aired. Said a South Carolina man: "If I want to see a Russian, then I will buy a Russian television set."

Figure 5.5.   Student unedited recall protocols for the German newspaper article text. (*cont.*)

Code #26

The article here describes the reactions of the people of the Soviet Union and the United States to the exchange of messages that Pres. Reagen and Soviet Leader Gorbichev exchanged on New Years Day. Both were televised on each others television broadcasts and this paper recorded the reactions.

The first one was from a citizen from Moscow who said that to his knowledge, he was happy lucky and the Soviet land was the same. Pravda, the official government newspaper, critisezed Reagen for his 'Star Wars' Strategic Defense Initiative program and the escalation of arms in the U.S. military. A citizen of the Capital of South Carolina said he didn't care and when he saw his first Soviet he would go buy a Soviet television to watch programs on.

Code #30

The Soviet people listened to Regan w/ both ears. his 5 minute message said he was coming to the Soviet Union to visit. One Soviet guy said "he thought it was good and we could word together." He didn't want to be named. Provda criticized the Strategic Defense Initive program. I think the message was telecast during the Rose-bowl, in Pasadina, California. Another Russian said Reagan & Gorbachev were both concerned with death after peace.

Code #6

One citizen of the Soviet Union thinks that President Reagan's speech to the USSR and Mr. Gorbachev's speech to the USA was something positive. He feels that the speech from a U.S. president is a change from the usual propaganda. he feels that such an exchange should take place more often.

Most Russian citizens were astonished at the fact that they would see Western journalism on T.V.

One unidentified person said that he things Reagan is a fair, peace-loving man. He thinks Reagan and Gorbachev are serious about creating an opportunity for peace. Reagen even said that there is no alternative to peace.

The state newspapers had big headlines about Reagan's speech. Most of the criticism was directed toward the US's "Star Wars" program-

At the same time Reagen was speaking to the Soviets, Mr. Gorbachev was speaking to the Americans. Mr. Gorbachev's speech was during the Rose Bowl parade in California.

One man in North Carolina said that if he wanted to see Soviet TV he would have bought his TV in the USSR.

Code #9

This article discussed the speeches made by the American and Soviet presidents on New Year's day in each man's opposite country.

One Soviet man said that the Russian people listened with one ear to what Reagan said.

Another said he felt that Reagan is a smart man and realizes that peace and cooperation are the most important things in the world today.

Reagan's message was played in the middle of the day when not everyone was watching TV.

In America, Gorbachev's speech interrupted the Rose Bowl parade for 15 minutes. Some viewers complained about the interruption. Said one man from South Carolina (or was it North Carolina?), "If I want to see a Russian, I'll go buy a Russian television!"

Code #20

A 79 year old soviet guy names Alexander was talking about a speech Reagan made to Soviets on New Year's Day. He said that he thinks the Soviets only hear the U.S. President with one ear. He thought it was a good idea though for Reagan to do that. Many soviet citizens didn't know it was on though. Some people in Moscow were interviewed and asked what they thought about Reagan. One man said he thought he believed in the whites, freedom & working together. He was glad that Reagan wanted to visit their country.

The two newspapers ran Reagan's & Gorbechov's speech side by side on the front page. *Pravda* criticized Reagan and the Military circle & said the U.S. wants to spread war throughout the world.

In America on New Year's Day, the Rose Bowl Parade in Pasadena was interrupted for Gorbechov's 5 minute speech. The T.V. stations got lots of phone calls from angry people. One man from Spartanburg, South Carolina said that if he wanted to watch a Russian, he would have bought a Russian T.V.

Code #15

The 79 year old Kisaklow said "the Soviet people hear with a single ear what President Reagan has to say." He was speaking in favor of President Reagan's brodcast on Soviet TV. The majority of the Soviet people knew about the brodcast, seeing on T.V. or reading the newspapers. They were surprised to see Western journalists around.

One unidentified Soviet citizen said of Reagan "He knows that peace and working together are the only important things. Another Soviet citizen also said Reagan was for Peace.

The Soviet Communist party, Pravda, and the news services were not as supportive. Pravda criticized Reagan, saying "His SDI defense is in danger of bringing the world into war.

In America, people were not as impressed with seeing Premier Gorbachev. The brodcast broke into the Rose Bowl brodcast for 5 minutes. And as one person from Spartanburg South Carolina said "If I'd wanted to see Russians, I'd have bought a Russian T.V."

Code #31

Alexander Klitkaw a 79 year old russion comments on the new years program that had president Reagan adress the Soviet people on Soviet T.V. He said it was good to hear what the president said right from him.

At this time in the capital city Moscow, western journalists were abuzz asking questions about how the Soviet people reacted to the adress.

The reaction to Reagan's adress was good and the people asked seem to be glad to hear Reagan calling for peace. One young Soviet who asked to remain unnamed said that he was glad for what the president said and felt that peace an working together were of the utmost importance. Others commented that surely the only way to gain peace was to work together.

The Soviet paper pravada was synical about Reagan's speech and asked how the President could be sincere when he still was pushing for the S.D.I. and other space weapons. In the U.S. it was said that the five minute broadcast came during the Rose Bowl in Pasadena and one man from South Carolina commented that if he wanted to see a Russian on T.V. he would buy a Russian T.V. Set.

Code #32

The article began by saying that the russian people will lisen to the presidtnt of the United States to see what he has to say. The first man interviewed, whoose name is unknown, said he was glad to hear that our president wants peace and feels it is the only way. The other man thinks that Reagen and Gorbachev should meet more often and seriously discuss the important issues. Both the Party Paper Pravda and the Govenment paper critized the american star wars defense system saying that increases the danger of War. During and/or after the Rose bowl on new year's day Gorbachev gave his T.V. broadcast and they asked a man what he felt about it. This saublöde arschloch said if he wanted to see a russian he would buy a russian T.V.

Prior knowledge also seemed to influence students' ability to correctly interpret syntactic features in the text. Students appeared to interject their own opinions and perceptions of the topic when attempting to decipher the syntactic relationships in sentences. For example, the clause "das amerikanische SDI-Projekt, mit dem "militaristische Kreise" in den USA die Gefahr eines Krieges über die Welt brächten" is variously interpreted as "there is a 'military crisis' in the United States that Reagan might spread throughout the world" by Subject 18 and "the United States wants to spread war throughout the world" by Subject 20. Another student interpreted this sentence as "it [the SDI-Project] increases the danger of war" (Subject 32).

Not only prior political biases or knowledge impacted students' recalls, but also their perceptions of the U.S. and the Union of Soviet Socialist Republics and the people who live there. This knowledge surfaced the most often in students' references to television. Subject 28, in particular, allowed prior perceptions to invade the recall when s/he wrote "Soviets say they like their country but they think our TV is the best in the world" and "Americans say it is bad the Soviets can see our TV." Other students interjected information about the broadcast by stating that "most Americans were watching the Rose Bowl" (Subject 18) and that "they all watched the Rose Bowl." These embellishments also reveal that the students had allowed their prior knowledge of the popularity of the Rose Bowl to infiltrate their recalls.

These findings with regard to background knowledge reinforce the conclusions stated earlier. Although prior knowledge had a profound impact on students' recall abilities, that impact was not as positive nor as facilitative as previous studies in this area have indicated. In many cases, nonspecific and vague background knowledge was inappropriately applied to the text, to such an extent that readers' comprehension of the text was grossly distorted. Thus, these findings imply that prior knowledge, if inappropriately applied, may well impede rather than facilitate comprehension.

Intratextual perceptions of the text were determined by students' initial decisions concerning the content of the text. Those initial decisions seemed to come primarily from students' prior knowledge and opinions about the topic of the text. As a result, students' intratextual perceptions of the text reflect the prior knowledge employed by them to comprehend the text. For example, when students applied background information about Reagan, Gorbachev, and the "summit meeting" to help them interpret the text, their entire recall conformed to this initial interpretation. Therefore, with regard to the newspaper article, students' intratextual perceptions of the text coincided closely with the kinds of prior knowledge they brought to bear on the text.

Although prior knowledge was certainly the most pervasive handicap for students, they also encountered difficulties in other areas. Syntactic feature recognition, in particular, seemed to plague many students' recalls. The most frequently misinterpreted sentence came at the end of the text: "Wenn ich einen

Table 5.2. Student recalls for the German newspaper article text according to subject number and instructional level and categorized according to text-driven and knowledge-driven elements.

LEVEL I Student Code	Word Recognition	Phonemic/Graphemic Features	Syntactic Feature Recognition	Intratextual Perceptions	Metacognition	Prior Knowledge
11	"Sehen"-rendered as "listen" probably because of the context—you both listen to and see a TV.	"Eigenen" translated as "einen" and interpreted as "one ear."	Student writes "only one ear." Only was probably added to support the belief that one as opposed to both ears were used. Possibly student interpreted "Ich halte ihn" as "he expected different from Mr. Reagan"—however this doesn't account for the "different." This may simply have been added to make sense with the "expected" part. This statement is hooked up with another (correctly recalled sentence) to give it more credibility. "Einen Russen" is translated as "Russians" (in the plural).		The student writes "the results of this by the public of countrys was this. . ." Obviously the student is trying to recall the outcome of the talks by using this introduction.	

147

LEVEL I Student Code	Word Recognition	Phonemic/Graphemic Features	Synctactic Feature Recognition	Intratextual Perceptions	Metacognition	Prior Knowledge
			"Will" is translated in past tense as "wanted." "Dann kaufe ich" is translated in past subjunctive: "I would have bought."			
14				Student's understanding of the two names of the papers leads him/her to believe that all persons quoted in the text were quoted in the two papers. Thus, student writes: "They got quotes from a young man, a soldier and a person in South Carolina." Student just hooks these three people together to make a coherent statement. Reference to soldier is probably gleaned from statements about "militaristische Kreise" and the "SDI Projekt" as	Student uses question mark when trying to recall the name of the newspaper "Isweltia?" This indicates s/he is not sure of the name or perhaps the spelling of the newspaper.	There does not seem to be anything directly in the text to support the student's claim that "Reagan visited a base"—(the text does mention that he wants to visit Russia, but not necessarily a base.) Student probably had prior knowledge of another or similar visit that Reagan made and this causes him/her to perceive the text in this way.

29

Student ignores "Um-zug" (parade) or sim-ply doesn't recognize it.

well as student's prior perception that the text is about Reagan visiting a "base."

The structure "They mentioned something . . ." shows use of metacognitive strategies.

Student uses metacognition in saying that "they talked about a 5-minute long some-thing during the Rose Bowl." This shows that the student knows something took place at that time, but wasn't able to deter-mine exactly what it was.

Student sees USSR and US and assumes it is about their relations—which is a very loose interpreta-tion of what the text is about, based more on student's prior knowledge than his/her comprehension of the text itself.

Student also states that "they mentioned something about the arms build-up." This was not explicitly in the text and only hinted at through such things as "die militaristische Kreise," etc.

LEVEL II

Student Code	Word Recognition	Phonemic/Graphemic Features	Syntactic Feature Recognition	Intratextual Perceptions	Metacognition	Prior Knowledge
13		Student sees "Bürger" (citizen) and tries to link this with something familiar so says "They ate a burger." This is also evidence of prior knowledge interference.	Student misunderstands who asked the Russian people about the broadcast. Student thought "The Russian asked people . . ." when really western journalists asked the questions. Student only recognizes that they "talked about American people in California," nothing about the context is understood.	Somehow the student gets the idea that the Russians think the broadcast "was very good for U.S. television." It seems like student is just fabricating something that fits his/her limited perception of the text.		
17	"Zeitung" interpreted as "magazines."		Date comes from a complete misunderstanding of "79-jährige" as "1979." Possibly the student thought that the questions posed to the Russians by Western journalists were really from President Reagan. Student apparently mixes up "Fernsehan-"	Somehow student gets the idea that Reagan "asked the Russians a question in 1979." Student perceives the interviewed Russian as saying "he likes to be a Russian and will stay a Russian." There doesn't really seem to be any information in the text to support this claim at all.		Seems that prior knowledge probably influenced the student in inferring that one of those interviewed said "he (Reagan) should not go on with the SDI project." The text just said that the SDI project was dangerous—only by implication could it be interpreted that it should be stopped.

"US-Präsident" is interpreted as "The President and the American people." Perhaps student interpreted US to mean Americans.

"Austausch" is interpreted as "communication," which is acceptable in this context.

stalten," "Russen," and "russischen Fernseher" to get this interpretation: "If he wanted to see Russian programs he would go buy a Russian TV." "Programs" is also included in the sentence incorrectly.

Student seems to recognize a few words but jumbles up their syntactic links, e.g., "gefallen habe" gets hooked up with "unser Land" so student thinks the text says: "Soviets say they like their country."

Then references to "Fernseh" and "die wichtigsten Dinge in der Welt" get interpreted together to mean "but they think our TV is the best in the world." This perception of the text pervades the rest of the student's recall.

Student obviously isn't quite sure about the connection between the Rose Bowl, the New Year's program and the speeches, so student just states "The New Year's program was also shown."

Student writes "they think our TV is the best in the world," which could be prior bias that our life (including TV) is better than the Russians'. Student probably brought this viewpoint to the text.

Probably prior knowledge of the popularity of the Rose Bowl leads student to write that "they all watched the Rose Bowl."

LEVEL II

Student Code	Word Recognition	Phonemic/Graphemic Features	Syntactic Feature Recognition	Intratextual Perceptions	Metacognition	Prior Knowledge
			The student writes: "They all watched the Rose Bowl except for a 5-minute interruption by Gorbachev." This probably comes from student's perception that the broadcast wasn't well-received and, therefore, that people didn't watch the broadcast.			
28	"Spartanburg, SC" is interpreted as "Spartan, NC." "Ich" is interpreted as "we" (probably to mean all Americans).	"Wenn" is translated as "when" not if.	Student seems to mix up both the syntax and the recognition of some words to interpret "Wenn ich einen Russen sehen will, dann kaufe ich mir einen russischen Fernseher" as "when we watch Russian TV we're Russian watchers."	Perhaps from the poor reception of the broadcast or perhaps from some negative sentences like "Die meisten Sowjetbürger waren gar nicht über die . . . TV-sendung unterrichtet," student gets the idea that "Americans say it is bad the Soviets can see our TV."		

Student Code	Word Recognition	Phonemic/Graphemic Features	Syntactic Feature Recognition	Intratextual Perceptions	Metacognition	Prior Knowledge
18	"sehr überrascht" is somehow misinterpreted as "very quiet."	"Kreise" is interpreted as "crisis," which doesn't effect the interpretation much.	Student doesn't get the syntax correct and translates "der Weiß, daß Friede und Zusammenarbeit die wichtigsten Dinge in der Welt sind" as "The right, trying for peace and working together and the best thing for the world." Nonetheless, the essence of the sentence is there. Student interprets "militaristische Kreise in den USA die Gefahr eines Krieges über die Welt brächten," as "a 'military crisis' in the U.S. that Reagan might spread throughout the world."		Student uses a very interesting convention; s/he makes a general summary statement to begin the recall and then draws a line after that and starts to recall specifics from the text. After the opening statement the student tries to use the same conventions as the original text, e.g., quotation marks, paragraph divisions, etc.	Though summit meeting is nowhere mentioned in the text the student concludes after seeing references to Reagan and Gorbachev that this is what the text is about. It is likely that the influence of prior knowledge causes the student to have this perception of the text. Student interjects "proposed" before SDI project—even though this isn't explicitly in the text. This indicates his/her prior knowledge of the topic. The student's perception that "there is a 'military crisis' . . . that Reagan might spread" indicates a certain bias against Reagan that may be due to prior knowledge of him as a leader.

LEVEL III

Student Code	Word Recognition	Phonemic/Graphemic Features	Syntactic Feature Recognition	Intratextual Perceptions	Metacognition	Prior Knowledge
						Prior knowledge of the Rose Bowl perhaps prompts the student to say "most Americans were watching the Rose Bowl," even though this wasn't stated in the text.
26	Student isn't sure how to interpret "glück-lich," so includes both "happy" and "lucky."	Student interprets "wenn" as "when" rather than if.	Student misrecognizes "der weiß" and "Ich bin sehr glücklich, daß er unser Land be-suchen will" as "to his knowledge, he was happy, lucky and the Soviet land was the same." It is not clear where student gets the idea of the Soviet land being the same—possibly from "gleich (zeitig)" included later in the text. Student also confuses the syntax of "wenn ich einen Russen sehen will, dann kaufe ich	Student gets the idea that the man in South Carolina "didn't care"—when really he cared so much he called into the TV sta-tion.	Student gives a gener-al overview describing the basic content of the text: "The article describes the reactions of the people of the Soviet Union and the United States . . ." This demonstrates a general understanding, but s/he thinks the whole text is only about the reactions of the people.	

30	Student interprets "eigenen Ohren" as "both ears." Student neglects to include "Umzug" (parade) when referring to the Rose Bowl.	"Streben nach Frieden" is interpreted as "Sterben nach Frieden," therefore, student states that Reagan and Gorbachev are "concerned with death after peace" rather than with striving for peace.	mir einen russischen Fernseher" as "when he saw his first Soviet, he would go buy a Soviet television to watch programs on." Apparently the tense confuses student as well as the word "wenn." The student puts the sentence in the past tense, when actually it is in the future tense.	Student uses a meta-cognitive strategy: "I think the message was to telecast . . ." to show his/her uncertainty and also to show that s/he is trying to fit the text together logically. The student knows something was broadcast but isn't sure if it was broadcasted during the Rose Bowl.
			Student slightly confuses who is for "Zusammenarbeit" (working together). S/he interpreted it as "we could work together" when really it is Reagan who is for working together. Student either isn't aware that there are two messages or confuses which one was broadcast when.	

LEVEL IV Student Code	Word Recognition	Phonemic/Graphemic Features	Syntactic Feature Recognition	Intratextual Perceptions	Metacognition	Prior Knowledge
6	"Informationen" possibly misrecognized as "propaganda." "Friede und Zusammenarbeit die wichtigen Dinge . . . sind" translated as "peaceloving." "Parteizeitung" and "Regierungszeitung" translated as "state newspapers." Student mistook "South Carolina" for "North Carolina." "Russen" mistaken for "Soviet TV"—(possibly believed to be an adjective). "Einen russischen Fernseher" thought to be a "TV in the USSR."	"Fähigen" translated as "fair." "Angesprochen" possibly misread as (an)gesehen"—"that they would see Western journalism on T.V."	Respective speeches seen as "something positive"—gleaned from text of first paragraph—but not stated per se. Student misconnects the words in the second sentence to get "the speech from a U.S. president is a change from the usual propaganda." Student thinks that the broadcasts occurred simultaneously: "At the same time Reagan was speaking to the Soviets . . ." "Wenn ich einen Russen sehen will . . ." translated in past subjunctive.			
9		"Mit eigenen Ohren" is interpreted as "mit einem Ohr"—("with one ear").	Student assumes that "Reagan's message was played in the middle of the day		Student made reference to the "man from South Carolina" but in parentheses says "(or	

20	"Gleichzeitig" is taken to mean "side by side" rather than simultaneously. "Sehen" is interpreted in context of TV as "watch" rather than see.	"Mit eigenen Ohren" is interpreted as "mit einem Ohren," so student thinks the Soviets only hear the U.S. "with one ear." "Der weiß" is interpreted as "the Whites" rather than as a relative clause, so student writes "he believed in the Whites . . ." Student goes beyond the text in rendering "in den USA die Gefahr eines Krieges über die Welt brächten" as "the US wants to spread war throughout the world." Student doesn't recognize present tense and so recalls the whole last sentence in the past tense: "If he wanted to watch a Russian, he would have bought a Russian TV."	was watching" rather than that it was very poorly advertised in the newspapers, etc. This is not an implausible explanation but it is not really stated in text. Student adds something to the sense of the sentence "Kislakow strahlte: Das Sowjetvolk . . ." by rendering this as "He said that he thinks the Soviets . . ." This weakens the original force of the message.	na?)," indicating that s/he is using metacognitive strategies to reconstruct the text. Student keeps relatively the same paragraph structure as the original text. Overall, student has a good recall of this text but does not use the same voice or any textual conventions to facilitate his/her recall. In fact, the tendency is to use more complex structures than what is in the text. Student's perception that "the U.S. wants to spread war throughout the world" could be due to the influence of prior knowledge.

LEVEL V

Student Code	Word Recognition	Phonemic/Graphemic Features	Syntactic Feature Recognition	Intratextual Perceptions	Metacognition	Prior Knowledge
15	"Strahlte" is interpreted as "speaking." Student misrecognizes "angesprochen" as "angesehen" and interprets the sentence as "they were surprised to see Western journalist around." "Parteizeitung Prawda" is misinterpreted as "the Soviet Comunist party, Pravda," by the student.	"Mit eigenen Ohren is misinterpreted as "with a single ear."	Student doesn't see or misidentifies "gar nicht über die verabredete TV-Sendung unterrichtet" and recalls this as "the majority of the Soviet people knew about the broadcast." This is also possibly a misunderstanding of the syntax of the sentence (i.e., student doesn't recognize the passive voice). "Die wichtigsten Dinge in der Welt" is interpreted to be "the only important things" rather than "the most important things." "Einen Russen" is translated in the plural as "Russians." ". . . dann kaufe ich mir . . ." is interpreted in the past subjunctive tense "I'd have bought . . ."	"Der Rentner freute sich vor allem über . . ." is interpreted as "He was speaking in favor of President Reagan's broadcast . . ." This is an abbreviated interpretation of this sentence.	Student uses transition sentence summing up the main ideas to introduce the third paragraph: "The Soviet Pravda the Communist party Pravda and the news services were not as supportive." This shows that student has gotten the gist of the paragraph and is attempting to relate it to the text as a whole. Student also uses a summary statement to introduce the final paragraph: "In America, people were not as impressed with seeing Premier Gorbachev." S/he then continues with specific information on the text.	

"Parteizeitung Prav-ada" as "the Soviet paper pravada."

"Umzug" (parade) is overlooked or ignored by the student.

be interpreted as "cynical."

tifies the comments of the first Soviet interviewed, but takes that same material and uses it in a modified form for the other person interviewed. It is also possible that the two references to "peace" make the reader think they were saying the same thing.

recall by including such words as "a-buzz."

prior knowledge when s/he writes "he (Reagan) still was pushing for SDI and other space weapons." "Pushing" probably comes from student's personal view of Reagan, while "other weapons" could be student's prior knowledge of the topic.

"Das Sowjetvolk hört mit eigenen Ohren, was der US-Präsident sagt" as "it was good to hear what the president said right from him."

Student just adds to the Soviet papers' criticisms of President Reagan when s/he writes: "how by writing the President could be sincere, when he was still pushing for the SDI and other space weapons." This isn't listed anywhere in the text but could be implied by the tone in which it was written.

Student perceives the telephone calls as being solicited rather than volunteered and shows this through "They asked a man . . ."

Student begins recall with "The article began by saying . . ." to show that s/he identifies the kind of text being read.

Student isn't sure if it is during or after Gorbachev's speech that the callers call, so s/he shows this ambiguity by saying "during/and/ or after."

Student has very strong feelings about the man from South Carolina who commented on the broadcast and refers to him as this "saublöde arschloch" (Interestingly enough the student keeps his/her comments in German.)

32

Student neglects to include Umzug (parade) when mentioning the Rose Bowl.

Student interprets "hört" in the future as "will hear" and seems to ignore subsequent references to the past tense.

Student writes "the first man interviewed, whose name is unknown . . ." It isn't clear if the student understands that the man didn't want his name

159

LEVEL V

Student Code	Word Recognition	Phonemic/Graphemic Features	Syntactic Feature Recognition	Intratextual Perceptions	Metacognition	Prior Knowledge
			mentioned or whether he thinks his name wasn't available.			
			Student interprets "keine alternative zum Frieden" as "the only way." The essense is similar but it conveys a stronger message.			
			Student slightly misinterprets the sentence about "Reagan and Gorbatschow sei es offenbar ernst mit dem Streben nach Frieden" as "Reagan and Gorbachav should meet more often and seriously discuss important issues."			
			Student strengthens the meaning of the statement "die Gefahr eines Krieges über die Welt brächten" by writing "it increases the danger of war."			

Russen sehen will, dann kaufe ich mir einen russischen Fernseher" [If I want to see a Russian, then I will buy myself a Russian TV set]. Several students interpreted the sentence as subjunctive, past tense, or a combination of both, (e.g., Subjects 20, 15, 11, and 6). Other students across all levels produced very unique interpretations of this section. For example, Subject 28 recalled this sentence as "when we watch Russian TV we're Russian watchers," while Subject 26 wrote "when he saw his first Soviet he would go buy a Soviet television to watch programs on." Another student interpreted this clause as "if he wanted to see Russian programs, he would go buy a Russian TV" (Subject 17). In all cases, the students attempted to reconstruct the sentence in a semantically logical way, but, nonetheless, failed to tap the actual meaning.

The phonemic and graphemic similarities of certain words, as well as word recognition in general, was an additional source of difficulty for some students. The word "eigenen" [only] was commonly misinterpreted on the basis of graphemic similarity as "einen" [one] (Subjects 11, 9, and 20) or "einzig" [single] (Subject 15). The word "Streben" [striving] also caused graphemic/phonemic recognition problems for students who interpreted the word as "Sterben" [death]. As a result, students believed that one portion of the text described the "death after peace" ("Sterben nach Frieden") instead of the correct phrase "striving after peace" ("Streben nach Frieden") (Subject 20).

Misinterpretations of both words and syntactic features led some students to misunderstand one critical passage in the text. The sophisticated syntax in the sentence: "Ich halte ihn für einen fähigen Mann, der weiss, dass Friede und Zusammenarbeit die wichtigsten Dinge in der Welt sind" [I consider him a capable man, who knows that peace and cooperation are the most important things in the world] yielded several erroneous interpretations. Especially problematic in the sentence was the relative clause construction, "der weiss" [who knows], which students took to be an article with a noun. For example, Subject 18 wrote "I take him for a fair man, *the right* trying for peace . . . ;" likewise Subject 20 wrote "he believed in *the whites*, freedom & working together" [emphasis added]. In both cases, the students relied more on microlevel textual features (i.e., word-level interpretation), rather than attending to more macrolevel features like syntax. Prior biases concerning race may have also influenced Subject 20's interpretation of the sentence. These examples clearly show how several factors in the constructivist model are activated simultaneously to promote the comprehension process.

The students' recalls were also rich in metacognitive strategies. One common technique was for the students to use summary statements in the recall. For example, Subject 18 wrote a general summary of the article, then drew a line in the middle of the page and began recalling specific information from the text. Likewise, Subject 15 used a summary sentence to introduce both the third and the final paragraphs of his/her recall, that is, "The Soviet Communist party, Pravda, and the news services were not as supportive." and "In America, people were not as impressed with seeing Premier Gorbachev.'' This strategy clearly indicates that the student understood how the information in these paragraphs related to the text as a whole.

Other students used metacognitive techniques to express ambiguity or uncertainty about various aspects of the text. Subject 30, for example, wrote ''I think the message was telecast during the Rose-bowl . . .'' to show that s/he was not sure when the message was broadcast. Another student put a question mark after the name of the paper, ''Isweltia?'' to indicate doubt about the name or perhaps the spelling of the paper. Likewise, Subject 32 expressed uncertainty by adding ''During and/or after the Rose bowl . . .'' to the recall. This varied and frequent use of metacognition on the part of the students emphasizes that they do take the reading task seriously and are monitoring their comprehension as they proceed through the text. As such, metacognition is an important component of the comprehension process for readers because it demands that they reevaluate and reflect on their interpretations of the text.

The analysis of the students' recalls demonstrates beyond a doubt that various text-driven and knowledge-driven elements interact with each other to develop an understanding. All factors are indispensable to the comprehension process. With the newspaper article, syntactic feature misinterpretations, phonemic/graphemic similarities, and the misrecognition of certain words caused students considerable comprehension problems. Yet, simultaneously, students employed various knowledge-driven strategies to promote the comprehension process. The impact of knowledge, however, proved to be an even more significant factor in their recall of the newspaper article. Although certain elements in the reading process seem to interact more vigorously at certain times than others, all of them contribute to the reader's evolving perception of texts.

Table 5.3 lists data generated by college-level subjects reading the texts in Spanish discussed in Chapter Four (see Figures 4.16–4.21 for the actual recalls). Elements in the recalls of some of the subjects are categorized, like the ones above, according to text-driven and knowledge-driven elements. The data in Table 5.3 serve to validate and expand the German language data above. The Spanish subjects, too, draw on various knowledge sources in order to understand in their second language.

The recalls for the Spanish texts also reveal how the various factors in L2 comprehension interact to yield understanding. The influence of background knowledge on the recalls of the four texts is discussed at length in Chapter Four. The focus of this discussion is how the other components of the model impact comprehension.

In the ''Armas Nucleares'' text word recognition is a significant problem for the student. For example, ''aseguran'' is translated as ''thinks'' and ''el ministro español'' is interpreted as ''the Spanish ambassador.'' Unraveling the syntax of this text also proves problematic for the student. The sentence ''Fuentes españolas aseguran que Estados Unidos está presionando en lo nuclear, exagerando

Table 5.3. Student recalls for the Spanish texts according to subject number and instructional level and categorized according to text-driven and knowledge-driven elements.

			"Armas Nucleares"			
Student Code	Word Recognition	Phonemic/Graphemic Features	Syntactic Feature Recognition	Intratextual Perceptions	Metacognition	Prior Knowledge
11-12	"Anticipan" is interpreted as "thinks." "El ministro español" is interpreted as "ambassador."		"Fuentes españolas aseguran que Estados Unidos está presionando en lo nuclear . . ." is interpreted as "The Spanish population thinks that the United States relies too heavily on nuclear weapons." "El próximo día 28 existe una última posibilidad, dentro del presente mes, . . . que George Shultz y el ministro español de Asuntos Exteriores . . ." is translated as ". . . In 28 days George Shultz and the Spanish ambassador in New York will meet to discuss the use of nuclear weapons in Spain."			

"Pinochet al filo de las Urnas"

Student Code	Word Recognition	Phonemic/Graphemic Features	Syntactic Feature Recognition	Intratextual Perceptions	Metacognition	Prior Knowledge
11-2	"anticipan" is interpreted as "is expected."		"Con el recuerdo de las protestas de 1983 y 1984 . . . estrategia militar" is interpreted as "There were protests in 1983 & 1984 because of the militaristic government." "Las encuestas anticipan una elección pareja con el triunfo de la oposición en Santiago . . ." is translated as "An election is coming up soon and it is expected that the dictator presently in office will be defeated."	Student thinks the text is about "politics in Chile."		Student's belief that it is a "militaristic government" may be due to prior knowledge of Chilean politics.

"La Uva"

Student Code	Word Recognition	Phonemic/Graphemic Features	Syntactic Feature Recognition	Intratextual Perceptions	Metacognition	Prior Knowledge
15-12					Student indicates uncertainty about his/her interpretation by adding a question mark after the word "seeds (?)."	

Student adds a parenthetical comment: "for the table (to eat)" to describe what is meant by table grapes.

Student writes "along with two other places" to indicate that s/he remembers that two other provinces were given but that the names of the provinces cannot be recalled.

"Regreso al Futuro"

Student Code	Word Recognition	Phonemic/Graphemic Features	Syntactic Feature Recognition	Intratextual Perceptions	Metacognition	Prior Knowledge
11-2	"Proyecta" is interpreted as "filmed."		"Es lo mejor que la Florida le ofrece al turista . . ." is interpreted as "In Florida, there are many places to tour." The noun "turista" is translated as a verb "to tour."	Student perceives the text to be about tourist places in Florida instead of about the Space Center and sites.	Student writes "a movie . . ." to indicate that s/he remembers something about a movie but can't remember the title.	Student writes "In July, 1969, we launched the Apollo ll rocket," probably because of prior knowledge of the subject. Student also writes "the NASA space center, which has a museum." Even though there is no mention of a museum in the text, the student probably has prior knowledge that a museum exists.

				Prior knowledge of U.S. and Soviet competition in space may have prompted student to write "The Soviets are also in a race with us in space."
				Student includes information about "the space shuttle disaster," which is not in the text, probably because of prior knowledge of this incident.
11-17	"hace referencia" is interpreted as "geared to."	". . . entre los que pueden verse edificios de compañías como Grumman . . ." is interpreted as "Also of interest are space related corporations that people tour such as Grumman . . ."	Student sees the article as a discussion of Florida and its highlights.	Student is unsure of the date so writes "July? 1969" to signify this uncertainty.
15-15			Student correctly perceives the text as an "article." Student just remembers isolated facts from the recall and is not able to give any substantive information about the text.	The student demonstrates uncertainty about the topic of the text by stating that "The article appears to be about . . ."

su importancia real . . ." is rendered as "The Spanish population thinks that the United States relies too heavily on nuclear weapons." Likewise, syntactic problems surface in the sentence "El próximo día 28 existe una última posibilidad, dentro del presente mes . . . que George Schultz y el ministro español de Asuntos Exteriores . . .", which the student interprets as "In 28 days George Schultz and the Spanish ambassador in New York, will meet to discuss the use of nuclear weapons in Spain." Obviously, different factors are interacting to contribute to the students' comprehension problems.

The "Pinochet" text also illustrates how students enlist different components of the model to achieve understanding. Subject 11-2 is highly influenced by his/her intratextual perception of the text. The student believes that the text is "about politics in Chile" and uses this framework to interpret what is read. S/he even goes so far as to state this belief at the onset of the recall process. The student also encounters some word recognition problems in the text, for example, "anticipan" is interpreted as "is expected." As with the "Armas Nucleares" text, the student has difficulty sorting out syntactic connections. For example, "Con el recuerdo de las protestas de 1983 y 1984, . . . estrategia militar" is interpreted as "There were protests in 1983 & 1984 because of the militaristic government." The student's belief that the government is "militaristic" also shows evidence of prior knowledge or bias about Chilean politics infiltrating the recall. Once again, several text-based and knowledge-based elements operate together to account for the student's comprehension of the text.

In the "La Uva" text few comprehension problems surface for Subject 15-12. The recall is exemplary in the amount of detail that is remembered. The structure of the recall is also closely aligned with the organization of the original text. The student has obviously perceived the text the way the author intended and has successfully used word recognition and syntax clues to interpret the text accurately. Perhaps even more important is the student's rich use of metacognition to recall the text. Subject 15-12 includes both question marks and parenthetical comments in his/her recall of the text. The question mark after "2 or 3 small seeds(?)" reveals that the student is uncertain whether this word has been correctly interpreted or not. Even though the translation is correct, the student's question mark indicates that s/he has reflected on the interpretation and challenged his/her comprehension process. Subject 15-12 also employed metacognition to indicate that two additional provinces famous for wine production were remembered but the actual names of those places could not be recalled when s/he wrote: "In Spain the main producing areas are Alraute along with two other places." Later in the recall the student used a parenthetical comment to embellish the text. This comment revealed that s/he truly understood what was meant by "grapes . . . for the table," namely that they are "(to eat)." Although few comprehension errors appeared in the student's recall, various elements, nonetheless, interacted to promote comprehension. In this instance, the student employed the factors successfully to achieve a very high level of comprehension.

The text "Regreso al futuro" also presented students with some interesting comprehension problems. One of the major difficulties encountered by students with the text was their initial perception of the topic. Subject 11-2, for example, believed that the text was about Florida where "there are many places to tour." This perception pervaded the student's recall and determined the course of subsequent comprehension. Interestingly enough Subject 11-17 recalled approximately the same information from the text (i.e., "Florida is a tourist state with such highlights as . . ."), but did not allow it to steer him/her off track. As a result, an appropriate textual perception is built by Subject 11-17, while an inappropriate perception ensues for Subject 11-2.

Metacognitive strategies are also employed by the students when recalling this text. Most notable are Subject 11-2's use of an ellipsis after "a movie . . ." to indicate that something about a movie had been remembered but the title could not be recalled. Likewise, Subject 11-7 used a question mark after "July?" to demonstrate uncertainty about the month in which the first moon landing took place. In a more general way, Subject 15-15 reveals uncertainty about the topic of the text by initiating the recall with "This article appears to be about . . ." In so doing, the student indicates that s/he is hesitant to commit to any single interpretation of the text probably because so little can be recalled from the text anyway. In fact, Subject 15-15 subsequently reveals that only isolated facts about the text have been comprehended and the student has difficulty integrating these facts into a coherent recall. This use of metacognition reveals that metacognition does play an important role in the recall process, because it signals student reflection about comprehension capabilities.

Word recognition and syntax difficulties also appear in the students' recall of the "Regreso al futuro" text. For example, the word "proyecta" is misinterpreted as "filmed" by subject 11-2, probably on the basis of confusion with the English cognate "project." In addition, Subject 11-2 encounters syntactic difficulty when the noun "turista" is rendered as the verb "to tour." A more serious syntactic problem arises for Subject 11-17 when the sentence ". . . entre los que pueden verse edificios de compañías como Grumman . . ." is translated as "Also of interest are space related corporations that people tour, such as Grumman . . ." Although meaning is not really obscured with this interpretation, it, nonetheless, illustrates that an inability to recognize syntactic features accurately can impede the comprehension process.

A THEORY OF SECOND LANGUAGE READING

A glance at the syntheses in the previous section as well as others indicates that problems or inaccuracies in second language text processing may be differentially linked to second language literacy development. These syntheses reveal that certain kinds of errors may be characteristic of certain stages of progression.

Figure 5.6. Theoretical distribution of reading factors.

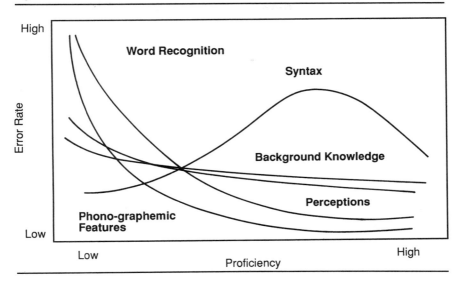

At any rate, the data are sufficiently consistent and voluminous to generate a formal theory of second language reading.

Before positing a theory based on such syntheses, however, a set of assumptions should be outlined. First, this formal statement of second language literacy theory assumes that second language text processing abilities develop over time. In other words, they are not learned as unitary entities. Second, this theory assumes that the abilities exhibit different facets of all features of text processing over time. This presupposes an interactive, multidimensional dynamic of literacy elements—not a linear one in which each element is gradually replaced by the next. Third, the theory assumes that errors in understanding can reveal development in literacy (parallel to observed phenomena in oral language development). Fourth, the theory assumes commonalities in second language text processing between and among literate learners and languages. Fourth, the theory assumes no definite terminus; that is, no reader would ever be 100 percent proficient with a 0-percent error rate; concomitantly, no first language literate reader would be 0-percent proficient with a 100 percent error rate.

Figure 5.6 illustrates a multifactor theory of second language literacy. The x-axis is labeled "proficiency" and portrays a continuum of increasing abilities in second language reading. This axis does not indicate particular *units* along the scale. Succinctly, the origin of the axes indicates no prior exposure to literacy in the language with the horizontal axis representing growth in knowledge of the language. The y-axis is labeled "error rate." It indicates a continuum of errors from the origin (whereby there can be, technically, no errors because there is, technically, no "knowledge" of the language) to some indeterminate point along the vertical axis. Hypothetical distributions of factors involved in second language text processing are plotted against each other according to the axes.

The three language-based features used as organizing principles above, word recognition, phonemic/graphemic features, and syntactic feature recognition, are described as curvilinear relationships. Word recognition, represented as an exponential curve, posits that in the early stages of proficiency errors that can be attributed to vocabulary difficulties are fairly common. As proficiency increases, however, the curve drops rather precipitously and levels off toward the 0-percent mark as development occurs. In like manner, the phonemic/graphemic confusions' curve starts in a similar area, but drops much more quickly and sooner than the word recognition curve. This curve posits that problems in understanding related to sound and word-shape features quickly diminish as proficiency increases.

Syntax, however, behaves in a different fashion from the other text–based features. In fact, it has a normal-curve shape. The error function illustrated in the syntax curve is one that is relatively stable for a period of time and then steadily increases. The increase in syntactic errors seems to develop as a function of greater exposure and growth in the language. In other words, as knowledge of the language increases (x-axis), so does risk taking and the potential for misusing and misunderstanding (y-axis) complex syntactic forms. As proficiency develops further, of course, the error rate begins to decline.

Two of the knowledge-driven aspects, background knowledge, and intratextual perceptions, are also described by exponential curves. They illustrate that the rate of errors due to both content knowledge and knowledge constructed during comprehension decreases as proficiency increases. This rate, however, is never as high as initial word-based error rates and never as low as word-based error rates in later stages of proficiency; simultaneously, error rates attributed to knowledge-driven aspects are higher in the initial stages of proficiency than error rates in syntax; there is, however, crossover in the curves as proficiency increases.

This crossover attempts to concretize the interaction of knowledge and language as proficiency develops. In initial stages, whatever knowledge a reader may bring to a task may override linguistic knowledge; hence, there are relatively more knowledge-based errors (that may also contribute to the word-based errors discussed above) than syntax errors. As a reader's linguistic knowledge grows, however, it begins to override knowledge-driven inferencing. In other words, a reader begins to rely more on the *language* and less on what he/she *thinks* the language contains.

The syntheses from the previous section provide a perspective on metacognition that is different from the other features. Metacognitive activity is present in all of the levels of subjects synthesized above. In addition, "error rate" is not a valid concept in this regard. Subjects seem to use these strategies or they do not.

Therefore, metacognition is included in the formal statement of the theory, but recognized, as it should be, as an individual learner characteristic.

This theory attempts to provide a picture of the development of second language reading proficiency. In order to be tested, studies that reveal subject performance in all of the facets of the theory, across time, must be conducted. The first step will be to establish appropriate measures for each of the variables. After data are collected path analysis techniques will determine whether the relationships suggested in the theory and illustrated by Figure 5.6 accurately reflect the development of second language reading proficiency.

CONCLUSION

The analysis of recall protocols for texts in German and Spanish integrated with other types of data indicate that text-driven and knowledge–driven factors contribute to learner's comprehension processes in unique, yet predictable, ways. The theory attempts to capture and hypothesize about the potential relationships between and interactions among the factors listed. Future research will determine the viability of the theory—whether it adequately describes and predicts the process of reading in a second language.

The factors in second language text comprehension listed here and their relationships are not meant to be the exclusive domain of theory and research. In fact, the analyses presented in this chapter also provide pedagogical tools. The next chapter turns to pedagogy and, among other things, presents a teaching method that draws heavily on protocol analysis for making appropriate instructional decisions.

6

Classroom Factors in Second Language Reading Comprehension: How is Comprehension Taught and Learned?

INTRODUCTION

Perhaps the words "taught" and "learned" in the title of this chapter are a bit overstated. "Taught" within the context of this chapter refers to external performances of teachers when they engage with students in activities centered around written texts. "Learned," within the same context, also refers to externals—that is, to the external performances of students in demonstrating that they have read the text assigned to them. These caveats regarding the topics of teaching and learning are important to the extent that they communicate that research has not yet firmly established *how* to teach comprehension (or for that matter *whether* it is teachable). Neither has research provided substantial insights into the process of second language learning. Nonetheless, there are acts that are called "teaching" and there are acts that are called "learning" and it is to these acts or performances that this chapter turns its attention.

"Classroom factors" refer to immediate contextual characteristics that in large part determine the kind, quality, and amount of learning that takes place. Clearly, there are no generic classrooms. There are bilingual classrooms, and immersion classrooms; second language and foreign language classrooms. The kind of reading instruction and learning that takes place in the former classrooms with children is very different from that which happens with older learners in second and foreign language classrooms. Recalling the outline of *who* second language learners are (Chapter One) implies that the "reading lesson" will look very different from program context to program context.

Second language reading lessons in bilingual and immersion settings have not been investigated. While test scores consistently reveal that learners in such environments can attain equivalent scores in the languages in which they receive instruction, *how* instruction gets played out is unclear. A critical factor in instruction is rooted in the literacy vs. nonliteracy of second language readers. Bilingual and immersion scholars have made an error in their "selling" of particular program designs. That error lies in the statement that the learning is the same in immersion and bilingual settings as in monolingual settings—that learning is just in another language.

That learning, however, is characterized by a process that is different from that which is found in a monolingual setting. It is precisely in the reading lesson where this difference becomes abundantly clear. In a monolingual setting, the point of departure for reading is the child's oral vocabulary. In other words, children are taught to learn to read words with which they are already familiar in their spoken form. In a bilingual/immersion setting, however, the school, through the teacher, has to provide oral vocabulary first and then can teach the written forms. What this means is that when children from a monolingual setting approach reading they have already spent five or six years practicing and learning an extensive oral vocabulary; children in bilingual settings, however, must, in a sense, begin again building a set of oral renderings of previously held concepts, followed by learning these words in printed form. With children in all of these settings, many of the processes are identical. Children are developing their own sense of language, learning to recognize words and to pronounce them, learning their meanings, and learning how they fit together. In a very real sense, interference from literate skills in their native language does not exist. Thus, reading lessons in such classrooms look very similar to monolingual settings for reading instruction. Admittedly, these statements are much too vague. Yet until classroom-oriented investigations are undertaken, the only reliable evidence for how lessons are conducted will come from monolingual settings.

Interestingly, there is also little, if any, generalizable empirical evidence regarding the instruction of reading in second and foreign language classrooms. In traditional foreign language classrooms, it is assumed that students can read and, that, as noted in Chapter One, since reading is just a slower form of first language reading, reading *instruction* per se really does not exist. Until observational studies are conducted that focus specifically on the teaching and the learning of reading in real L2 classroom contexts, investigators are forced to rely on more indirect evidence such as what foreign language "methods" textbooks have to say or on what scholars have published on the how-to of teaching reading. The other danger of so few observational studies is that researchers have very little knowledge of how students go about "reading in a second language" in an instructional setting. While research might give some indication of how individual readers cope with individual texts, how that act of reading gets played out in individual classrooms by groups of students remains unexplored territory.

This chapter targets these issues specifically. First, it recalls some traditional "methods" for reading instruction. Second, it analyzes the role of reading and reading exercises in commonly used methods textbooks. Third, it posits a view of second language reading in classroom settings that suggests that comprehension of L2 texts, rather than being genuine, may be a part of the great "pretend" of classroom life.

A PORTRAIT OF A L2 READING LESSON

L2 reading lessons as they are reported tend to follow a rather consistent pattern. It is important to keep in mind that the materials used for L2 reading lessons are more often than not artificially constructed. That means that they are written with the intent of illustrating particular grammatical and syntactic features as well as carefully chosen lexical items. Authors of such materials generally carefully gloss uncommon words in the text. In addition, these authors often provide important introductory material for the student. This introductory material, generally cultural in nature, is frequently written in English and also uses a comparison contrast structure—comparing the learners' L1 culture with some cultural feature or aspect that they will read about. These features, then, provide the entre for the teacher.

Swaffar (1991) notes in a recent study evaluating reading materials in L2 texts that all of the texts investigated:

> state in their introductions that students should practice skimming, scanning, reading for main ideas, and recognition of implicit as well as explicit information. However, regardless of such advice, most reading is, as stated earlier, restricted to short, glossed, texts. Such texts appear to have been written to illustrate the language and subject matter of the particular chapter. Simplified or not, their very brevity encourages reliance on command of lexical and syntactic detail, micro- rather than macro-strategies. Without exercises that encourage alternative reading styles, FL students, particularly those with limited proficiency, tend to read word for word. (p. 259)

The findings of her study further reveal that authentic texts appear significantly less often in L2 textbooks than do edited texts, written expressly to illustrate chapter goals.

Teachers "introduce" the reading selection by referring to the cultural material provided by the author of the textbook or they provide their own set of introductory material. Swaffar (forthcoming) discovered, however, that despite including cultural notes, few texts afford "students regular opportunity to explore authentic cultural information, texts that reflect a cross section of cultural values or texts that present cultural values different from those in the United States" (pp. 264, 266). This initial phase of the reading lesson may take place in a class period before the students are asked to read. This phase generally takes no more than eight minutes and is usually done in the native language of the student. Teachers then "preteach" the vocabulary. This act of "preteaching" consists of pronouncing the words for the students and then having the students pronounce the words in response as they look at the English translations. More sophisticated preteaching techniques include asking students to use the new words in sentences of their own in order to check whether they have an appropriate meaning. In other words, this activity is to avoid the pitfalls of seeing the translation of "können" [to be able] in German as "can" and listening to students produce the sentence "Meine Mutter könnt im Summer Gemüse" [My mother cans vegetables in the summer].

In general, students are then assigned the reading selection for homework and asked to write out the comprehension questions. It is fairly well known that students use the principle of least resistance as most human beings do. As a result, they perform a quick matching exercise on the questions and paragraphs in the text and are quickly finished with their homework assignments (Hosenfeld, 1977). Despite the valiant efforts of most materials designers the relationship between the text and the questions on the text are generally so translucent as to make the task of "answering comprehension questions" extremely simple.

In class, activities take the form of oral reading and then questions and answers. With oral reading a round robin format is generally employed with teachers calling on students in a random order to recite. During this activity teachers call students' attention to pronunciation errors. Next, teachers focus on the content questions asked in the textbook. They may quiz the students formally or informally on vocabulary words and ask the content questions. When this part of the lesson is maintained in the target language, the teacher is satisfied when the students answer with grammatically correct utterances. A variation on this sequence is asking the relevant content questions after the oral rendering of each section.

Where the grammar exercises fit in—either before the reading selection or after—is probably the most variable portion of most lessons. Either the reading selection serves as the foundation for the learning of these structures or the selection becomes the reinforcement of the structures. In either way, the reading text is frequently seen as the buttress for lexical and syntactic learning—not as a provider of new content information for the student.

Of course, new content information comes into play in the upper levels of language learning in culture and literature courses. These courses are in general not seen as language acquisition courses and, therefore, the instructional strategies such as vocabulary preteaching, syntactic support, and direct content questions, are phased out or eliminated almost entirely. This type of classroom event will be the focus of a later section. For the moment, this discussion will continue to focus on earlier stages of language learning.

THE ROOTS OF THE GENERIC

The description of these generic L2 classrooms comes partly from anecdotal descriptions, but also to a large extent from L2 methods textbooks; in other words, from those textbooks that ostensibly teach teachers how to teach. Despite variations between foreign and second language classrooms, due principally to a lack of a *lingua franca* in many second language classrooms, the two classroom types are more similar than different. There are vocabulary exercises, there are direct content questions, and there are syntactic exercises derived from or based on texts.

As argued earlier, the strands of these similarities may be traced to authors on methodology. Their works fall into two categories. The first category, which may have the largest impact, is that of methods textbooks since a majority of second language teachers throughout the world have had some type of professional training or certification. Generally speaking, then, in the "methods course" teachers are introduced to an array of instructional strategies that are supposed to "work." The second category consists of clinical pieces written about teaching reading. As documented in Chapter Two, these articles constitute at least two-thirds of what is written on second language reading. Frequently, a collection of these articles replaces the methods text.

AN ANALYSIS OF "READING METHODS"

For purposes of this analysis, a number of methods texts were analyzed: Allen and Valette (1979), *Classroom Techniques: Foreign Languages and English as a Second Language*; Bowen, Madsen, and Hilferty (1985), *TESOL Techniques and Procedures*; Chastain (1988), *Developing Second Language Skills: Theory and Practice*; Omaggio (1986), *Teaching Language in Context*; Paulston and Bruder (1975), *Teaching English as a Second Language: Techniques and Procedures*; and Rivers (1981), *Teaching Foreign-Language Skills*. Figure 6.1 provides a view of the relative amount of material devoted to reading within the course of these texts. The percentage of page space devoted to reading ranges from 4.6 percent of the entire book to a high of almost 20 percent. This figure would indicate that (using the rule of thumb that the textbook is the curriculum and that most courses meet on the average 30 hours) most trained teachers have had between one hour and six hours of instruction in the teaching of reading. Even if this figure is doubled or tripled it could hardly be expected to be significant. Of course, these figures do not indicate how many reading-specific methods courses there may be in teacher education programs. An educated guess would argue for very few.

The next area to probe is the nature of the instructional strategies offered by

Figure 6.1. Percentage of pages devoted to reading instruction in six methods textbooks.

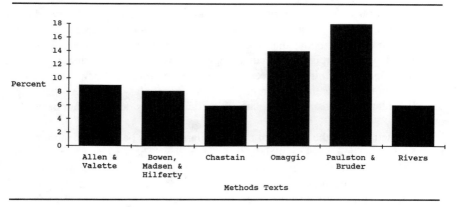

the traditional methods books. When examining methods textbooks, two aspects are of particular importance. The first is what the authors tell the reader about a particular process. In other words, how they provide a definition or an explanation of a process. All methods books should explicitly define language processes such as speaking, listening, writing, reading, and culture learning. These definitions should provide the backdrop for the instructional strategies to be introduced and encouraged on the part of teachers. Should and explicitly are important words in this discussion. *Should* is used because it implies that it is possible to find methods "cookbooks" that provide no theoretical frameworks for the suggestions they make; *explicitly* is used because there are methods publications that send subliminal messages about the nature of the process about which they are making pedagogical suggestions.

Several of the methods books chosen for analysis do provide explicit definitions of reading. Omaggio (1986) states:

> [r]eading is an active process involving . . . (1) the individual's knowledge of the linguistic code, (2) cognitive skills of various types, and (3) the individual's knowledge of the world. (p. 121)

Allen and Valette (1979) argue:

> Reading is more than just assigning foreign language sounds to the written words; it requires the comprehension of what is written. (p. 249)

Rivers (1981) offers a parallel definition:

> A student who stands up in class and enunciates . . . the sounds symbolized by the printed . . . marks . . . may be considered to be "reading." . . . The student must also be taught to derive meaning from the word combinations in the text and to do

this in a consecutive fashion at a reasonable speed, without necessarily vocalizing what is being read. This is *reading for comprehension*. (p. 261)

These definitions choose to legitimize oral reading as reading and to underline a one way process which is reading as gaining meaning from the text. Paulston and Bruder (1975) define reading as "decoding meaning—lexical, structural, and cultural—from graphic symbols" (p. 158). Bowen et al. provide no definition.

In contrast to the frameworks listed above is that offered by Chastain. Chastain (1988) explains:

Reading is a process involving the activation of relevant knowledge and related language skills to accomplish an exchange of information from one person to another . . . recent researchers in reading describe the process in a way that implies an active reader intent upon using background knowledge and skills to recreate the writer's intended meaning. (p. 216)

He adds:

The reading goal is to read for meaning or to recreate the writer's meaning. Reading to improve pronunciation, practice grammatical forms, and study vocabulary does not constitute reading at all because, by definition, reading involves comprehension. When readers are not comprehending, they are not reading. (p. 217)

The difference between Chastain's theoretical view and that of the others is striking. In a sense it is unfair to assail other writers whose books are older than Chastain's. But two points are extremely important. First, reading research could have been consulted by the other authors to bring them to a more enlightened view when they authored their books. Second, the other texts have widespread use in teacher education programs in North America and, hence, widespread influence.

The other point that needs examination is the nature of the instructional strategies that are suggested. Figure 6.2 outlines them.

Several things unify the methods texts, making them, in fact, indistinguishable. First of all, four of the six posit *stages* in the reading process, stemming from letters to words to sentences or from sound symbol activities to guided practice to independence or from decoding to interpretation. Interestingly, none of these indicate the research base from which the stages cited were generated. A second interesting point is that a minority of the texts advocate structured materials. In other words, the use of authentic materials is suggested more often than materials deliberately reflecting particular grammatical structures. A third distinguishing feature is the consistent nature of the activities listed: oral reading, prereading vocabulary study, skimming and scanning, and teacher prequestions.

Figure 6.2. Types of instructional strategies advocated in the six methods textbooks.

	Rivers	Chastain	Allen & Vallette	Bowen	Paulston & Bruder	Omaggio
Stages	●		●	●		●
Oral/Aural Base	●		●	●	●	
Assumptions about reading		●			●	
Advocates structured materials	●		●			
Activities:						
oral reading	●		●	●	●	
vocabulary study		●		●	●	
skimming and scanning				●	●	●
SQ3R				●		
prequestions		●		●	●	●

Instructional strategies outlined above actually are described and exemplified in a vacuum, so to speak. The nature of a methods book is to make suggestions for the teacher to employ. A methods book per se cannot offer the flavor of life in a classroom when a variety of personal and interpersonal variables come into play and interact with each other. This interaction of activities, teachers, students, materials, and personalities develops into unique classroom events.

The classroom reading event has not been thoroughly investigated. A portrait of the generic sequence of events was drawn from anecdotes and evidence from methods textbooks; what happens in real-life classrooms, however, when interactions are negotiated, that is, when students are more linguistically proficient and, therefore, more able and willing to participate in content-oriented instruction is virtually uninvestigated. Yet, experience, anecdotes, an analysis of student outcomes, *and* general classroom-based research in conjunction with research cited in Chapter Two, lead to some interesting hypotheses.

STUDENTS CAST IN THE ROLE OF READERS

Ethnographic approaches to the study of classroom processes have highlighted the importance of teacher mediation in the construction of meaning (Golden, 1985, 1988). Put another way, as highlighted in Chapters Two and Four, the interpretation of text is most often filtered through a teacher's perspective with little regard for the manner in which students have reconstructed and, frequently, misunderstood the text (Bernhardt, 1985, 1989). Research in second language text comprehension has underlined how frequently students misunderstand foreign language texts. Interestingly, second language readers often exhibit extraordinary competence in grammar and vocabulary and use these competencies to "retell" a story, but, simultaneously, as noted in Chapter Four these same readers cannot attach any genuine "meaning" to a text.

Educational ethnographers have isolated a construct termed "procedural display" (Bloome, 1985) that provides insights into the frequent mismatch between teacher perceptions and student understandings of texts. Bloome (1985) notes:

> Procedural display can be compared to a group of actors who have memorized their roles and who enact a play for each others' benefit without necessarily knowing what happens in the play or what it means. In a lesson, teachers and students may enact their roles, say what "needs" to be said to each other, move through and complete the lesson, without necessarily knowing or acquiring the academic intent underlying the lesson. Simply put, procedural display occurs when teachers and students are displaying to each other that they are "getting the lesson done" which is not at all the same thing as substantive engagement in some academic content. (n.p.)

The thesis of the latter portion of this chapter is that some of the frustrations and difficulties that characterize student/L2 text—especially L2 literary text—interaction may stem directly from the classroom phenomenon of procedural display. Students quickly learn how to "get the lesson done" by displaying their knowledge of vocabulary; simultaneously, teachers allow them to display that knowledge since they (teachers) tend to be particularly sensitive to the anxiety-laden situation of foreign language learning.

Procedural display is a concept being researched in first language literacy as well as in classroom process research. These research domains have underlined the importance of the concept of procedural display toward understanding educational situations in general. Such research seeks to clarify hair-raising news reports about children who graduate from high school and who are not able to read. It asks "How is this possible? Are teachers that uncaring and that bad? Are kids that unwilling to learn? Are parents so unobservant and uncaring that they do not notice that their children are not learning?" The answers to these questions have to be "no." Teachers are basically good-spirited people who play out particular instructional techniques like the ones suggested earlier in this chapter. These instructional techniques communicate what *counts* as reading.

Bloome (1985) provides the example of what counts as reading. He states: "Raising one's hand to answer a comprehension question or looking at the textbook while another student reads aloud may be a set of behavioral displays agreed upon by the teacher and students to count as reading" (n.p.). In fact, a small number of classroom studies have recently pointed out that students often learn how to *behave* in classroom situations without necessarily learning academic content. For example, DeStefano, Pepinsky, and Sanders (1982) studied reading lessons in a first grade classroom. They found that although the students learned how to behave in classroom lessons (e.g., how to respond to questions), they did not learn how to use or interpret printed discourse for meaning. In other words, the students learned how to "look literate."

There is a corollary to these observations in second language classrooms. To reiterate some of the arguments made in Chapter Four, recent research in L2 reading comprehension has been examining an intrapersonal dimension—one that examines how individual readers reconstruct the foreign language texts they encounter. Studies utilizing both narrative and expository prose have indicated that grammatical competence or even conversational competence are not adequate predictors of the ability to understand a written text; rather, personal experiences or background with the text topic are. In conducting this research, students are asked to read authentic passages. These students tend to know a lot of vocabulary and are able to recall a text, but rarely are they able to explain the *intent* of a story. An example might buttress the point; an honor student in German explained that the Wolfgang Borchert story "Das Brot" is about a man on a diet who sneaks to his kitchen for a piece of bread in the middle of the night and his wife catches him. [For readers who do not know the story, "Das Brot" or "The Bread," is a story about a married couple in war-ridden Germany who have nothing left to eat but a bit of bread.]

The previous discourse implies that students such as the one noted above potentially engage with their teachers in procedural display. They enact the classroom scenario most probably by answering questions on texts and taking grammar tests. In so doing, they can appear to be "literate." Foreign language students are rarely asked to display nonteacher-mediated understanding as documented by the "Methods" discussion above. If students can perform the tasks that teachers give them, they are certified as having successfully completed "a lesson." In addition, it can be argued that this type of situation is not anomalous, but rather, characteristic. The extent to which it is characteristic needs to be investigated. Ethnographic-sociolinguistic methodologies will provide the lenses through which to view this particular phenomenon.

One of the questions such research should address is how the phenomenon of procedural display occurs. In other words, what sorts of unique procedures are displayed by teachers and students in foreign language classrooms when they confront written materials?

L2 LANGUAGE TEACHING AND PROCEDURAL DISPLAY

In order to begin to address the question of procedural display in second language classrooms, the nature of teaching a foreign language in general and a literary text in particular needs to be probed. A 1981 study of teaching found that "the primary concern of teachers is *maintaining the flow of ongoing classroom activities* rather than thinking about students' instructional needs and adapting lessons accordingly'' (Duffy & Anderson, 1981). At that time, teachers were described as "utilitarian, technical and activity oriented, and practical- and survival-oriented" (n.p.). Bloome (1985) calls this the need to get through the lesson. These results stem from observations of elementary and junior high school classrooms and, therefore, are not completely generalizable. But, these findings might be highly descriptive of what foreign language teachers do, too, in light of the great similarities in methods used.

Obviously, if a teacher believes that learning can only occur through conversational interaction, then silence is not golden—it's a death knell. This belief clarifies the above statement that students are rarely given an opportunity to utter a nonteacher-mediated response. Teachers are so sensitive to silence, and are, moreover, so hypersensitive to the difficulties that students have in speaking foreign languages, that they help them in every way possible. Further, the good student, the one who is praised, is the one who says *something . . . anything*. After all, that is the student who helps the teacher through the lesson.

Corollary to the notion of maintaining the flow of classroom activities is the *fear of lesson breakdown*. This fear of lesson breakdown is partly responsible for why teachers mediate and feed answers all the time. When teachers are trained they are—and perhaps mistakenly so—socialized into believing that the good teacher is the "prepared" teacher. Therefore, teachers arm themselves with activities and the activities drive the lesson. Thus, the good or successful student is one who helps to drive the lesson forward. A student who reveals that he/she has not understood is the student who helps lead to a lesson breakdown. This phenomenon is one of the reasons why learners who have difficulties receive the least amount of teacher attention—these learners tend to stop lessons. In other words, these students are not socially cooperative; they are mean-spirited; therefore, teachers tend to ignore them.

But the nature of studenting needs to be considered, too. Specifically, these comments focus on studenting in a literature class. The understanding of authentic texts is probably the most difficult task students try to accomplish. It is much more difficult than learning to role play, much more intimidating than giving an oral report, and much more challenging than figuring out the difference between *ser* and *estar* in Spanish or the Subjunctive I vs. the Subjunctive II in German. The reason for this is that with those other tasks, students have previous knowledge, skills, and resources, to draw upon. When they approach authentic texts, however, the only resource these students have consists of some linguistic skills. They have nouns, and verbs, and a concept of structure. But, they have none of the implicit knowledge that the native speaking group possesses for whom the text was intended as discussed in previous chapters. Foreign language teachers ask students to accomplish tasks for which the students have minimal, if any, appropriate resources.

These comments need to be placed into the perspective of a classroom as a cooperative social event. Students want to be cooperative particularly in foreign language classrooms when most of them elect to be there. They also know that teachers expect them to be cooperative. Hence, students are frequently presented with the *task of being cooperative in a setting in which they do not understand what is transpiring*. But, they do know how to behave in classrooms so they can enact appropriate procedures.

Students display these procedures in a number of ways. Some examples are enlightening. A graduate student in social studies education, for example, in a Beginning Chinese class said this:

> What my Chinese teacher wants most is for us to say something. I've picked up a couple of words and I just say them when she looks at me. She seems really happy that I'm trying to say something. But I don't know what she's talking about. I just try to stick with the class and then hope I can understand the homework.

Some high school German teachers admitted this:

> In order to "survive" literature courses, they would go to the library to secondary literature in English and find a line from the text which was frequently commented on. They would then translate the author's comment into German and, consequently, be prepared to say *something* in literature class . . .

. . . *anything* despite its relevance or irrelevance to the classroom discussion. In other words, this was a strategy to be cooperative. These same teachers admitted that the "literature" experience could be so frustrating that being prepared to make one comment was all they could manage.

When asked about the classroom foreign language experience, most students say that the first and foremost rule of those classrooms is verbal participation. The *content* of the participation is basically irrelevant. Participation is viewed as cooperation. The task of students is to find some way of displaying their cooperation with the teacher.

SUMMARY

Bloome (1985) suggested that when teachers and students display to each other that they are "getting the lesson done" they are not necessarily "substantive[ly] engage[d] in some academic content" (n.p.). This may possibly explain how students can be performing adequately and simultaneously not understand anything or how they can engage in 2–5 years of foreign language instruction and still not appreciate a literary text.

Of course, this idea is not in the exclusive domain of foreign language. Charles M. Schulz, Peanuts creator, focused on exactly the same theme in one of his cartoons in 1988. Lucy writes: "Tess of the D'Urbervilles by Laurel N.

Hardy.'' Charlie Brown explains: ''That's Thomas Hardy.'' She replies ''Really?'' He responds with: ''I can't believe you read this whole book.'' Lucy: ''I read the first word 'on.' '' Charlie then questions: ''How can you write a book report if you've only read the first word?'' ''No problem'' says Lucy, and writes ''Right from the first word I knew this was going to be a good book.'' The final exchange between them illustrates the principle behind procedural display. Charlie says: ''I can see you're going to be a lover of great literature'' to which Lucy responds: ''Those who can't do, fake it!''

The importance of understanding literature to the development of literacy in general and cultural knowledge in specific must not be forgotten or underestimated. It is in literary texts that the implicit knowledge structures, and the unstated cultural heritage, that *all* learners need if they are to develop usable, authentic language skills are found. An understanding of how learners approach these texts, whether their teachers are aware of these approaches, and whether these approaches merely facilitate the facade of understanding as evidenced by Lucy's approach or the development of real understanding must be developed.

PRINCIPLES OF SECOND LANGUAGE
READING INSTRUCTION

The message communicated by the methods textbooks discussed in an earlier portion of this chapter is that reading instruction, like other instructional activities, consists of a series of teacher-directed activities and tasks to be completed by the learner. In this view, the interaction of teacher-led activities and student task-completion yields reading competencies. Critically, however, such procedures risk allowing students to hide in an instructional setting, displaying knowledge, or in Schulz' words, ''to fake it.'' The final section of this chapter is focused on instructional principles designed to reduce significantly the possibility that student behaviors mask their actual understandings.

Reading Development in a Second Language is a book about principled language research and instruction. Therefore, instructional suggestions are made in terms of principles not in terms of activities. There are two reasons for this. First, the concept of principles is more theoretically consistent with reading as a cognitive and as a social process because predetermined activities or tasks imply a generic processor in a generic situation. Second, the concept of principle is also more theoretically consistent with the knowledge that large numbers of second language readers are also literate in their first language, and have well-developed ideas about the whole notion of reading as a meaning-centered process. That is, they already believe that written texts are ''supposed to make sense.''

What follows, then, is a set of instructional principles derived from the theory and research set forth in previous chapters. These principles embody fundamental assumptions about the act of reading in a second language.

Principle One

Principle One is characterized as allowing students to develop some understanding of a text. This principle is rooted in adult (defined here as post pubescent) cognitive theory. Adults have well-developed beliefs and understandings about the world. They do not suspend these beliefs, knowledges, and understandings simply because they operate in a second language. These features of readers are integral to the readers themselves and are available. When teachers try to maintain control of the development of text understanding, they run the risk of forcing students into a dual-process. One part of the process consists of the meaning developed by the individual reader; the other part consists of what the teacher wants.

Principle Two

Principle Two is characterized as working from students' understanding of L2 texts. This principle implies that a teacher should not pretend to anticipate which portions of a text students will find problematic. It also implies that a teacher should not have pre-ordained "activities" that supposedly foster comprehension. Rather, principled teaching lies in a *strategic* teacher rather than in a *prepared* teacher in the usual sense. Strategic teaching implies an instructor who analyzes student behaviors "on-line" during instruction, rather than one who is "activity-driven," fearful of being interrupted by student interpretations.

Principle Three

The third principle of theoretically-grounded, research-based reading instruction is that reader misunderstandings can arise from a variety of sources both text-based and knowledge-based in nature. The word *variety* is important since a high probability exists that misunderstandings can be rooted in "previously learned" material as well as in so-called "new" material. In other words, relying on inappropriate assumptions about what students already "know," potentially leads to misanalyses of student difficulties. Because students have learned and understood a concept under one set of conditions, does not mean students can necessarily use the same concept under a different set of conditions. This principle implies that the analysis of student understandings needs to encompass a broad spectrum of possible problem sources.

Principle Four

Reading instruction should be, fourth, focused on individual readers and individual understandings. In other words, anticipating average difficulties across the mean of students implies, once again, the generic rather than the particular.

Principle Five

Principle Five is that second language reading instruction, based on the previous four principles, should be direct. Direct means that once a teacher has completed analyses of student understandings, instruction should deal specifically with problematic portions of a text; that is, teachers need to return to an "explication de texte" mode, explaining specific comprehension problems. These problems may be text-driven (some grammatical feature that needs explanation) or they may be knowledge-driven (some lack of cultural knowledge or the misuse of another kind of knowledge). Ultimately, it is the teacher who possesses the appropriate and accurate knowledge sources needed to equip students to interpret texts in a culturally appropriate manner.

The principles imply a teacher who is simultaneously in and out of direct control of her classroom. On the one hand, instruction needs to be student-centered to provide the teacher with appropriate diagnostic material without the initial intervention of the teacher's "best judgment." On the other hand, instruction needs to be teacher-controlled so that students are not forced into "faking it." Rather, students need to be given the resources they need as individuals to cope with second language texts.

THE RECALL PROTOCOL PROCEDURE

The previous chapters have indicated that the preferred method of investigating foreign language readers' comprehension processes is through the qualitative analysis of student recall. Not surprisingly, then, the preferred method of second language reading instruction draws heavily on the use of recall data as well as on its analysis also illustrated in previous sections. The final portion of this chapter, then, reviews the use of student recall data as an instructional device. The following chapter, Chapter Seven, explains the use of this same procedure in a testing situation.

Briefly, the immediate recall protocol procedure involves the following steps:

1. Select an unglossed text (perhaps 200 words).
2. Tell students that they may read the text as often as they like and that when they are finished you will ask them to write down everything that they remember from the text.
3. Give students sufficient time to read the text several times.
4. Ask the students to put the text out of sight and to write down everything that they remember in English.
5. Collect the protocols written by the students.
6. Use these student generated data as the basis for a future lesson plan that addresses:
   (a) cultural features

(b)   conceptual features
(c)   grammatical features that seem to interfere with comprehension (Bernhardt, 1983, p. 108).

Any instructional sequence needs to be contextualized. Reading is only one of four skills involved in typical second language programs. In other words, at best, it may receive one-fourth to one-third of instructional attention. The sequence outlined above may take on any number of variants. The sequence may be begun at the end of a class period for 10 minutes, the teacher may then design a lesson in her planning time, and then instruction continues in a subsequent hour for an appropriate amount of time. Similarly, the whole sequence may be used to fill a class hour with an immediate analysis of student understandings by asking one student to read his/her recall and then having other students participate in the analysis. The intention here is, once again, not to provide yet another "method" that works, but rather to outline a set of principles and a set of procedures that are consistent with those principles.

This procedure has been utilized by a number of scholars in a number of ways. It has been used by Wells (1986) for testing purposes, by Bernhardt and James (1987) in listening comprehension, and by Berkemeyer (1989) for instructional purposes.

Berkemeyer comments:

> The immediate recall protocol demands that the reader comprehend the text well enough to be able to recall it in a coherent and logical manner. More importantly, this procedure allows misunderstandings or gaps in comprehension to surface; a feature that other methods of evaluation cannot offer. (p. 131)

She continues:

> [immediate recall] can serve an extremely valuable diagnostic function. . . . [it] is useful for classroom teachers because it reveals in a direct way the information that they most want and need to know—i.e., how meaning is being constructed and what factors, whether textual or extratextual, are impeding reading comprehension. (p. 136)

SUMMARY

The bandwagon approach to language teaching inevitably reinforces the idea that the new *replaces* the old. The intention of this chapter was to review the old and to understand its roots.

Clearly, second language students for centuries have learned to read; no argument is made here that the past has been *wrong*, yet, past procedures characterized by a teacher-centered view on instructional strategies have possibly helped to mask student understandings. The present has much to offer. New research approaches have provided new data on how second language learners approach texts. The present and the future need to integrate this new knowledge into instruction. The set of principles and procedures outlined here provide a format for integration.

7

Assessing Second Language Reading Comprehension

INTRODUCTION

This chapter explores the links between teaching, learning, and assessment. The introduction of the alternative teaching strategy using immediate recall discussed in Chapter Six implies or mandates an alternative assessment strategy. Indeed, one of the goals of this chapter is to introduce such a strategy along with practicalities of scoring, among other factors.

At the outset, however, it is important to set the stage for the final act so to speak. "So to speak" is used deliberately, for assessment is infrequently the final act and very frequently Act One or even the prologue to the event of teaching and learning reading. Clearly, this is not an unusual phenomenon in education—the fact that testing drives the curriculum is discussed and lamented, but rarely remedied. The theory and the teaching and testing strategies set forth in this book imply that contemporary standardized and classroom testing of reading comprehension, that is, tests in their current conceptualization that place readers on a generic measuring stick, has little, if any link to validity. The argument presented calls for, to use Fanselow's (1987) term, "breaking the rules," by propelling the second language teaching field out of the black hole of traditional conceptualizations into a realm of realism that focuses on *real* readers with *real* texts.

This view on assessment, measurement, and reading is not unique to second language reading. In fact, assessment in reading has been characterized as a "dilemma" (Pearson & Valencia, 1987). That dilemma is characterized as "the conflict between newly emerging views of the reading process and the model of the reading process that underlies . . . current assessment practices and procedures" (p. 3). The research-based views of the reading process delineated in the previous chapters indicate that reading comprehension is constructive in nature and that it entails an active process of relating new or incoming information to information already stored in memory. This associative process implies the taking of multiple linguistic and conceptual units and building them into "understandings." Yet, this view on reading "bears little resemblance to that model which underlies most of our current reading assessment schemes" (pp. 6–7). In fact, most such schemes involve short passages about unfamiliar topics "that rarely approximate authentic texts and literal-level, direct content questions in multiple-choice formats. Rarely are readers provided with real reading tasks with which they are asked to apply or use knowledge that they gain from texts" (p. 7). Indeed, these characterizations are accurate syntheses of the nature of assessment in second language reading.

Rather than taking this assertion at face value, the following pages discuss, in detail, factors that need to be considered in either the development of or the administration of an appropriate and useful assessment device. This discussion necessarily entails comments about validity and reliability as well as other concerns in testing. It also entails a discussion of the relationship between the theory presented in Chapters Three and Four and assessment as well as that between instruction (Chapter Six) and assessment. In addition, these pages will review popular "tests" of reading comprehension, such as cloze, multiple choice, and short answer. Finally, in parallel to Chapter Six, this chapter ends with an assessment mechanism attached to the instructional procedure of immediate recall protocol.

MEASUREMENT CONCERNS: APPROPRIATENESS AND MEANINGFULNESS

The most important feature of a test is its validity. In fact, a joint commission of the American Psychological Association, the American Educational Research Association, and the National Council of Mathematics Educators agreed in 1985 on the following:

> Validity is the most important consideration in test evaluation. The concept refers to the appropriateness, meaningfulness and usefulness of the specific inferences made from test scores. . . . Validity . . . is a unitary concept. Although evidence may be accumulated in many ways, validity always refers to the degree to which that evidence supports the inferences that are made from test scores. (n.p.)

Appropriateness and meaningfulness are important words. They imply that a successful test must match as closely as possible what is known about a process at any point in time. This is technically termed "construct validity." Messick (1988) comments:

> The heart of the unified view of validity is that appropriateness, meaningfulness, and usefulness of score-based inferences are inseparable and that the unifying force is empirically grounded construct interpretation. Thus, from the perspective of

validity as a unified concept, all educational and psychological measurement should be construct-referenced because construct interpretation undergirds all score-based inferences—not just those related to interpretive meaningfulness but also the content- and criterion-related inferences specific to applied decisions and actions based on test scores. As a consequence, although construct-related evidence may not be the whole of validity, there can be no validity without it. That is, there is no way to judge responsibly the appropriateness, meaningfulness, and usefulness of the score inferences in the absence of evidence as to what the scores mean. (p. 35)

Placing Messick's (1988) comments within the context of the arguments in this book, implies developing a conceptualization of second language reading performance that is grounded in the evidence and theory presented in Chapters Two, Three, Four, and Five. Specifically, those discussions argue that the reader-based model posited in Chapters Three and Four suggests that an assessment mechanism must incorporate a sense of the individual reader—not a "generic" reader; must include an adequate description of textual features; must provide an understanding of *how* and *what* readers select from texts for processing; and, finally, must indicate how culturally accurate the reconstruction of a text is. These requirements mandate a new conceptualization of both test construction and interpretation. This new conceptualization entails a number of facets.

First of all, if a test is to adequately assess second language reading ability it must acknowledge the status of the reader's knowledge base. This means recognizing readers' interests and expertises as well as their attitudes and intentions toward the second language. It is important to reiterate at this juncture that this book is principally focused on adult readers of a second language. As noted several times throughout these pages and most especially in Chapter Four, these readers carry with them into the reading experience a wealth of life experiences as well as experience with literacy that then interacts with their abilities with the language for comprehension purposes.

Second, a successful assessment mechanism must be integrative in nature. A valid test of reading must examine the extent to which a text actually communicates a coherent message to the reader. Critical in this regard is that comprehension is a constructive construct—not one that is a sum of a number of discrete points. The discussion in both Chapters Three and Four indicated that second language readers are frequently able to handle units of language as separate entities and that this ability does not necessarily transfer to comprehension; the converse also seems to be true at times. Second language readers sometimes appear to have little ability at handling individual units of language, but, nevertheless, are able to achieve impressive understandings. Any appropriate measurement mechanism must be able to balance these two phenomena and neither overestimate nor underestimate the ability being measured. In the next section of this chapter, space will be devoted to an analysis of standard assessment measures such as cloze and direct content questioning. This analysis indicates that these types of tests can become entrapped in precisely this dilemma.

Third, a successful assessment mechanism for second language reading comprehension must provide in-depth information on *how* readers cope with text while, at the same time, providing quantifiable data for large-scale comparison and contrast. This last statement may sound like a bit of a contradiction. How can an instrument simultaneously reflect individual interpretations of text *and* provide a generalizable score for comprehension? Indeed, the issue is problematic. The words of Messick (1988) are applicable again:

> [T]he process of construct validation seems complicated and vague. But the appearance of complexity and vagueness stems from its enormous flexibility and generality. Test validation in the construct framework is integrated with hypothesis testing and with all of the philosophical and empirical means by which scientific theories are evaluated. Thus, construct validation embraces all of the statistical, experimental, rational, and rhetorical methods of marshalling evidence to support the inference that observed consistency in test performance has circumscribed meaning. With respect to the generality of the process, the development of evidence to support an inferential leap from an observed consistency to a construct or theory that accounts for that consistency is a generic concern of all science. (p. 41)

Messick alludes here to the relationship between validity and reliability. Clearly, any appropriate and useful measurement schema must reflect the nature of the process it purports to measure *and* it must do so consistently—that is, in a nonidiosyncratic fashion.

Messick (1988) ultimately terms the pursuit of construct validation:

> a never-ending one, as the ever-expanding development of a mosaic of research evidence where at any moment new findings or new credible assumptions may dictate a change in construct interpretation, theory, or measurement. But just because a process is never-ending does not mean that it should not have a beginning. (p. 41)

This book is an attempt to heed Messick's comment. Defining and refining the construct of second language text comprehension is a difficult, exciting, and frustrating task. The principal source of frustration has been the lack of attempts to bring appropriate research evidence to bear on the definition of constructs. Unfortunately, the field of foreign language education abounds in these negative examples. The continuation of the use of the second language as a response measure even after considerable evidence was generated that indicated that scores were reflections of language performance rather than of language understanding is one example. Another is the foreign language proficiency movement that adopted a framework of reading proficiency yet neither investigated its roots, researched its implications, nor accommodated counter-evidence. Yet a third example is of scholars who admit to the lack of construct validity in the measures that they use, but for reasons of efficiency choose to use them anyway (Lange, 1988).

While issues of validity are at the forefront of this chapter, they are not meant to mask the importance of reliability. Reliability is a measure of consistency; that is, whether a measuring device measures a construct in the same way from context to context. Understandably, if measures are not reliable, they obscure the construct they measure and, hence, obstruct validity. This means that any valid measure must, of course, be reliable. For this reason, the first part of this chapter attended principally to validity.

This chapter now turns to conventional methods of assessing second language reading comprehension. These methods will be discussed in terms of the construct they purport to measure as well as in terms of how they are scored, and what they require on the part of the test taker.

POPULAR PERSPECTIVES ON ASSESSING SECOND LANGUAGE READING

The model in Figure 7.1 should be a familiar one at this point in the book. This is the model discussed as the most common theory of instruction and materials development for second language reading. To reiterate, this view holds that the act of reading involves taking a text, applying lexical and syntactic knowledge to it, and then assessing whether the lexical and syntactic knowledge were used "correctly." This view on reading as a construct consisting of vocabulary words and syntactic patterns is also implicit in many assessment schemes. It is reflected in instruction with "prereading vocabulary" and grammatical practice followed by a question-answer methodology in some form or in cloze tests, for example. Ultimately, the focus of the assessment is on the knowledge of vocabulary and sentence structure. It is important to reiterate the content of Chapter Three at this juncture: the knowledge of words and of how words can be related to each other is a necessary yet insufficient prerequisite for understanding.

The perspective in Figure 7.1 gets played out in a number of commonly used techniques for measuring second language reading abilities. The focus in this next section is on the most frequently used techniques, namely cloze, multiple-choice questions, and direct content questions.

Cloze

In Chapter Two, the research on cloze in second language was reviewed and analyzed. It is not the task of this section to review that literature once again, but rather it is the purpose to lead the reader to think about cloze in a bit more depth.

Figure 7.1.   Comprehension: A text-based perspective.

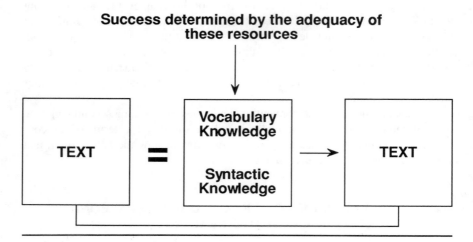

Perhaps the best tactic is to look at a cloze text. The following is taken from a high school social studies textbook cited in a book on reading in the content area (Roe, Stoodt, & Burns, 1987).

> Rocks exposed to the atmosphere slowly change. Air, water, and materials _____ living things can react _____ minerals in rock to _____ or even remove them. _____ is the process by _____ rocks change to soil. _____ may result from both _____ and physical action in _____.

The task before the reader is to fill in the exact words from the original text. If the reader can perform this task with at least 50 percent accuracy he may be rated as "fully competent" to read the passage.

Since validity is the most important feature of any assessment mechanism, it is important to begin the discussion there. The research cited in Chapter Two indicates that cloze testing possesses concurrent validity. That is, it correlates highly with other language proficiency measures (Lange & Clausing, 1981). In other words, achievement in cloze testing directly relates to achievement in other tests such as grammar and even sentence repetition tasks. A caveat must be inserted here, however. For scores on a cloze test to generate high correlations with scores on other measures, exact word scoring must be used. In other words, in the above example, *alter* must be used rather than *change* for a point to be awarded. If acceptable word scoring is permitted, then the correlation between a cloze test score and other tests decreases, therefore, changing its concurrent validity.

Another important question surrounds face validity. Face validity refers to the appearance of validity or "looking like a test." While some psychometricians dismiss face validity as a serious concern, many do acknowledge that a test should "look valid and be acceptable to the test taker and the public generally" (Angoff, 1988, p. 24). A cloze test is hardly face valid since it is rare during reading that a reader has pencil in hand filling in words. Concomitantly, another factor is reader attitude toward cloze tests. Shohamy (1982) found that learners have a strong aversion to cloze testing since they feel defeated from the beginning. (To reiterate, a failing grade of 50 percent is an extremely high score on a cloze test.)

Yet these issues of concurrent and face validity are trivial within the context of considering construct validity or the extent to which a cloze test accurately and adequately reflects the actual process of reading in a second language. To this extent, cloze testing is profoundly inadequate. The inadequacy lies in the relationship between being able to insert a word in a clause and the ability to understand the concepts held within a text. In the sentence "_____ is the process by _____ rocks change to soil" it would seem that using *erosion* to fill the first blank would indicate that the reader has understood. In traditional scoring, however, the answer of *erosion* would be wrong since the original passage contained the word *weathering*. While it may well be true that the text's author used the word weathering to avoid an overuse of the word erosion or vice versa, expecting a reader to come up with the synonym in a language not his own forces an additional productive capacity on the reader that is not part of the reading process. The second blank in the sentence provides an illustration of the converse. Does the ability to generate the terms "by which" indicate understanding of the process in the passage—which would be an indication of comprehension—or rather does it indicate a sense of a rather conventional English formula *by which*. From the cloze passage, it is impossible to make this judgement.

Another point about "nonnativeness" and productive ability is critical here, too. The material in Chapter Four indicates that it is possible for a nonnative reader to have considerable topic knowledge. That reader might be an archeology student, for example. That reader may have a well-established concept of *erosion*, may know that that is what the passage is about, and may not have an extra synonym. In other words, he may have the concept and not the word; the understanding and not the performance ability. In this case, cloze testing is a vocabulary exercise, not an assessment of reading.

A final point is that cloze testing has been found to measure information only within clause boundaries (Kamil et al., 1986; Shanahan, Kamil, & Tobin, 1982). In other words, it focuses a reader's attention on individual words to the detriment of a global understanding of text. In fact, identical scores are generated in cloze passages even when they are presented to readers as randomized sentences within paragraphs (Markham, 1985). In the end, this is probably the most damning feature of cloze testing. It clearly has little if anything to do with a reader's understanding of a piece of connected discourse.

Multiple-Choice Tests and True/False

True/false and multiple-choice tests, for example, are also problematic. For instance, they are often not passage-dependent. The following item provides an appropriate example.

The passage indicates that the reason most Americans do not know another language is:

1. They possess genetic defects that disable language learning abilities.
2. There are few opportunities for learning other languages in American schools and universities.
3. There is rarely an immediate need to know another language since the U.S. is very large and basically self-sufficient.
4. Second languages are prohibited.

Clearly, one does not need to read the passage in order to choose the correct answer "c." The absurdity of choice "a" and the falsity of "b" and "d" make it clear to the test taker what the answer has to be.

The above example is not meant to be so inane as to be meaningless. Many tests, even formally and professionally developed ones, fall into the passage independence category. In a 1975 study conducted on multiple-choice questions in standardized reading tests in the native language, Pyrczak found no significant difference between the scores of students who read a passage and selected an answer to comprehension questions and scores of students who simply selected a, b, c, or d in answer to the same comprehension questions without reading the text. Pyrczak (1975) cited three reasons for the results: (a) prior knowledge; (b) the "interrelatedness" of the questions; and (c) the general construction of multiple-choice tests. In a later publication, Pyrczak and Axelrod (1976) concluded that teachers should pretest a test before administering it, in order to determine whether it is indeed passage dependent. They concluded that if reading tests are passage independent and students do not have to read carefully to perform at criterion level, the testing system defeats the purpose of reading instruction. Foreign language studies that have included multiple-choice items in their published reports have fallen prey to the same difficulty. Jarvis and Jensen (1982) and Barnett (1986) are two examples.

In a major study investigating the quantity and quality of information gained from prose, Meyer (1985) deals with the difficulty of test construction. She points to the subjective nature of designing comprehension questions, stating that interrater reliability is rarely high since there is general disagreement on the determination of the "most important parts of the text."

Similar problems exist in the testing of reading in a foreign language. Valette (1977) speaks to the problem of prior knowledge and passage independence, arguing that tests should not turn into logical thinking and problem solving. The problem of interrelatedness cited by Pyrczak (1975) is even more pronounced in a foreign language. Since students' vocabularies are limited, test makers often do not have the freedom of using synonyms or the time to recombine structures and words carefully to express concepts in passages or to provide useful distractors. They are forced essentially to repeat sections of passages and the test can become merely a word recognition and matching exercise.

Hosenfeld (1977) illustrates this problem in her study of reading/grammar tasks. When students were asked to self-report on what they did to complete reading assignments for homework, almost all reported that they did not bother reading for information. Rather, they sought out grammatical cues and performed grammatical operations from the cues.

Direct Content Questions

Direct content questions have been alluded to twice in preceding chapters. Both of these instances refer to the fundamental problems in this type of assessment schema. In Chapter Two, Richterich's and Chancerel's (1980) statement regarding a question always implying its answer should be reiterated. If the question, *How many inches of rainfall is there annually in Southern Ontario?*, is posed, the answer can only be given in some quantitative sense. In other words, the question delimits the answer. The second mention of the nature of direct questioning is in Chapter Six concerning instruction. The chapter illustrated in part the interaction of reader, questioner, and questions. When the questioner asks the following about *Das Brot* (The Bread), *Have you any experience with starvation or with wartime for that matter?*, a reader probably rejects his view of the story as the trials and tribulations of dieting and shifts his understanding. This shifting of understanding is the result of the *question* not the *text*.

Summary

The intention of this section on popular perspectives in assessment is to outline some of the issues related to the validity of the schemas mentioned. Clearly, there is no perfect assessment schema—one that will accurately measure all processes involved in second language text comprehension. Unfortunately, in the professional literature there is little if any reference to these problematic areas. Students are assessed for placement purposes, for achievement purposes, and for empirical research purposes. Yet, scant attention is paid to the validity of these assessments. Parallel to arguments made earlier in this book, in order to approach any aspect of language teaching, in this case reading comprehension, with a set of theoretically grounded and data-driven principles, a method of assessment needs to be developed that reflects a contemporary knowledge base.

AN ALTERNATIVE: USING IMMEDIATE RECALL PROTOCOLS

The suggested measure of reading comprehension in this book is immediate recall. As noted in Chapter Five, recall is a common measure for the assessment of comprehension in L1 research. Considered to be the "most straightforward assessment of the result of the text-reader interaction" (Johnston, 1983, p. 54), recall reveals "something about the organization of stored information, about some of the retrieval strategies used by readers, and reveals the method of reconstruction which [the reader] employs to encode information in a text" (Bernhardt, 1983, p. 31). Hayes and Flower (1980), who have studied the use of recall protocols in writing, point to the "richness of recall data," explaining that the data reflect how subjects analyze information, and how they think about it (p. 2). More recently, Hayes (1989) has described protocol analysis as "cognitive psychology's most powerful tool for tracking psychological processes" (p. 69).

This tracking capability enables several things to happen at once. First, recall can show where a lack of grammar is interfering with the communication between text and reader, while not focusing a reader's attention on linguistic elements in texts. Second, generating recall data does not influence a reader's understanding of a text. As noted earlier in the chapter, when questions are administered, an additional interaction takes place among texts, reader, questioner, and among the questions themselves. In other words, questions form another "text" for comprehension. It is, therefore, extremely difficult to pinpoint how a reader encodes information apart from the *additional* input he or she receives from questions. In other words, a free recall measure provides a purer measure of comprehension, uncomplicated by linguistic performance and tester interference.

Suggesting the use of recall is not totally new on the second language scene. In the early 1970s "recall score" (see Chapter Two) started to be listed as a dependent variable in a number of studies. Three features of recall are unique to this book and its author. First, a recall protocol should be written in the native language of its author. As noted earlier, although this recommendation has been made by different researchers it seems to have been unheeded. Second, unique to this discussion is the suggested use of recall in nonresearch settings, that is, as a "test" or in large scale assessment studies. Third, the measure is linked to an instructional strategy, thereby enabling it to maintain content validity. The next section of this chapter discusses and provides the practicalities of scoring recall protocols. It also looks toward the future by commenting on possibilities and potentials for recall in large-scale assessment. In addition, it includes data from a validation study in order to document concurrent validity.

SCORING SYSTEMS

Meyer's System

There are a number of methods for scoring recalls. The base scoring instrument frequently used is Meyer's (1985) recall protocol scoring system, which is based on Grices' (1975) case grammar. The Meyer system identifies the structural characteristics as well as lexical units of a passage. The procedure helps to assess the relationship between passage type and level of performance. Moreover, because the system arranges the idea units hierarchically, its use provides an illustration of not only which lexical and relational units are remembered, but also from which portion of the structure those units are recalled.

Procedures for the development of a recall protocol scoring template within this system are undertaken in the following manner. First, top level structure is determined (e.g., comparison-contrast); second, macrostructural relationships are determined by looking for relationships with lexical items such as "because" and "therefore"; third, the microstructural level is composed which consists of lexical predicates and role arguments or "referential indices." Figure 7.2 provides a sample passage for discussion and illustration. Figure 7.3 illustrates the structural characteristics of the passage.

Once the structure is devised, it is transposed into a scoring instrument by listing all lexical items, roles and relationships on graph paper, with higher level ideas placed to the left and lower level ideas to the right. Figure 7.4 is the actual scoring instrument. The scoring template is then paper-clipped to a score sheet, so that the idea units mentioned by each subject can be recorded chronologically into a subject's scoring column.

Role arguments are recorded as they occur in the recall protocol. Lexical predicates are recorded somewhat more loosely: If at least two referential indices are scored, and if those are recorded as in the same role as in the original passage, then the lexical predicate to which they corresponded is also recorded as present. Moreover, if a subject indicates an awareness of the presence of a particular role, but does not remember the lexical item (e.g., John hid *something*), only the role relationship is scored as present. In addition, inferences are circled but not scored.

Figure 7.2.   French general interest article text.

NOUVEAU HOBBY DES JEUNES: OBSERVER LES ASTRES

En 1969, ils étaient 700. Certains d'entre eux n'avaient que des jumelles. Aujourd'hui, ils sont plus de 7000 à fouiller chaque soir (ou presque) le ciel de France avec des télescopes. En deux ans, il s'est vendu en France plus de 4000 télescopes de 10 à 20 000 F pièce et des milliers de lunettes de 50 à 90 mm. En 1969, les amateurs recevaient un petit bulletin. Aujourd'hui, leur association édite un luxueux magazine, lu par 50 000 fanatiques dans le Benelux. A la Foire de Paris, cette année encore, ils auront un stand et un planétarium. Voici comment fonctionne l'Association française d' astronomie et ce que les jeunes ou les vieux peuvent en attendre.

ET D'ABORD, QU'APPORTE L'ASTRONOMIE?

Quand on observe le ciel dans une lunette, on se détache du monde. C'est un traitement souverain contre la neurasthénie et les soucis quotidiens. L'astronomie permet de fantastiques voyages immobiles. Le ciel grouille de vie silencieuse. Il y a des milliards de choses passionnantes à observer: Saturne (on ne sait pas à quoi sert son anneau), la végétation de Mars (qui change de couleur avec les tempêtes de poussière et de sable), les cratères de la Lune, les galaxies loin taines (habitées?), etc.

Photographier le ciel est un hobby en pleine expansion. Dans ce domaine, les "sujets" ne manquent pas et on peut même avoir la chance de réussir une photo qui aidera les savants à résoudre quelque énigme. On peut débuter dans l'astronomie avec une simple paire de jumelles (de 400 à 800 F), avec une lunette (de 500 à 15 000 F), avec une télescope que l'on a construit soi-même (prix de revient:de 800 à 1 300 F pour un 200mm). Faire partie d'un club permet de se passer de matériel, mais surtout d'apprendre les BA BA du métier.

As is true for L1 scoring, any reasonable paraphrasing of lexical units is judged as present in the protocol. Because the protocols and scoring instruments are written and scored in a language different from that of the original passage, interpretation of lexical units is relatively liberal. A score within this system is defined as the total number of lexical predicates and role arguments marked.

This system as described has a number of advantages. It divides a text not only into units but also provides a mechanism for scoring the relationship between and among those units. It has also consistently provided reliable scores as well as scores that appear to reflect the manner in which subjects recall text, the operationalization of comprehension in many studies. In addition to providing a valid and reliable score, the system lends itself to qualitative analysis since different portions of the text can be highlighted and analyzed and compared with other portions of the text.

There are two principal disadvantages to the Meyer recall protocol system both of which center on efficiency. The first disadvantage is the time involved in developing a scoring template from the text hierarchy. Such development has traditionally taken between 25 and 50 hours per 250-word text. This development time does not include initial training time. It refers only to the amount of time spent with analyzing the text, dividing it into appropriate lexical predicates

Figure 7.3. Structural characteristics of the French general interest article text according to Meyer's system.

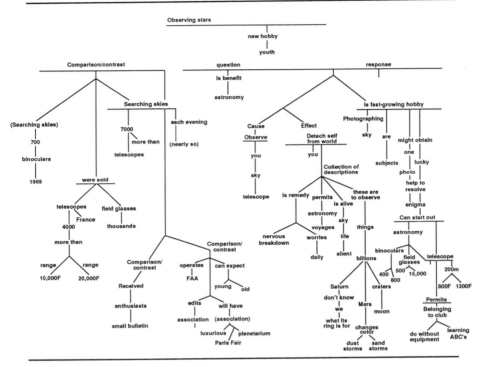

and role relationships, and then checking the developer's reliability and validity with another developer. The second disadvantage stems from the time involved in scoring itself. Each unit must be scored chronologically and decisions must be made regarding the presence or absence of complete relationships in which case either full or partial credit is given. Recent estimates have it that each student protocol, depending upon how much information is contained in it, takes one-half hour to one hour for scoring using materials illustrated in the previous figures.

Such time commitments as well as the expertise needed in instrument development make it difficult to justify the use of such a procedure even in research, let alone in classroom environments. Clearly, the use of such a procedure at a classroom level is prohibitive. There is a need, therefore, of developing alternative methods of scoring recall protocols that, nevertheless, provide the same quality data without the concomitant time and training commitment. The following section of this chapter describes just such an attempt.

Figure 7.4. Scoring template for the French general interest article text according to the Meyer system.

1	Comparison/ contrast: response: question, answer
2	OBSERVING STARS
3	description: equivalent
4	HOBBY
5	description
6	NEW
7	benefactive
8	YOUTH
9	Comparison/contrast
10	SEARCHING SKIES
11	agent
12	7,000
13	description: specific
14	MORE THAN
15	description: manner
16	TODAY
17	description: setting-location
18	FRANCE
19	description: manner
20	EACH EVENING
21	description: manner
22	(OR NEARLY SO)
23	description: attribution
24	TELESCOPES
25	Comparison/contrast
26	(Searching Skies)
27	agent
28	700
29	description: time-setting
30	1969
31	description: attribution
32	HAD BINOCULARS
33	agent
34	SOME
35	description: manner
36	ONLY
37	description
38	WERE SOLD
39	patient
40	TELESCOPES
41	description: time-setting
42	IN TWO YEARS
43	description: specific
44	4,000
45	description: specific
46	MORE THAN
47	range
48	10,000 FRANCS
49	20,000 FRANCS

204

50	patient
51	FIELD GLASSES
52	description: specific
53	THOUSANDS
54	description: setting-location
55	FRANCE
56	range
57	50mm
58	90mm
59	Collection: comparison/contrast
60	HOW OPERATES
61	patient
62	FRENCH ASTRONOMICAL ASSOCIATION
63	CAN EXPECT
64	patient
65	YOUNG
66	OLD
67	Comparison/contrast
68	RECEIVED
69	agent
70	ENTHUSIASTS (AMATEURS)
71	patient
72	SMALL BULLETIN
73	description: setting-time
74	IN 1969
75	Collection
76	EDITS (PUBLISHES)
77	agent
78	ASSOCIATION
79	patient
80	MAGAZINE
81	description: setting-time
82	TODAY
83	description: attribution
84	LUXURIOUS
85	benefactive
86	50,000 ENTHUSIASTS
87	description: attribution
88	BENELUX
89	WILL HAVE
90	agent
91	THEY
92	patient
93	STAND
94	PLANETARIUM
95	description: attribution
96	PARIS FAIR
97	description: manner
98	THIS YEAR

99	AGAIN
100	Response: question
101	IS BENEFIT
102	description: attribution
103	ASTRONOMY
104	Causation: covariance, antecedent
105	OBSERVES
106	agent
107	YOU (ONE)
108	patient
109	SKY
110	description: manner
111	TELESCOPE
112	Causation: covariance, consequent
113	DETACH SELF FROM WORLD
114	patient
115	YOU (ONE)
116	Collection of descriptions
117	IS SOVEREIGN REMEDY
118	patient
119	NERVOUS BREAKDOWNS
120	DAILY WORRIES
121	PERMITS
122	agent
123	ASTRONOMY
124	patient
125	VOYAGES
126	description: attribution
127	STATIONARY
128	description: attribution
129	FANTASTIC
130	Collection of descriptions
131	IS ALIVE
132	patient
133	SKY
134	description: attribution
135	LIFE
136	description: attribution
137	SILENT
138	THERE ARE TO OBSERVE
139	patient
140	THINGS
141	description: attribution
142	THRILLING
143	description: specific
144	BILLIONS
145	Collection of descriptions: equivalent
146	SATURN
147	description: attribution

148	DON'T KNOW
149	agent
150	WE
151	patient
152	WHAT ITS RING IS FOR
153	VEGETATION
154	description: setting location
155	MARS
156	description: attribution
157	CHANGES COLOR
158	description: attribution
159	DUST STORMS
160	SANDSTORMS
161	CRATERS
162	description: setting location
163	MOON
164	GALAXIES
165	description: setting location
166	DISTANT
167	description: attribution
168	INHABITED?
169	Response: response
170	IS FAST GROWING HOBBY
171	patient
172	PHOTOGRAPHING THE SKY
173	Collection of descriptions
174	ARE PLENTIFUL
175	patient
176	SUBJECTS
177	MIGHT OBTAIN
178	agent
179	ONE
180	description: attribution
181	LUCKY
182	patient
183	PHOTO
184	description: attribution
185	WILL HELP TO RESOLVE
186	patient
187	ENIGMA
188	benefactive
189	SCIENTISTS
190	CAN START OUT
191	agent
192	ONE
193	description: manner
194	ASTRONOMY
195	Collection of descriptions
196	PAIR OF BINOCULARS

Figure 7.4.   Scoring template for the French general interest article text according to the Meyer system. (*cont.*)

197	description: attribution
198	SIMPLE
199	range
200	400F
201	800F
202	FIELD GLASSES
203	range
204	500F
205	15,000F
206	TELESCOPE
207	description: attribution
208	CAN CONSTRUCT ONESELF
209	patient
210	200M
211	range
212	800F
213	1300F
214	Description
215	PERMITS
216	agent
217	BELONGING TO CLUB
218	patient (collection)
219	TO DO WITHOUT EQUIPMENT (BUT ESPECIALLY)
220	TO LEARN
221	patient
222	ABC'S (FUNDAMENTALS, BASICS)
223	description: attribution
224	TRADE
225	
226	
227	
228	
229	
230	
231	
232	
233	

Other Systems

Among reasonable alternative systems are a simple propositional analysis and a weighted one posited by Johnson (1970). A simple propositional analysis system is based on pausal units or breath groups. In other words, a "pausal unit" is one that has a pause on each end of it during normally paced oral reading. A weighted propositional system is also based on pausal units. It, however, takes an additional step in development in that raters must rank each pausal unit in terms of its salience to the message of the text.

In order to analyze these other systems, the same texts and student protocols used in Allen et al. (1988) were used. Since they had already been scored by two independent raters using the Meyer system, they were appropriate for cross-validation. The German newspaper article entitled "Reagan kam bei den Russen an" (Figure 5.4) and the German business letter text (Figure 5.2) were used.

In order to develop the unweighted or simple propositional analysis system, three fluent readers of German were asked to read each text to themselves and to mark all those places in the text where they paused. As noted in most L1 research, pausal unit endings are generally found at the end of a syntactically related unit such as *in the morning* or *The old man / was happy/ above all/ about the information/ which he obtained/ recently*. The three readers provided almost 100 percent overlap in their pausal units—the only inconsistency was the tendency of one reader to have slightly longer units. In this case, the more narrow units were chosen. Figure 7.5 illustrates the individual propositions that were determined by this process for the newspaper text. These propositions are listed on the left side, forming 127 total propositions. This should be compared with the total of 160 lines of text included for the same text under the Meyer system (Figure 7.6).

In order to conduct a cross-validation, the newspaper article, "Reagan kam bei den Russen an," and the business letter were rescored using the simple propositional analysis system. The correlation between between the scores generated on the newspaper article was .96 and on the business letter .54. The newspaper article scores were encouraging. The scores generated using the simpler method for the business letter were not as encouraging.

The next step in the process was to weight each proposition according to the method suggested by Johnson (1970). The process begins in the same manner as above. The text is divided into pausal units. Next, two fluent readers are asked to divide the text into four levels: the lowest level being the least important 25 percent of the propositions in a text, the next level being the next least important 25 percent, and so forth. In other words, the lowest 25 percent are considered to be of value *1*, the next, *2*, the next *3*, and the highest or most important information, *4*. The *4* level information maintains the thread of a text in a telegraphic style.

This method was also used with the newspaper article. Because of the brevity of the business letter, only three levels of information were used: level *1* being the least important and level *3*, the most. Reliability using only three levels was a little lower, approximately 85 percent. Where disagreements occurred, the raters compromised. Figure 7.5 also illustrates the values awarded each proposition of the Reagan and Gorbachev text.

The scores on the recall protocols were then recalculated using the weighted analysis system. The correlation between the original Meyer scores and the weighted scores on the newspaper article is .96 and on the business letter .85.

Figure 7.5. Scoring instrument based on pausal units for the German newspaper article text.

Proposition	Value	1	2	3	4	5	6	7	8	9	10	11	12	13
							Subjects							
Reagan	3													
an . . . kam	1													
bei den Russen	4													
DW	1													
Washington/Moskau	1													
der 79järhige	1													
AK	1			*						*				
strahlte:	3													
Das SV	4									*		*	*	
hört	4			*						*		*	*	
mit eigenen Ohren	1													
was . . . sagt	2			*						*	*			
der US P.	4			*						*	*			
Der Rentner	2													
freute sich über	4	*					*							
vor allem	1													
bisher nicht zugängliche	1													
Informationen	3													
die . . . erhalten hatte	2													
durch die Neujahrsgebot	4	*	*							*				
von RR	3	*	*							*				
im sowjetischen Fernsehen	2	*								*				
Es wäre gut	3	*					*							
fuhr er fort	1						*							
wenn	3						*							
ein solcher Austausch	4			*				*						
öfter	4	*					*							
stattfände	4	*					*							
K gehörte	2													
zu denjenigen	2													
die Austrahlung	2													
der R Rede	2													
zufällig	1													
die . . . mitererlebt hatten	2													
Denn	2													
die meisten SB	4						*	*						
waren . . . unterrichtet	4						*	*						
gar nicht	4	*					*							
über die TV Sendung	2	*					*							

Proposition	Value	1	2	3	4	5	6	7	8	9	10	11	12	13
verabredete	1	*						*						
Weder . . . noch	2		*											
in der Programmvorschau	1		*											
der Fsill	1		*											
TagesZt.	2		*											
war . . . angekündigt worden	3		*											
das Ereignis	3		*											
FG	3		*	*										
im Moskauer SZ	2		*	*			*	*						
zeigten sich	3	*	*			*	*							
sehr überrascht	4		*	*			*	*						
als sie	3		*											
von westlichten Journalisten	2	*	*	*			*							
darauf angesprochen wurden	4		*											
Ein junger Mann	3		*					*		*				
in der sowjetischen Hauptstadt	2													
antwortete auf die Frage	3													
wie ihm . . . habe gefallen	4		*							*				
Reagan	3		*				*			*				
Ich halte ihn	2		*	*			*	*					*	
für einen fähigen Mann	4		*	*			*	*		*			*	
der weiß	2			*				*		*			*	
dass Frieden	3		*	*			*	*		*			*	
und Zusammenarbeit	3		*	*						*	*		*	
die wichtigsten Dinge	3		*					*		*			*	
in der Welt sind	1		*					*		*			*	
Ich bin sehr glücklich	4		*	*					*					
dass er . . . besuchen will	3		*	*	*				*			*		
unser Land	3		*	*	*				*			*		
Seinen Namen	3	*	*				*		*			*		
wollte er	2	*	*				*		*			*		
jedoch	3	*	*				*		*			*		
nicht nennen	3	*	*				*		*			*		
Ein anderer MB	3		*		*									
meinte	3		*				*	*						
R & G	3		*			*	*	*					*	
sei es offenbar ernst	4		*				*	*					*	
nach Frieden	4		*				*						*	
Die Ansprache	1													
des amer. P.	1													
habe gezeigt	1													
da	2													
er teilt	2													
die sow. An.	2						*							

211

Figure 7.5. Scoring instrument based on pausal units for the German newspaper article text. (*cont.*)

Proposition	Value	1	2	3	4	5	6	7	8	9	10	11	12	13
es gebe	1	*					*							
keine Alternative	3	*					*							
zum Frieden	3	*												
In der PZ Prawda	3		*				*		*		*			
und in der RZ Is. .	3	*					*		*					
waren . . . zu lesen	4						*		*					
die gleichzeitig ausgestrahlten R.	4													
der mächtigsten Manner der Welt	1													
auf der Titelseeite	2													
Die P.	4	*	*				*	*						
kritisierte	4	*	*				*	*	*		*			
das amer. SDI-P	4	*	*			*	*	*	*					
mit dem militär. Kreise	2	*	*				*	*	*		*			
in den USA	2	*	*				*	*			*			
die Gefahr eines K.	4	*	*					*						
über die Welt	3	*	*								*			
brachten	2	*	*											
Als das NJP	4						*		*	*	*			
in den VS	1						*							
mit dem alljährlich	1													
in Pasadena (K) stattfindenden	1				*				*					
berühmten RBU	3	*	*		*	*	*	*	*	*	*			
fur die fünfminutige Fernsehrede	4								*		*		*	
des sow. Partei. G.	4		*					*	*	*			*	
unterbrochen worden war	4	*						*	*	*	*			
griffen	2		*								*			
einige Zuschauer	2	*	*								*			
erbost	2	*	*						*		*			
zum Telephon	2	*	*							*				
und beschwerten sich	4	*	*							*				
bei den FSA	4	*	*							*				
Wenn . . . dann	1	*	*	*	*		*	*		*	*	*	*	
einen R. sehen	1	*	*	*	*		*			*	*	*		
ich will	1	*	*	*	*		*	*		*	*	*		
kaufe ich mir	1		*	*	*		*	*		*	*	*		
einen R. FS.	1	*							*	*	*			
sagte einen Burger	1		*	*					*	*	*			
in Spartanburg	1	*												
im BS SC	1	*			*	*		*		*	*			

212

Figure 7.6.   Scoring template for the German newspaper article text according to the Meyer system.

```
 1   Comparison: adversative
 2   "ARRIVED WITH" (achieved favorable response)
 3       agent
 4       REAGAN
 5       patient
 6       RUSSIANS
 7       range
 8       WASHINGTON/MOSKAU
 9       GREETING
10           agent
11           RONALD REAGAN
12           description: manner
13           SOVIET TELEVISION
14           description
15           NEW YEAR'S
16   Causation: covariance, antecedent
17       WAS NOT ANNOUNCED
18           patient
19           EVENT
20               description: setting location
21               TV GUIDE
22                   description: attribution
23                   NEWSPAPER
24                   description: setting location
25                   DAILY NEWSPAPER
26   Causation: covariance, consequent
27       APPEARED TO BE VERY SURPRISED
28           patient
29           PASSERSBY
30               description: setting location
31               CENTER OF MOSCOW
32               description: manner
33               ASKED BY JOURNALISTS
34   Response (Comparison adversative)
35   ARE HEARING WITH OWN EARS
36       agent
37       SOVIET PEOPLES
38       patient
39       WHAT U.S. PRESIDENT IS SAYING
40   Collection of responses
41       GLOWED
42           patient
43           ALEXANDER KISLAKOW
44               description: specific
45               79–YEAR OLD
46               Collection: explanation
47               HAVING INFORMATION PREVIOUSLY UNAVAILABLE
48               patient
49               RETIRED MAN
```

50	description: manner
51	NEW YEAR'S GREETING
52	description: attribution
53	RONALD REAGAN
54	description: manner
55	SOVIET TELEVISION
56	Causation: covariance, consequent
57	WOULD BE GOOD
58	Causation: covariance, antecedent
59	TOOK PLACE MORE OFTEN
60	patient
61	SUCH AN EXCHANGE
62	PLEASED
63	patient
64	YOUNG MAN
65	description: attribution
66	DIDN'T WANT TO GIVE NAME
67	description: equivalent
68	CONSIDER TO BE CAPABLE
69	agent
70	I
71	patient
72	RONALD REAGAN
73	description: attribution
74	FREEDOM MOST IMPORTANT
75	COOPERATION MOST IMPORTANT
76	Causation: covariance, consequent
77	AM VERY HAPPY
78	Causation: covariance, antecedent
79	WANTS TO VISIT OUR COUNTRY
80	agent
81	description: attribution
82	MAINTAINED THAT SERIOUS IN STRIVING FOR PEACE
83	agent
84	ANOTHER CITIZEN
85	description: attribution
86	MOSCOW
87	patient
88	REAGAN
89	patient
90	GORBATSCHOW
91	description: manner
92	OBVIOUSLY
93	Description: equivalent
94	SHOWED
95	agent
96	SPEECH
97	description: attribution
98	AMERICAN PRESIDENT

99	patient
100	THAT HE SHARED SOVIET OPINION
101	description: equivalent
102	NO ALTERNATIVE TO PEACE
103	(Comparison: adversative)
104	WERE ON TITLE PAGE
105	description: attribution
106	NEWSPAPER
107	description: attribution
108	PARTY
109	description: equivalent
110	PRAVDA
111	description: attribution
112	PAPER
113	description: attribution
114	GOVERNMENT
115	description: equivalent
116	ISWESTIJA
117	patient
118	GIVEN SPEECHES
119	description: attribution
120	TWO MOST POWERFUL MEN IN WORLD
121	description: adversative
122	CRITICIZED
123	agent
124	PRAVDA
125	patient
126	AMERICAN SDI PROJECT
127	description: equivalent
128	BRINGING INTO DANGER OF WAR
129	agent
130	U.S. "MILITARY CIRCLES"
131	patient
132	ENTIRE WORLD
133	Comparison: adversative
134	PRESENTATION
135	agent
136	SOVIET PARTY CHIEF
137	description: equivalent
138	GORBATSCHOW
139	patient
140	U.S.
141	Causation: covariance, antecedent
142	INTERRUPTED
143	agent
144	NEW YEAR'S GREETING
145	patient
146	ROSE BOWL PARADE
147	description: setting

Figure 7.6.   Scoring template for the German newspaper article text according to the Meyer system. (*cont.*)

148	PASADENA (CALIFORNIA)
149	description: specific
150	15 MINUTE
151	Causation: covariance, consequent
152	COMPLAINED
153	description:
	equivalent
154	GRABBED PHONE ANGRILY
155	agent
156	SOME LISTENERS
157	patient
158	TELEVISION STATIONS
159	Causation: covariance, antecedent
160	WANT TO SEE RUSSIAN
161	description: consequent
162	WILL BUY A RUSSIAN T.V. SET
163	agent
164	CITIZEN OF SPARTANBURG
165	description: setting location
166	SOUTH CAROLINA
167	
168	
169	
170	

Advantages—Efficiency

Clearly, there is enough overlap in the scores to argue that both systems are tapping the same behavior. Hence, the more efficient system becomes the better. Scoring time per protocol using either the weighted or the unweighted system is approximately 10 minutes. This efficiency is gained by not having to make specific decisions about awarding full or partial credit for full lexical predicates. In addition, it is easier to see the propositions broken into pausal units than it is to see those listed in the Meyer hierarchy.

The instruments listed in Figure 7.5 also illustrate another important point. This type of scoring lends itself to the use of a computer spread sheet. A spread sheet is arranged in a column and row format. This means it is suited to storing lists, such as propositions, which can be seen on the left, as well as lists of names, such as students or subjects, which can be listed at the top. Spread sheets can also sort information alphabetically and numerically as well as provide

Table 7.1. Mean Scores for the German Newspaper
Article Text According to Levels of Propositions in the
Text and Levels of German Instruction.

	Table of Means Subjects	Mean
Propositions		
Level 1	7	5
2	7	3.9714
3	7	6.4286
4	7	6.6286
Level of Instruction		
German 1	7	1.9643
2	7	2.0714
3	7	5.3571
4	7	10.0714
5	7	8.0714

calculations. In other words, the spread sheet can automatically tally the value of
the propositions. This means that the scorer merely has to make tick marks
regarding whether the proposition is in the protocol or not. The spread sheet
program calculates the score.

Advantages—Qualitative Information

A final advantage to a spread sheet format is its ability to sort information
numerically. This ability links to the final portion of the validation project: Can
qualitative data be easily gleaned from the recall protocol scoring format? Since a
spread sheet can sort according to numerical values, it can generate data *per level
of proposition* and, therefore, conveniently delineate which readers are gathering
which types of information from a text. It can answer questions such as *What
types of information are the best readers gathering? Are certain readers reading
more from one type of proposition than from another?*

In order to test out the effectiveness of this type of information, scores
according to subject group and level of information were calculated. The means
are listed in Table 7.1. Level *A* refers to the four levels of propositions within the
text "Reagan kam bei den Russen an." Level *B* refers to the five levels of
German students who participated. Analysis of Variance indicates that there are
significant main effects for Level of Proposition and for Level of Subjects.
Validating the original data, discussed in Chapter Three, the means ascend in the
same sequence: B1, B2, B3, B5, B4. That is, the Level Four students scored

higher than the Level Five, etc. These data reflect the same sequence for the total number of propositions gathered across all subjects and across all five levels of instruction.

The main effect for Level of Proposition is, however, the variable of interest at the moment. Across all the subjects, the mean number of Level One propositions was 5; for Level Two propositions, 3.97; for Level Three propositions, 6.4; and for Level Four propositions, 6.6. The significant difference is found between Level Two propositions and the other sets of propositions. In other words, despite level of instruction or proficiency, the least number of propositions is gathered from Level Two information.

This preliminary finding is interesting and needs to be explored as the development of reading proficiency is investigated. An examination of Level Two propositions reveals that these propositions provide redundant information within the text. That information includes redundancies such as "U.S. President" for Reagan and "the two superpowers" for the US and the USSR. Clearly, this type of information can be lost in memory since it is not necessary for comprehension. Interestingly, all readers regardless of proficiency level treated these redundant propositions as such. In these data, readers are behaving in ways consonant with their L1 behaviors. The quality of the information they are gathering is good. They simply gather ever more pieces of information from a text as proficiency increases.

RECALL PROTOCOL SCORES
AS APPROPRIATE AND MEANINGFUL

This summary needs to return to the measurement concepts of appropriateness and meaningfulness. Critical questions that need to be answered in this chapter are *Does recall in the native language reflect the construct of second language comprehension as it is currently understood from both a theoretical and from an empirical perspective? Do scores generated from recall reflect previous measures of language proficiency? Does a recall test look like a comprehension test? Are the scores from recall useful and interpretable; in other words, do they provide rich information?*

Obviously, the author concludes that the answers to these questions are "yes." The use of immediate recall protocol for operationalizing comprehension is generally not assailed. In broader terms, discussions in Chapters Three and Four as well as Chapter Five indicate that recall is compatible with the theory of second language reading posited in this book.

Other facets of measurement to which the procedure discussed must be responsive, such as reliability and cost-effectiveness, seem to be satisfactory. Messick (1988) would indicate that validation procedures are eternal and ongoing. Hence, the use of the phrase "seem to be."

The answer to the final question is of great importance—*is the information useful?* It is true that scholars have been generating "appropriate" scores for years. Many respond with *What do they mean?* since a score is a score is a score. A critical advantage to the assessment procedure outlined in this chapter is that it provides qualitative information. This information is critical toward new insights into the comprehension processes of second language readers that lead to principled language instruction.

8

Recommendations for Theory, Research, Curriculum, and Instruction

INTRODUCTION

Reading Development in a Second Language posits a theory of second language reading. As such, it must withstand conventional tests of "theories." Stern (1983) lists six qualities that "theory development should cultivate in order to meet . . . serious criticism" (p. 27). These qualities are: usefulness and applicability; explicitness; coherence and consistency; comprehensiveness; explanatory power and verifiability; and simplicity and clarity. The first part of this chapter concerns precisely these issues.

The second part of this chapter discusses research directions in second language literacy. Findings and conclusions from findings are not static entities. They should be continuously reexamined. In like manner, traditional research designs and conventional conceptions of research questions need to be refined and developed.

These sections on theory and research lead then to the final portion of the chapter: their implications for curriculum, materials, instruction, and teacher education. It is in these latter domains that theory and research are translated into principled practice.

TESTS OF A THEORY

Stern (1983) writes that a theory:

> refers to the systematic study of the thought related to a topic or activity. . . . A theory offers a system of thought, a method of analysis and synthesis, or a conceptual framework in which to place different observations, phenomena, or activities. (pp. 25–26).

The previous pages attempted to analyze and to synthesize data generated by second language readers and to place them within a model. As theory development, it must be tested according to the following criteria.

Usefulness and Applicability

Any learning theory must be grounded in the real world of a learning context peopled by teachers and students. The real world grounding provides the test for both usefulness and applicability.

The theory set forth in this book is useful on several counts. First, it was developed from real learners, and hence, applies to real learners. In fact, the primary data sets outlined in this book were collected from learners of French, German, and Spanish at the high school level (Chapter Three, for example), and from learners of French, German, and Spanish at the college level (Chapter Four, for example). In addition, the learners were all in traditional secondary or postsecondary second language programs. Second, the theory accounts for classroom behavior (Chapters Three, Four, and Six, for example). In other words, the data were collected in intact classrooms, and are, therefore, reflective of learner behavior within an instructional setting. Third, the theory accounts for individual reactions to second language texts. That is, the research methodologies employed, most prominently immediate recall, allow for the making of rather fine distinctions between and among individual responses to second language texts. In these ways, the theory "helps make sense of planning, decision making, and practice" (Stern, p. 27).

Explicitness

This theory attempts to be explicit in that it lists and delineates its assumptions through the reader-based model illustrated in Chapter One. In addition, it defines each dimension of the phenomenon known as "reading in a second language" (Chapters Three and Four); furthermore, it describes and posits the ways in which these dimensions interact with each other (Chapter Five).

Coherence and Consistency

Coherence mandates that there be no inner contradictions in the theory. A way of thinking about coherence is to question whether text-driven elements in reading as well as knowledge-driven elements and their interactions are described in reasonable and logical ways. In Stern's words, "All parts should fit together in a manner which can be explained. It is this ordering of the data or ideas and the logical relationship between them that is likely to distinguish a good theory from a poor one'' (p. 28).

Consistency mandates that the theoretical framework, namely, a socio-cognitive perspective, be explicit throughout. It also requires that the term *sociocognitive* be defined in the same manner throughout these pages. Consistency also implies that any suggestions for learning and instruction follow from the arguments as outlined; that is, that the suggestions in Chapters Six and Seven acknowledge text-driven and knowledge-driven aspects of reading as well as the integrative nature of the process they unite to create.

Comprehensiveness

According to Stern, a theory must be broad in nature. Broadness allows it to account for a wide range of observations under an array of conditions. The theory of second language reading presented here is applicable to both natural and instructed language learning contexts. It also includes issues of cross-linguistic processing.

The theory has two specific limitations. First, it principally emphasizes learners who are already literate in a first language. Second, the instructional strategies suggested are primarily applicable in classrooms with learners who share a first language with the teacher.

Explanatory Power and Verifiability

Support for the theory lies in anecdotal classroom experience (Chapter Six) as well as in the data base on second language reading itself (Chapter Two). The theory sheds light on *why* certain research findings have been observed as well as *why* learners react to second language texts as they do (Chapter Five).

The question of verifiability targets the extent to which additional second language reading data generated under different conditions provide further documentation for the theory. In summary, the theory presented in this book ''must not merely lead from claim to counterclaim'' (p. 30).

Simplicity and Clarity

The theory presented is basically stated with four dimensions: reader dimensions, text dimensions, the interaction of those dimensions, the product of them. In addition, the theory is clarified through the use of concrete examples and through visual support (Chapter Five, for example). In this way, it ''aims at being simple, economical, and parsimonious'' (Stern, 1983).

Recommendations

The evaluation of these qualities is conducted ultimately by other theorists and researchers. Perhaps the most critical test of all, however, is whether practitioners find a theory meaningful and satisfying.

Two data sets are missing in the theory as it is presented in these pages. First, the theory is not buttressed at the present time by retrospective learner reports. It needs to be expanded and modified to accommodate such data. Second, teacher-generated data, for the most part, are excluded. Data from teachers as former learners who bring their own learning strategies to the instructional process should be included. In addition, data should be generated from teachers as theory builders who have personal conceptualizations of the reading process as well as of the content of texts. Both of these facets of teachers impinge upon the comprehension products of learners.

RESEARCH DIRECTIONS

"The surest avenue to improve educational practice will occur through the application of knowledge derived from careful research" (Kamil, Langer, & Shanahan, 1985, p. ix). This statement by Kamil and colleagues states the overriding purpose in this book as well as its aspirations for the future. Principled language instruction evolves from a sound knowledge of learners as learners, of learners in the act of accomplishing language tasks, of teachers as learners, as well as of teachers as designers of learning tasks. All four of these areas need further data and theory development.

The introductory statement in this section uses the adjective *careful* before research. The word careful is critical. The discussion in Chapter Two highlighted that much of the extant research was either ill-conceived or simply not carefully done. A research community can almost forgive ill-conceived research. New research methodologies, new technologies, and new theories provide new perspectives that, ultimately, make some research pieces appear to be naive. Carefulness is a different issue. The second language research community needs to be responsive to new data. This lack of responsiveness is evident in second language literacy studies that continued to use cloze even after published data indicated that cloze was wholly inappropriate for reading assessment; that insisted on using the production of a second language as a response measure for comprehension after data indicated that patterns of response depended upon language of elicitation and that insisted on treating second language readers as monolithic generic groups when data indicated that there are language-specific processing strategies. These situations point to research that is conducted for purposes other than for the development of an empirical understanding of second language literacy.

Recommendations

First, more basic research is needed. The purpose of basic research is to facilitate the development of theory as well as to verify and substantiate current theory. Basic research and theory development are critical first steps toward applied research and theory. Application without appropriate basic knowledge inevitably leads toward the claims and counter-claims Stern (1983) alluded to earlier.

This is not, however, a naive call for more basic research. Basic research should have the following characteristics. First, it should be conducted on second language readers delineated by native language group. Language specific data should lead toward a resolution of the question of language-specific processing. Second, basic research should only use authentic materials. A significant amount of previous research has probed readers using texts that have little or no relationship to texts that readers might encounter in an authentic situation. This leads to a knowledge of how readers read anomalous texts and no knowledge of how they cope with real texts. Third, second language literacy research needs to collect data from readers under a variety of conditions. That is, data need to reflect readers' processes under high and low topic knowledge conditions, from a variety of cognitive and affective stances, and while accomplishing different reading goals (studying for a test versus casual entertainment reading versus collecting evidence for a written term paper). Each one of these conditions and circumstances implies a potentially different set of processing strategies and concomitant different sets of performance data.

Fourth, multiple measures need to be collected on each subject involved in a study. There is no perfect measure of reading comprehension. Every measure is flawed; each measure provides one perspective. Therefore, multiple measures are necessary to provide a more than unidimensional picture. Multiple measures might consist of recall protocol scores, grammatical achievement test scores, time delay recall, coupled with delayed direct questioning, a responsive writing, or a retrospective interview. The point is that principled theory development requires fairly extensive knowledge of readers as multifaceted, multiproficient learners.

Fifth, research studies need to display their substeps. A glance through the charts in Chapter Two that outlined research studies indicates that some of the outlines are incomplete. In fact, in some published research studies subject groups or their tasks or the responses to the tasks were not discernible from the report. Whether the fault lies with ill-prepared researchers or unschooled editors, it is clear that progress in second language literacy research demands full disclosure. The 10-page report is no longer a legitimate form of communication in second language reading research: the process itself is so complex and the information needed for interpreting results so multifaceted that traditional page constraints impede rather than facilitate research-generated knowledge. Validity and reliability information, texts and tests, as well as scoring and analysis information are minimal expectations for appropriate research.

Sixth, refined methodology and analysis procedures are critical, too. Some of the research methods used by the author and colleagues in this book were principally recall protocol and eye movement. Other methods that have yet to be extensively tapped in second language research are retrospection and online introspection or think-alouds. The data analysis procedures used in this book were fairly conventional correlational and analysis of variance measures. Researchers need to begin to use more sophisticated statistical techniques, such as multiple regression. Multiple regression accommodates individual scores rather than group scores, providing a more individualized picture of second language text processing. Other techniques, such as path analysis and causal modeling (suggested in Chapter Five), will provide greater insight into factors that predict or contribute to second language text processing proficiency. At the same time, the qualitative model used in Chapters Four and Five for protocol analysis has only six dimensions. Additional qualitative analysis models should be developed to tap other learner dimensions such as affective stance and attitude.

Seventh, second language literacy research should recognize itself as an entity distinct from first language literacy research. The slavish adherence to first language literacy research designs, questions, and materials has forced the second language literacy field to relive many of the former's mistakes. The argument was made in Chapter One that second language literacy is not a less-skilled, less-accurate form of first language literacy, but rather, a different phenomenon. Therefore, certain research questions, designs, and types of tasks are unique to second language, and the field should demand that they be explored.

These six recommendations are meant to exemplify—not to be exclusive. Research is a process; it has evolutionary stages that change, grow, and accommodate new information. Second language reading research needs to push itself and to expand its goals and intentions so that it becomes more theoretically viable and principled.

CURRICULUM AND INSTRUCTION

The relationship between theory and practice in second language reading is an unhappy one at best. The theory and data presented throughout these pages provide an enormously complex picture of reading in a second language; the conventional practice of both teaching and assessing second language reading as outlined in Chapters Six and Seven is simplistic at best.

An underlying theme in this book is that practice must be responsive to theory and research. The intention, however, is not to simply display an array of research results, but also to provide practical ways in which to apply them. Yet, the principles outlined for teaching and for assessment are local-level suggestions. They do not characterize systemic changes. It is in systemic change guided by research that dramatic developments will be found.

Recommendations

First, the expectations of the second language reading curriculum need to change. Adult learners are more than capable of reading adult texts and should be expected to do so. Syntactically simplified prose on simplistic topics should not be tolerated either by students or teachers. Admittedly, of course, adult learners who are not already literate in a language and those learners who must cope with orthographies completely distinct from their own should be paced differently. The expectations should allow, however, for the qualitative and quantitative gaining of increasing amounts of information from authentic texts: not just the hope of someday reading something "real."

Second, materials used in the curriculum need to change. The 1980s saw a concern for the use of increased amounts of authentic materials in classrooms. The 1990s should see an end to the debate: Textbooks should consist of authentic materials of interest to learners in comparable age ranges. Topics of texts should be topics of concern to native readers in those age ranges and educational levels. Because reading materials provide the most significant source of cultural materials, it is critical that learners learn how to cope with these materials early in their instruction.

Culture teaching and its implications are important to consider at this juncture. If materials are constantly sanitized versions of both the language and the culture of the language, how can students be expected to learn to understand a second language? In other words, materials may be constructed in such a way that they are basically removed from the reality of the culture a student is trying to learn. In such a situation, it is hardly surprising that many students emerge from language programs in an alingual and monocultural state.

Third, materials need to be recycled. Conventional approaches to instruction and assessment outlined in Chapters Six and Seven take a componential approach to reading. Generally speaking, a text is read or a text is used in assessment, and teachers and learners move to the next lesson. Research, however, indicates that the principal distinction characterizing development is that reading is not an either/or matter of understanding. Rather, as readers progress in proficiency they are capable of garnering ever-increasing amounts of information. Thus, materials should be re-read at times in the curriculum so that students are permitted to get those ever-increasing amounts of information.

Fourth, materials should be developed in such a way that learners are required to do something with the materials—not just "read" them. In the real world, reading is rarely for pure entertainment. When it is, readers may choose to share "the great book they read last weekend," but they also do not tell every detail of a plot because they do not want to spoil another reader's prospective interest. In the real world, reading plays many functions. Readers use information to form opinions, to write papers and reports, to guide them in making decisions. In other words, reading materials should be related to specific tasks so that reading has some purpose.

Fifth, inservice teachers need to reconceptualize the reading process; preservice teachers need to receive alternative reading instruction methods. Chapter Six indicated that training methods were fairly consistent over a wide array of methods textbooks. The theory and research reported in this book indicate that reading instruction should not be "controlled" in the conventional sense of designing and carrying out lessons. Teachers need to learn to take on a facilitative not a directive role in the initial phases of reading instruction and a directive role in later stages of reading instruction. Teachers need to see reading not as one of the "four skills," but rather as a form of cultural exploration.

These recommendations, too, parallel to the ones offered for theory and research, are meant to exemplify, not to be exclusive. Curriculum and instruction are also processes that change and grow and are responsive to contextual needs. The second language reading curriculum as well as the manner in which that curriculum is implemented should take principled steps to involve new research and insight in order to improve student learning.

SUMMARY

Reading Development in a Second Language: Theoretical, Research, and Classroom Perspectives is meant to be a contribution to second language acquisition in general and to second language reading research and instruction in particular. It is not meant to replace or to supersede the writings of other scholars. It is clear that context effects are so great that to pretend to present "the answer" is arrogant at best and harmful at worst. This book does offer *a* principled approach to theory, research, and instruction in second language reading. The field can only dream of ultimately locating *the* approach.

References

Adams, M.J. (1980). Failures to comprehend and levels of processing in reading. In R.J. Spiro, B.C. Bruce, & W.F. Brewer (Eds.), *Theoretical issues in reading comprehension: Perspectives from cognitive psychology, linguistics, artificial intelligence and education* (pp. 11–32). Hillsdale, NJ: Lawrence Erlbaum.

Adams, S.J. (1982). Scripts and the recognition of unfamiliar vocabulary: Enhancing second language reading skills. *Modern Language Journal, 66*, 155–159.

Alderson, J.C., & Urquhart, A. H. (Eds.). (1984). *Reading in a foreign language.* New York: Longman.

Alderson, J.C., & Urquhart, A.H. (1988). This test is unfair: I'm not an economist. In P.C. Carrell, J. Devine, & D.E. Eskey (Eds.), *Interactive approaches to second language reading* (pp. 168–182). Cambridge: Cambridge University Press.

Allen, E.D., Bernhardt, E.B., Berry, M.T., & Demel, M. (1988). Comprehension and text genre: Analysis of secondary school foreign language readers. *Modern Language Journal, 72*(2), 163–172.

Allen, E D., & Valette, R.M. (1979). *Classroom techniques: Foreign languages and English as a second language.* New York: Harcourt Brace Jovanovich.

American Psychological Association. (1985). *Standards for educational and psychological testing.* Washington, DC: American Psychological Association.

Angoff, W.H. (1988). Validity: An evolving concept. In H. Wainer & H.S. Braun (Eds.), *Test validity* (pp. 19–32). Hillsdale, NJ: Lawrence Erlbaum.

Baldauf, R. B., Jr., Dawson, R. L. T., Prior, J., & Propst, I.K., Jr. (1980). Can matching cloze be used with secondary ESL pupils? *Journal of Reading, 23*, 435–440.

Barnett, M. (1986). Syntactic and lexical/semantic skill in foreign language reading: Importance and interaction. *Modern Language Journal, 70*, 343–349.

Barnett, M.A. (1988). Teaching reading strategies: How methodology affects language course articulation. *Foreign Language Annals, 21*(2), 109–119.

Barnitz, J.G. (1985). *Reading development of nonnative speakers of English.* Orlando, FL: Harcourt Brace Jovanovich.

Barrera, B.R., Valdes, G., & Cardenes, M. (1986). Analyzing the recall of students across different language-reading categories: A study of third-graders' Spanish-L1, English-L2, and English-L1 comprehension. In J.A. Niles & R.V. Lalik (Eds.), *Thirty-fifth yearbook of the National Reading Conference* (pp. 375–381). Rochester, NY: National Reading Conference.

Bean, T.W., Potter, T.C., & Clark, C. (1980). Selected semantic features of ESL materials and their effect on bilingual students' comprehension. In M. Kamil & A. Moe, (Eds.), *Perspectives on reading research and instruction: Twenty-ninth yearbook of the National Reading Conference* (pp. 1–5). Washington, DC: National Reading Conference.

Beaugrand, R. de. (1984). *Text production: Towards a science of composition.* Norwood, NJ: Ablex.

Beltran, A., Cabrera, M., & Coombe, C. (1989). *A Spanish replication of Allen, Bernhardt, Berry, and Demel.* Unpublished manuscript, The Ohio State University, Columbus, OH.

Bensoussan, M., & Ramraz, R. (1984a). Helping the poor to help themselves: A quantitative re-evaluation of the outcomes of an advanced reading comprehension program in English as a foreign language. *System, 12*, 61–66.

Bensoussan, M., & Ramraz, R. (1984b). Testing EFL reading comprehension using a multiple-choice rational cloze. *Modern Language Journal, 68*, 230–239.

Bensoussan, M., Sim, D., & Weiss, R. (1984). The effect of dictionary usage on EFL test performance compared with student and teacher attitudes and expectations. *Reading in a Foreign Language, 2*, 262–276.

Berger, R., & Haider, U. (Eds.). (1981). *Lesen in der Fremdsprache.* München: Kemmler and Hoch.

Berkemeyer, V.B. (1989). Qualitative analysis of immediate recall protocol data: Some classroom implications. *Die Unterrichtspraxis, 22*, 131–137.

Bernhardt, E.B. (1983). Three approaches to reading comprehension in intermediate German. *Modern Language Journal, 67*, 111–115.

Bernhardt, E.B. (1984). *Text processing strategies of native, non-native experienced, and non-native inexperienced readers of German: Findings and implications for the instruction of German as a foreign language.* Unpublished doctoral dissertation, The University of Minnesota, Minneapolis, MN.

Bernhardt, E.B. (1985). Reconstructions of literary texts by learners of German. In M. Heid (Ed.), *New Yorker Werkstattgespräch 1984: Literarische texte im Fremdsprachenunterricht* (pp. 255–289). München: Kemmler and Hoch.

Bernhardt, E.B. (1986a). Cognitive processes in L2: An examination of reading behaviors. In J. Lantolf & A. Labarca (Eds.), *Research in second language acquisition in the classroom setting* (pp. 35–51). Norwood, NJ: Ablex.

Bernhardt, E.B. (1986b). Reading in a foreign language. In B.H. Wing (Ed.), *Listening, reading, writing: Analysis and application* (pp. 93–115). Middlebury, VT: Northeast Conference on the Teaching of Foreign Languages.

Bernhardt, E.B. (1990). A model of L2 text reconstruction: The recall of literary text by learners of German. In A. Labarca & L. Bailey (Eds.), *Issues in L2: Theory as practice/practice as theory* (pp. 21–43). Norwood, NJ: Ablex.

Bernhardt, E.B., & Berkemeyer, V.B. (1988). Authentic texts and the high school German learner. *Die Unterrichtspraxis, 21*(1) 6–28.

Bernhardt, E.B., & James, C.J. (1987). The teaching and testing of comprehension in foreign language learning. In D.W. Birckbichler (Ed.), *Proficiency, policy and professionalism in foreign language education* (pp. 65–81). Lincolnwood, IL: National Textbook Company.

Bhatia, V.K. (1984). Syntactic discontinuity in legislative writing for academic legal purposes. In A. K. Pugh & J. M. Ulijn (Eds.), *Reading for professional purposes: Studies and practices in native and foreign languages* (pp. 90–96). London: Heinemann Educational Books.

Bialystok, E. (1983). Inferencing: Testing the 'hypothesis-testing' hypothesis. In H. Seliger (Ed.), *Classroom oriented research in second language acquisition* (pp. 104–124). Rowley, MA: Newbury House.

Blau, E.K. (1982). The effect of syntax on readability for ESL students in Puerto Rico. *TESOL Quarterly, 16*, 517–528.

Block, E. (1986). Comprehension strategies of non-proficient college readers. In J. A. Niles & R. V. Lalik (Eds.), *Thirty-fifth yearbook of the National Reading Conference* (pp. 344–352). Rochester, NY: National Reading Conference.

Bloome, D. (1985). *Procedural display.* Unpublished manuscript, University of Massachussetts, Amherst, MA.

Bloome, D., & Green, J. (1984). Directions in the sociolinguistic study of reading. In P.D. Pearson (Ed.), *Handbook of reading research* (pp. 395–421). New York: Longman.

Bormuth, J., Carr, J., Manning, J., & Pearson, P. D. (1970). Children's comprehension of between- and within-sentence syntactic structures. *Journal of Educational Psychology, 61*, 349–357.

Bowen, J.D., Madsen, H., & Hilferty, A. (1985). *TESOL techniques and procedures.* Rowley, MA: Newbury House.

Brown, J.D. (1984). A norm-referenced engineering reading test. In A.K. Pugh & J.M. Ulijn (Eds.), *Reading for professional purposes: Studies and practices in native and foreign languages.* Leuven, Belgium: Acco.

Brown, J.D., Yongpei, C., & Yinglong, W. (1984). An evaluation of native-speaker self-access reading materials in an EFL setting. *RELC Journal, 15*, 75–84.

Brown, T.L., & Haynes, M. (1985). Literacy background and reading development in a second language. In T.H. Carr (Ed.), *The development of reading skills* (pp. 19–34). San Francisco: Jossey-Bass.

Bruder, M.N., & Henderson, R.T. (1986). *Beginning reading in English as a second language.* Washington, DC: Center for Applied Linguistics.

Campbell, A.J. (1981). Language background and comprehension. *Reading Teacher, 35*, 10–14.

Carpenter, P., & Just, M. (1977). Reading comprehension as eyes see it. In M.A. Just & P.A. Carpenter (Eds.), *Cognitive processes in comprehension* (pp. 109–139). Hillsdale, NJ: Lawrence Erlbaum.

Carrell, P.L. (1983). Three components of background knowledge in reading comprehension. *Language Learning, 33*, 183–207.

Carrell, P. L. (1984a). Evidence of a formal schema in second language comprehension. *Language Learning, 34*, 87–112.

Carrell, P.L. (1984b). Inferencing in ESL: Presuppositions and implications of factive and implicative predicates. *Language Learning, 34*, 1–21.

Carrell, P.L. (1987). Content and formal schemata in ESL reading. *TESOL Quarterly, 21*(3), 461–481.

Carrell, P.L., Devine, J., & Eskey, D. (1988). *Interactive approaches to second language reading.* Cambridge: Cambridge University Press.

Carrell, P., & Wallace, B. (1983). Background knowledge: Context and familiarity in reading comprehension. In M.A. Clarke & J. Handscombe (Eds.), *On TESOL '82* (pp. 245–308). Washington, DC: TESOL.

Cates, G.T., & Swaffar, J. (1979). *Reading in a second language.* Washington, DC: Center for Applied Linguistics.

Chastain, K. (1988). *Developing second-language skills: Theory and practice* (3rd ed.). San Diego: Harcourt Brace Jovanovich.

Clarke, M.A. (1979). Reading in Spanish and English: Evidence from adult ESL students. *Language Learning, 29*, 121–150.

Clarke, M.A. (1980). The short circuit hypothesis of ESL reading: Or when language competence interferes with reading performance. *Modern Language Journal, 64*, 203–209.

Cohen, A., Glasman, H., Rosenbaum-Cohen, P., Ferrar, J., & Fine, J. (1979). Reading English for specialized purposes: Discourse analysis and the use of student informants. *TESOL Quarterly, 13*, 551–564.

Connor, U. (1981). The application of reading miscue analysis to diagnosis of English as a second language learners' reading skills. In C. W. Twyford, W. Diehl, & K. Feathers (Eds.), *Reading English as a second language: Moving from theory* (pp. 47–55). Bloomington, IN: Indiana University School of Education.

Connor, U. (1984). Recall of text: Differences between first and second language readers. *TESOL Quarterly, 18*, 239–255.

Cooper, M. (1984). Linguistic competence of practiced & unpracticed non-native readers of English. In J.C. Alderson & A.H. Urquhart (Eds.), *Reading in a foreign language* (pp. 122-135). London: Longman.

Cowan, J.R., & Sarmad, S. (1976). Reading performance of bilingual children according to type of school and home language. *Language Learning, 26*, 353–376.

Cziko, G.A. (1978). Differences in first- and second-language reading: The use of syntactic, semantic, and discourse constraints. *Canadian Modern Language Review/ La revue canadienne des langues vivantes, 34*, 473–489.

Cziko, G.A. (1980). Language competence and reading strategies: A comparison of first- and second-language readers. *Language Learning, 30*, 101–116.

Dank, M., & McEachern, W. (1979). A psycholinguistic description comparing the native language oral reading behavior of French immersion students with traditional English language students. *Canadian Modern Language Review/La revue canadienne des langues vivantes, 35*, 366–371.

Davies, A. (1984). Simple, simplified and simplification: What is authentic? In J.C. Alderson & A.H. Urquhart (Eds.), *Reading in a foreign language* (pp. 181–195). London: Longman.

Davis, J.N., Lange, D.L., & Samuels, S.J. (1988). Effects of text structure instruction on foreign language readers' recall of a scientific journal article. *Journal of Reading Behavior, 22*(3), 203–214.

DeFrancis, J. (1984). *The Chinese language: Fact and fantasy.* Honolulu: University of Hawaii Press.

DeStefano, J., Pepinsky, H., & Sanders, T. (1982). Discourse rules for literacy learning in a first grade classroom. In L.C. Wilkinson (Ed.), *Communicating in the classroom* (pp. 101–129). New York: Academic Press.

Devine, J. (1981). Developmental patterns in native and non-native reading acquisition.

In S. Hudelson (Ed.), *Learning to read in different languages* (pp. 103–114). Washington, DC: Center for Applied Linguistics.

Devine, J. (1984). ESL reader's internalized models of the reading process. In J. Handscombe, R. Orem, & B. Taylor (Eds.), *On TESOL '83* (pp. 95–108). Washington, DC: TESOL.

Devine, J. (1987). General language competence and adult second language reading. In J. Devine, P.L. Carrell, & D.E. Eskey (Eds.), *Research in reading in English as a second language* (pp. 73–86). Washington, DC: Teachers of English to Speakers of Other Languages.

Devine, J. (1988). A case study of two readers: Models of reading and reading performance. In P.C. Carrell, J. Devine, & D.E. Eskey (Eds.), *Interactive approaches to second language reading* (pp. 127–139). Cambridge: Cambridge University Press.

Devine, J., Carrell, P.L., & Eskey, D. (Eds.). (1987). *Research in reading English as a second language*. Washington, DC: TESOL.

Douglas, D. (1981). An exploratory study of bilingual reading proficiency. In S. Hudelson (Ed.), *Learning to read in different languages* (pp. 93–102). Washington, DC: Center for Applied Linguistics.

Dubin, F., Eskey, D., & Grabe, W. (Eds.). (1986). *Teaching second language reading for academic purposes*. Reading, MA: Addison-Wesley.

Duffy, G., & Anderson, L. (1981). *Final report: Conceptions of reading project*. Unpublished report, Institute for Research on Teaching, Michigan State University, East Lansing, MI.

Elley, W.B. (1984). Exploring the reading difficulties of second language learners and second-languages in Fiji. In J.C. Alderson & A.H. Urquhart (Eds.), *Reading in a foreign language* (pp. 281–297). London: Longman.

Elley, W.B., & Mangubhai, F. (1983). The impact of reading on second language learning. *Reading Research Quarterly, 19*, 53–67.

Everson, M.E. (1986). *The effect of word-unit spacing upon the reading strategies of native and non-native readers of Chinese: An eye-tracking study*. Unpublished doctoral dissertation, The Ohio State University, Columbus, OH.

Ewoldt, C. (1981). Factors which enable deaf readers to get meaning from print. In S. Hudelson (Ed.), *Learning to read in different languages* (pp. 45–53). Washington, DC: Center for Applied Linguistics.

Fanselow, J.F. (1987). *Breaking rules: Generating and exploring alternatives in language teaching*. New York: Longman.

Fry, G. (1988). *A French replication of Allen, Bernhardt, Berry, and Demel*. Unpublished manuscript, The Ohio State University, Columbus, OH.

Favreau, M., & Segalowitz, N.S. (1982). Second language reading in fluent bilinguals. *Applied Psycholinguistics, 3*, 329–341.

Favreau, M., Komoda, M.K., & Segalowitz, N. S. (1980). Second language reading: Implications of the word superiority effect in skilled bilinguals. *Canadian Journal of Psychology/Revue canadienne de psychologie, 34*, 370–380.

Feldman, D. (1978). A special reading system for second language learners. *TESOL Quarterly, 12*, 415–424.

Flick, W.C., & Anderson, J.I. (1980). Rhetorical difficulty in scientific English: A study in reading comprehension. *TESOL Quarterly, 14*, 345–51.

Fransson, A. (1984). Cramming or understanding? Effects of intrinsic and extrinsic motivation on approach to learning and test performance. In J.C. Alderson & A.H. Urquhart (Eds.), *Reading in a foreign language* (pp. 86–115). London: Longman.

Golden, J.M. (1985). Interpreting a tale: Three perspectives on text construction. *Poetics, 14*(6), 503–524.

Golden, J.M. (1988). The construction of a literary text in a story-reading lesson. In J.L. Green & J.O. Harker (Eds.), *Multiple perspective analysis of classroom discourse* (pp. 71–106). Norwood, NJ: Ablex.

Goodman, K.S. (1967). Reading: A psycholinguistic guessing game. *Journal of the Reading Specialist, 6*, 126–135.

Goodman, K. (Ed.). (1968). *The psycholinguistic nature of the reading process.* Detroit, MI: Wayne State University Press.

Goodman, K.S. (1969). Analysis of reading miscues: Applied psycho-linguistics. *Reading Research Quarterly, 5*, 9–30.

Goodman, K. (1971). Psycholinguistic universals in the reading process. In P. Pimsleur & T. Quinn (Eds.), *The psychology of second-language learning: Papers from the Second International Congress of Applied Linguistics.* Cambridge: Cambridge University Press.

Gough, P.B. (1972). One second of reading. In J.F. Kavanaugh & I.G. Mattingly (Ed.), *Language by eye and ear* (pp. 331–358). Cambridge: MIT Press.

Graesser, A.C., Haberlandt, K., & Koizumi, D. (1987). How is reading time influenced by knowledge-based references and world knowledge? In B.K. Britton & S.M. Glynn (Eds.), *Executive control processes in reading* (pp. 217–251). Hillsdale, NJ: Lawrence Erlbaum.

Grice, H.P. (1975). Implicature. In P. Cole & J. Morgan (Eds.), *Syntax and semantics Volume 3: Speech acts.* New York: Academic Press.

Grimes, J. E. (1975). *The thread of discourse.* The Hague: Mouton.

Groebel, L. (1979). A comparison of two strategies in the teaching of reading comprehension. *English Language Teaching Journal, 33*, 306–309.

Groebel, L. (1980). A comparison of students' reading comprehension in the native language with their reading comprehension in the target language. *English Language Teaching Journal, 35*, 54–59.

Grosse, C., & Hameyer, K. (1979). Dialect and reading interferences in second language perception and production. *Die Unterrichtspraxis, 12*, 52–60.

Guarino, R., & Perkins, K. (1986). Awareness of form class as a factor in ESL reading comprehension. *Language Learning, 36*, 77–82.

Guthrie, J.T., Seifert, M., & Mosberg, L. (1983). Research synthesis in reading: Topics, audiences, and citation rates. *Reading Research Quarterly, 19*(1), 16–27.

Hardyck, C.D. (1968). *The effect of subvocal speech on reading* (Contract No. OE-6-10-275). Berkeley, CA: University of California, Institute of Human Learning. (ERIC Document Reproduction Service No. ED 022 656).

Hare, V.C. (1982). Preassessment of topical knowledge: A validation and an extension. *Journal of Reading Behavior, 14*(1), 77–85.

Hatch, E., Polin, P., & Part, S. (1974). Acoustic scanning and syntactic processing: Three reading experiments: First and second language learners. *Journal of Reading Behavior, 6*, 275–85.

Hayes, E.B. (1988). Encoding strategies used by native and non-native readers of Chinese Mandarin. *Modern Language Journal, 72*(2), 188–195.

Hayes, J.R. (1989). *The complete problem solver*. Hillsdale, NJ: Lawrence Erlbaum.

Hayes, J.R., & Flower, L.S. (1980). Identifying the organization of writing processes. In L.W. Gregg & E.R. Steinberg (Eds.), *Cognitive processes in writing* (pp. 1–30). Hillsdale, NJ: Lawrence Erlbaum.

Haynes, M. (1981). Patterns and perils of guessing in second language reading. In J. Handscombe, R. Oren, & B. Taylor (Eds.), *On TESOL '83* (pp. 163–176). Washington, DC: TESOL.

Henning, G.H. (1975). Measuring foreign language reading comprehension. *Language Learning, 25*, 109–14.

Hill, J.K. (1981). Effective reading in a foreign language: An experimental reading course in English for overseas students. *English Language Teaching Journal, 35*, 270–281.

Hock, T.S., & Poh, L.C. (1979). The performance of a group of Malay-medium students in an English reading comprehension test. *RELC Journal, 10*, 81–87.

Hodes, P. (1981). Reading: A universal process. In S. Hudelson (Ed.), *Learning to read in different languages* (pp. 27–31). Washington, DC: Center for Applied Linguistics.

Homburg, T.J., & Spaan, M.C. (1982). ESL reading proficiency assessment: Testing strategies. In M. Hines & W. Rutherford (Eds.), *On TESOL '81* (pp. 25–33). Washington, DC: TESOL.

Hosenfeld, C. (1977). A preliminary investigation of the reading strategies of successful and nonsuccessful second language learners. *System, 5*, 110–123.

Hosenfeld, C. (1984). Case studies of ninth-grade readers. In J.C. Alderson & A.H. Urquhart (Eds.), *Reading in a foreign language* (pp. 231–244). London: Longman.

Hudelson, S. (Ed.). (1981). *Learning to read in different languages*. Washington, DC: Center for Applied Linguistics.

Hudson, T. (1982). The effects of induced schemata on the 'short circuit' in L2 reading: Non-decoding factors in L2 reading performance. *Language Learning, 32*, 1–32.

Huggins, A.W.F., & Adams, M.J. (1980). Syntactic aspects of reading comprehension. In R.J. Spiro, B.C. Bruce, & W.F. Brewer (Eds.), *Theoretical issues in reading comprehension: Perspectives from cognitive psychology, linguistics, artificial intelligence, and education* (pp. 87–112). Hillsdale, NJ: Lawrence Erlbaum Associates.

Irujo, S. (1986). Don't put your leg in your mouth: Transfer in the acquisition of idioms in a second language. *TESOL Quarterly, 20*, 287–304.

Jarvis, D.K., & Jensen, D.C. (1982). The effect of parallel translations on second language reading and syntax acquisition. *Modern Language Journal, 66*, 18–23.

Johnson, P. (1981). Effects on reading comprehension of language complexity and cultural background of a text. *TESOL Quarterly, 15*, 169–181.

Johnson, P. (1982). Effects on comprehension of building background knowledge. *TESOL Quarterly, 16*, 503–516.

Johnson, R.E. (1970). Recall of prose as a function of the structural importance of the linguistic units. *Journal of Verbal Learning and Verbal Behavior, 9*, 12–20.

Johnston, P.H. (1983). *Reading comprehension assessment: A cognitive basis*. Newark, DE: International Reading Association.

Just, M.A., & Carpenter, P.A. (1987). *The psychology of reading and language comprehension*. Boston: Allyn and Bacon.

Just, M.A., & Carpenter, P.A. (1980). A theory of reading: From eye fixations to comprehension. *Psychological Review, 87*, 329–354.

Kamil, M. (1984). Current traditions of reading research. In P.D. Pearson (Ed.), *Handbook of reading research* (pp. 39–62). New York: Longman.

Kamil, M.L., Langer, J.A., & Shanahan, T. (1985). *Understanding research in reading and writing.* Boston: Allyn and Bacon.

Kamil, M.L., Smith-Burke, M., & Rodriguez-Brown, F. (1986). The sensitivity of cloze to intersentential integration of information in Spanish bilingual populations. In J.A. Niles & R.V. Lalik (Eds.), *Thirty-fifth yearbook of the National Reading Conference* (pp. 334–338). Rochester, NY: National Reading Conference.

Kellerman, M. (1981). *The forgotten third skill: Reading a foreign language.* Oxford: Pergamon.

Kendall, J.R., Lajeunesse, G., Chmilar, P., Shapson, L.R., & Shapson, S.M. (1987). English reading skills of French immersion students in kindergarten and grades 1 and 2. *Reading Research Quarterly, 22*(2), 135–159.

Kintsch, W. (1974). *The representation of meaning in memory.* Hillsdale, NJ: Lawrence Erlbaum.

Kleinmann, H.H. (1987). The effect of computer-assisted instruction on ESL reading achievement. *Modern Language Journal, 71*(3), 267–276.

Koda, K. (1987). Cognitive strategy transfer in second language reading. In J. Devine, P.L. Carrell, & D.E. Eskey (Eds.), *Research in reading in English as a second language* (pp. 125–144). Washington, DC: TESOL.

LaBerge, D., & Samuels, S.J. (1974). Toward a theory of automatic information processing in reading. *Cognitive Psychology, 6*, 293–323.

Lange, D. (1988, December). *Assessing foreign language proficiency in higher education in the United States.* Paper presented at The American Association of Applied Linguistics, New Orleans, LA.

Lange, D.L., & Clausing, G. (1981). An examination of two methods of generating and scoring CLOZE tests with students of German on three levels. *Modern Language Journal, 65*(3), 254–261.

Langer, J.A. (1980). Relation between levels of prior knowledge and the organization of recall. In M.L. Kamil (Ed.), *Perspectives on Reading Research and Instruction: Twenty-ninth Yearbook of the National Reading Conference* (pp. 28-33). Rochester, NY: National Reading Conference.

Langer, J.A., & Nicolich, M. (1981). Prior knowledge and its relationship to comprehension. *Journal of Reading Behavior, 13*(4), 373–379.

Laufer-Dvorkin, B. (1981). "Intensive" versus "extensive" reading for improving university students' comprehension in English as a foreign language. *Journal of Reading, 25*(1), 40–43.

Lee, J.F. (1986a). Background knowledge and L2 reading. *Modern Language Journal, 70*, 350–354.

Lee, J.F. (1986b). On the use of the recall task to measure L2 reading comprehension. *Studies in Second Language Acquisition, 8*, 83–93.

Lee, J.F., & Musumeci, D. (1988). On hierarchies of reading skills and text types. *Modern Language Journal, 72*(2), 173–187.

Lutjeharms, M. (1985). Testing reading comprehension: An example from German for academic purposes. In J.M. Ulijn & A.K. Pugh (Eds.), *Reading for professional purposes: Methods and materials in teaching languages* (pp. 148–158). Leuven, Belgium: Acco.

Mackey, R., Barkman, B., & Jordan, R.R. (Eds.). (1979). *Reading in a second language.* Rowley, MA: Newbury House.

MacLean, M., & d'Anglejan, A. (1986). Rational cloze and retrospection: Insights into first and second language reading comprehension. *Canadian Modern Language Review/La revue canadienne des langues vivantes, 42,* 814–826.

Markham, P. (1985). The rational deletion cloze and global comprehension in German. *Language Learning, 35,* 423–430.

Massaro, D.W. (1984). Building and testing models of the reading process. In P. D. Pearson (Ed.), *Handbook of reading research* (pp. 111–146). New York: Longman.

McConkie, G.W., & Rayner, K. (1975). The span of the effective stimulus during a fixation in reading. *Perception and Psychophysics, 17,* 578–586.

McDougall, A., & Bruck, M. (1976). English reading within the French immersion program: A comparison of the effects of the introduction of English at different grade levels. *Language Learning, 26,* 37–44.

McLeod, B., & McLaughlin, B. (1986). Restructuring or automaticity? Reading in a second language. *Language Learning, 36,* 109–123.

Meara, P. (1984). Word recognition in foreign languages. In A.K. Pugh & J.M. Ulijn (Eds.), *Reading for professional purposes: Studies and practices in native and foreign languages* (pp. 97–105). London: Heinemann Educational Books.

Messick, S. (1988). The once and future issues of validity: Assessing the meaning and consequences of measurement. In H. Wainer & H.S. Braun (Eds.), *Test validity* (pp. 33–45). Hillsdale, NJ: Lawrence Erlbaum.

Meyer, B.J.F. (1985). Prose analysis: Purposes, procedures, and problems. In B.K. Britton & J.B. Black (Eds.), *Understanding expository text: A theoretical and practical handbook for analyzing explanatory text* (pp. 11–64). Hillsdale, NJ: Lawrence Erlbaum.

Mohammed, M.A.H., & Swales, J. M. (1984). Factors affecting the successful reading of technical instructions. *Reading in a Foreign Language, 2,* 206–217.

Mott, B. (1981). A miscue analysis of German speakers reading in German and English. In S. Hudelson (Ed.), *Learning to read in different languages* (pp. 54–68). Washington, DC: Center for Applied Linguistics.

Muchisky, D.M. (1983). Relationships between speech and reading among second language learners. *Language Learning, 33,* 77–102.

Mustapha, H., Nelson, P., & Thomas, J. (1985). Reading for specific purposes: The course for the faculty of earth sciences at King Abdulaziz University. In J.M. Ulijn & A.K. Pugh (Eds.), *Reading for professional purposes: Methods and materials in teaching languages* (pp. 236–246). Leuven, Belgium: Acco.

Narayanaswany, K.R. (1982). ESP for Islamic school-learners. *System, 10,* 159–170.

Nehr, M. (1984). Audio-lingual behaviour in learning to read foreign languages. In A.K. Pugh & J.M. Ulijn (Eds.), *Reading for professional purposes: Studies and practices in native and foreign languages* (pp. 82–89). London: Heinemann Educational Books.

Neville, M.H. (1979). An Englishwoman reads Spanish: Self-observation and speculation. *English Language Teaching Journal, 33,* 274–281.

Neville, M.H., & Pugh, A.K. (1975). An exploratory study of the application of time-compressed and time-expanded speech in the development of the English reading proficiency of foreign students. *English Language Teaching Journal, 29*, 320–329.

Nunan, D. (1985). Content familiarity and the perception of textual relationships in second language reading. *RELC Journal, 16*, 43–51.

Nuttall, C. (1982). *Teaching reading skills in a foreign language.* London: Heinemann Educational Books.

O'Flanagan, M.J.R. (1985). A program for teaching and learning to read professional texts in a second/foreign language at Siemens AG. In J. M. Ulijn & A. K. Pugh (Eds.), *Reading for professional purposes: Methods and materials in teaching languages* (pp. 211–222). Leuven, Belguim: Acco.

Olah, E. (1984). How special is special English? In A. K. Pugh & J. M. Ulijn (Eds.), *Reading for professional purposes: Studies and practices in native and foreign languages* (pp. 223–226). London: Heinemann Educational Books.

Oller, J.W., Jr. (1979). *Language tests at school: A pragmatic approach.* London: Longman.

Olshtain, E. (1982). English nominal compounds and the ESL/EFL reader. In M. Hines & W. Rutherford (Eds.), *On TESOL 81* (pp. 153–167). Washington, DC: TESOL.

Olson, D.R. (1981). Writing: The divorce of the author from the text. In B. M. Kroll & R. J. Vann (Eds.), *Exploring speaking-writing relationships: Connections and contrasts* (pp. 99–110). Urbana, IL: National Council of Teachers of English.

Omaggio, A.C. (1979). Pictures and second language comprehension: Do they help? *Foreign Language Annals, 12*, 107–116.

Omaggio, A.C. (1986). *Teaching language in context: Proficiency-oriented instruction.* Boston: Heinle & Heinle.

Padron, Y.N., & Waxman, H.C. (1988). The effect of ESL students' perceptions of their cognitive strategies on reading achievement. *TESOL Quarterly, 22*(1), 146–150.

Parry, K.J. (1987). Reading in a second culture. In J. Devine, P.L. Carrell, & D.E. Eskey (Eds.), *Research in reading in English as a second language* (pp. 59–70). Washington, DC: TESOL.

Patberg, J., Dewitz, P., & Samuels, S.J. (1981). The effect of context on the size of the perceptual unit used in word recognition. *Journal of Reading Behavior, 13*, 33–48.

Paulston, C.B., & Bruder, M.N. (1975). *Techniques and procedures in teaching English as a second language.* Cambridge, MA: Winthrop.

Pearson, P.D. (1975). The effects of grammatical complexity on children's comprehension, recall, and conception of certain grammatical relations. *Reading Research Quarterly, 10*, 155–192.

Pearson, P.D., & Valencia, S. (1987). Assessment, accountability and professional prerogative. In J.E. Readence & R.S. Baldwin (Eds.), *Research in literacy: Merging perspectives* (pp. 3–16). Rochester, NY: National Reading Conference.

Pederson, K. (1986). An experiment in computer assisted second-language reading. *Modern Language Journal, 70*, 36–41.

Perkins, K. (1983). Semantic constructivity in ESL reading comprehension. *TESOL Quarterly, 17*, 19–27.

Perkins, K. (1984). An analysis of four common item types used in testing EFL reading comprehension. *RELC Journal, 15*, 29–43.

Perkins, K. (1987). The relationship between nonverbal schematic concept formation and story comprehension. In J. Devine, P.L. Carrell, & D.E. Eskey (Eds.), *Research in reading in English as a second language* (pp. 151–171). Washington, DC: TESOL.

Perkins, K., & Angelis, P.J. (1985). Schematic concept formation: Concurrent validity for attained English as a second language reading comprehension? *Language Learning, 35*, 269–283.

Perkins, K., & Brutten, S.R. (1988). A behavioral anchoring analysis of three ESL reading comprehension tests. *TESOL Quarterly, 22*(4), 607–622.

Propst, I.K., Jr., & Baldauf, R.B., Jr. (1979). Using matching cloze tests for elementary ESL students. *Reading Teacher, 32*, 683–690.

Pugh, A.K. (1977). Implications of problems of language testing for the validity of speed reading courses. *System, 5*, 29–39.

Pugh, A.K., & Ulijn, J.M. (Eds.). (1984). *Reading for professional purposes: Studies and practices in native and foreign languages*. London: Heinemann Educational Books.

Pyrczak, F. (1975). Passage dependence of reading comprehension questions: Examples. *Journal of Reading, 18*, 308–311.

Pyrczak, F., & Axelrod, J. (1976). Determining the passage dependence of reading comprehension exercises: A call for replications. *Journal of Reading, 19*, 279-283.

Reeds, J. A., Winitz, H., & Garcia, P. A. (1977). A test of reading following comprehension training. *IRAL, 15*, 307–319.

Richterich, R., & Chancerel, J.L. (1980). *Identifying the needs of adults learning a foreign language* (2nd ed.). New York: Pergamon Press.

Rigg, P. (1978). The miscue-ESL project. In H.D. Brown, C. Yorio, & R. Crymes (Eds.), *On TESOL 77* (pp. 109–117). Washington, DC: TESOL.

Rivers, W.M. (1981). *Teaching foreign language skills* (2nd ed.). Chicago: University of Chicago Press.

Robbins, B. (1983). Language proficiency level and the comprehension of anaphoric subject pronouns by bilingual and monolingual children. In P. Larson, E.L. Judd, & D.S. Messerschmitt (Eds.), *On TESOL 84* (pp. 45–54). Washington, DC: TESOL.

Roe, B.D., Stoodt, B.D., & Burns, P.C. (1987). *Secondary school reading instruction: The content areas*. Boston: Houghton Mifflin.

Roller, C. M. (1988). Transfer of cognitive academic competence and L2 reading in a rural Zimbabwean primary school. *TESOL Quarterly, 22*(2), 303–328.

Romatowski, J. (1981). A study of oral reading in Polish and English: A psycholinguistic perspective. In S. Hudelson (Ed.), *Learning to read in different languages*. Washington, DC: Center for Applied Linguistics.

Rumelhart, D. (1977). Toward an interactive model of reading. In S. Dornic (Ed.), *Attention and performance I* (pp. 573–603). Hillsdale, NJ: Lawrence Erlbaum.

Sacco, S. (1984). *The development of the knowledge of orthographic redundancy by experienced and inexperienced nonnative adult readers of French*. Unpublished doctoral dissertation, The Ohio State University, Columbus, OH.

Samuels, S.J. (1977). Introduction to theoretical models of reading. In W. Otto, L.W. Peters, & N. Peters (Eds.), *Reading problems* (pp. 7–41). Boston: Addison-Wesley.

Samuels, S.J., & Kamil, M.L. (1984). Models of the reading process. In P.D. Pearson (Ed.), *Handbook of reading research* (pp. 185-224). New York: Longman.

Samuels, S.J., LaBerge, D., & Bremer, D. (1978). Units of word recognition: Evidence for developmental changes. *Journal of Verbal Learning and Verbal Behavior, 17*, 715–720.

Samuels, S.J., Miller, N., & Eisenberg, P. (1979). Practice effects on the unit of word recognition. *Journal of Educational Psychology, 71*, 514–520.

Sarig, G. (1987). High-level reading in the first and in the foreign language: Some comparative process data. In J. Devine, P.L. Carrell, & D.E. Eskey (Eds.), *Research in reading in English as a second language* (pp. 105–120). Washington, DC: TESOL.

Shanahan, T., Kamil, M., & Tobin, A. (1982). Cloze as a measure of intersentential comprehension. *Reading Research Quarterly, 17*, 229–255.

Shohamy, E. (1982). Affective considerations in language testing. *Modern Language Journal, 66*, 13–17.

Shohamy, E. (1984). Does the testing method make a difference? The case of reading comprehension. *Language Testing, 1*, 147–170.

Shulman, L. (1987). Presentation at The Ohio State University, Columbus, OH.

Sim, D., & Bensoussan, M. (1979). Control of contextualized function and content words as it affects EFL reading comprehension test scores. In R. Mackay, B. Barkman, & R.R. Jordan (Eds.), *Reading in a second language* (pp. 36–47). Rowley, MA: Newbury House.

Smith, F. (1971). *Understanding reading.* New York: Holt, Rinehart and Winston.

Spiro, R. J., Vispoel, W. P., Schmitz, J. G., Samarapungavan, A., & Boerger, A.E. (1987). Knowledge acquisition for application: Cognitive flexibility and transfer in complex content domains. In B.K. Britton & S.M. Glynn (Eds.), *Executive control processes in reading* (pp. 177–199). Hillsdale, NJ: Lawrence Erlbaum.

Stanley, R.M. (1984). The recognition of macrostructure: A pilot study. *Reading in a Foreign Language, 2*, 156–168.

Stanovich, K.E. (1980). Toward an interactive compensatory model of individual differences in the development of reading fluency. *Reading Research Quarterly, 16*, 32–71.

Steffensen, M.S. (1988). Changes in cohesion in the recall of native and foreign texts. In P.L. Carrell, J. Devine, & D.E. Eskey (Eds.), *Interactive approaches to second language reading* (pp. 140–151). Cambridge: Cambridge University Press.

Steffensen, M.S., Joag-Dev, C., & Anderson, R.C. (1979). A cross-cultural perspective on reading comprehension. *Reading Research Quarterly, 15*, 10–29.

Stern, H.H. (1983). *Fundamental concepts of language teaching.* London: Oxford University Press.

Strother, J.B., & Ulijn, J.M. (1987). Does syntactic rewriting affect English for science and technology text comprehension? In J. Devine, P.L. Carrell, & D.E. Eskey (Eds.), *Research in reading in English as a second language* (pp. 89–100). Washington, DC: TESOL.

Suarez, J. de. (1985). Using translation communicatively in ESP courses for science studies. In J.M. Ulijn & A.K. Pugh (Eds.), *Reading for professional purposes: Methods and materials in teaching languages* (pp. 56–68). Leuven, Belgium: Acco.

Swaffer, J.K. (1991). Language learning is more than learning language: Rethinking reading and writing tasks in textbooks for beginning language study. In B. Freed (Ed.), *Foreign language acquisition research and the classroom* (pp. 252–279). Lexington, MA: D.C. Heath.

Taglieber, C.K., Johnson, L.L., & Yarbrough, D.B. (1988). Effects of prereading activities on EFL reading by Brazilian college students. *TESOL Quarterly, 22*(3), 455–472.

Tang, B.A. (1974). A psycholinguistic study of the relationships between children's ethnic-linguistic attitudes and the effectiveness of methods used in second-language reading instruction. *TESOL Quarterly, 8*, 233–251.

Tatlonghari, M. (1984). Miscue analysis in an ESL context. *RELC Journal, 15*, 75–84.

Terry, P., Samuels, S.J., & LaBerge, D. (1976). The effects of letter degradation and letter spacing on word recognition. *Journal of Verbal Learning and Verbal Behavior, 15*, 577–585.

Twyford, C.W., Diehl, W., & Feathers, K. (Eds.). (1981). *Reading English as a second language: Moving from theory.* Bloomington, IN: Indiana University School of Education.

Ulijn, J.M., & Pugh, A.K. (Eds.). (1985). *Reading for professional purposes: Methods and materials in teaching languages.* Leuven, Belgium: Acco.

Urquhart, A. H. (1984). The effect of rhetorical ordering on readability. In J.C. Alderson & A.H. Urquhart (Eds.), *Reading in a foreign language* (pp. 160–175). London: Longman.

Valette, R.M. (1977). *Modern language testing.* New York: Harcourt Brace Jovanovich.

Van Dijk, T. A. (1979). Recalling and summarizing complex discourse. In W. Burghardt & K. Hoelker (Eds.), *Text processing: Papers in text analysis and text description* (pp. 49–118). Berlin: Walter de Gruyter.

Van Parreren, C.F., & Schouten-Van Parreren, M.C. (1981). Contextual guessing: A trainable reader strategy. *System, 15*, 235–241.

Wagner, D.A., Spratt, J.E., & Ezzaki, A. (1989). Does learning to read in a second language always put the child at a disadvantage? Some counter evidence from Morocco. *Applied Psycholinguistics, 10*, 31–48.

Walker, L. J. (1983). Word identification strategies in reading in a foreign language. *Foreign Language Annals, 16*, 293–299.

Wallace, C. (1986). *Learning to read in a multicultural society.* Oxford: Pergamon.

Waller, R. (1987). Typography and reading strategy. In B. K. Britton & S.M. Glynn (Eds.), *Executive control processes in reading* (pp. 81–106). Hillsdale, NJ: Lawrence Erlbaum.

Webber, B L. (1980). Syntax beyond the sentence: Anaphora. In R.J. Spiro, B.C. Bruce, & W.F. Brewer (Eds.), *Theoretical issues in reading comprehension: Perspectives from cognitive psychology, linguistics, artificial intelligence and education* (pp. 141–164). Hillsdale, NJ: Lawrence Erlbaum.

Webster's Seventh New Collegiate Dictionary. (1971). Springfield, MA: G.S.C. Merriam.

Wells, D. R. (1986). The assessment of foreign language reading comprehension: Refining the task. *Die Unterrichtspraxis, 19*, 178–184.

Wells, G. (1986). *The meaning makers: Children learning language and using language to learn.* Portsmouth, NH: Heinemann Educational Books.

Williams, D. (1981). Factors related to performance in reading English as a second language. *Language Learning, 31*, 31–50.

Yekovich, F.R., & Walker, C.H. (1987). The activation and use of scripted knowledge in reading about routine activities. In B.K. Britton & S.M. Glynn (Eds.), *Executive control processes in reading* (pp. 145–171). Hillsdale, NJ: Lawrence Erlbaum.

Zuck, L.V., & Zuck, J.G. (1984). The main idea: Specialist and nonspecialist judgments. In A.K. Pugh & J.M. Ulijn (Eds.), *Reading for professional purposes: Studies and practices in native and foreign languages* (pp. 130–135). London: Heinemann Educational Books.

Author Index

Subject Index